Tales·of· Inspiration

Leisure Entertainment Service Co., Inc.
(LESCO Distribution Group)
And
Dorchester Media LLC.

For Paul J. Gross,
a man who turned good ideas
into great things. Sorely missed
and deeply loved by family and
friends

Leisure Entertainment Service Co., Inc. (LESCO Distribution Group)
65 Richard Road Ivyland, PA 18974   www.leisureent.com

Published by special arrangement with Dorchester Media, LLC.

Copyright © 2006

Printed in the United States of America.

A Special LESCO Edition

FIRST TIME IN PAPERBACK

Dorchester Media is
a consumer magazine publisher.

Our Women's Romance Group of
eight titles includes the world's
largest and best selling women's
romance magazine, *True Story*.
True Story has a great history
(1919) and heritage and continues to
touch the heart, mind and soul of
readers by sharing everyday
experiences of romantic life.

In addition to *True Story*, sister
publications include *True Confessions*,
True Romance, and *True Love*.
Special collector magazines from
the substantial archive include
True Story Remember When.

For more information on all of
Dorchester Media publications, write
to Publisher, Dorchester Media,
333 Seventh Avenue, 11th Floor,
New York, N.Y. 10001.

We hope you enjoy the book.

Table Of Contents

An *Original* Publication of Dorchester Media, LLC.

ISBN:
First LESCO Edition Printing: February 2006
1-60016-006-9
Printed in the U.S.A.

Leisure Entertainment Service Co., Inc.
(LESCO Distribution Group)
65 Richard Road Ivyland, PA 18974
www.leisureent.com

TALES OF
INSPIRATION

GOD'S GREATEST GIFT

It seems as though it was such a short time ago, the night I walked into that motel room. I guess you might say that was the turning point in my life. I remember being dead tired, and I just wanted some pampering or loving, but, instead, I wound up surrounded by the faded walls, secondhand furniture, and a very saggy bed—alone.

I pulled the chain lock on the door and rechecked the knob. Then, I dropped my bags and the newspaper on the chair that sat forlornly in the corner. I checked the window locks and curtains for a second time. After kicking off my purple satin pumps, I stretched and walked softly into the bathroom, gripping the pink-flecked tiles slightly with my toes. *Well, enough exercise for one night,* I thought.

While steamy, hot water poured into the tub and bath salts frothed and foamed under its pressure, I undressed slowly, folding each piece of clothing carefully before resting it over a nearby chair. It seemed like my clothes never were hung in a closet or settled in scented drawers. They were just washed in motel sinks, folded, rolled, and ready to pack the next morning.

I winced as I took off my strapless violet gown. "This thing is getting too tight," I said to my reflection in the mirror, while tossing the gown over the chair with the other clothes. Somehow, I'd have to find the money to pick up a more fashionable outfit. This sort of thing had gone out of style years ago.

And my hair . . . my style was definitely out. I knew it, Stan, my road manager, knew it, and any fool who owned a TV knew it. But style cost money.

I sighed, poured a glass of wine, got the newspaper, and slipped into the hot water—a divine gift. I picked up the newspaper and held it above the suds. Springfield . . . I had been there before, several times at least. And come to think of it, even twenty years ago on the tour. I guessed it had been that long. I'd have to check my mother's scrapbook to be sure. I brought it with me since I had no permanent home, just traveling all the time. But then, why would I want to be reminded of anything that made me feel so much older?

My promotional picture was squirreled between the farm index and the 4-H winners at the county fair in Mom's scrapbook. "Rita Reynolds to entertain tonight."

That name always did seem so phony to me. Sometimes, I craved having someone on the road call me Becky, but that was a person I had to keep all to myself—the real me. Even so, the farmers and truckers who had made up the bulk of the audience at the armory that evening had been appreciative of my efforts. I could tell. Most of them were usually skeptical at first when they read my billing as a "famous songstress and stage beauty." Good old Stan, he could sure stretch the truth!

But the men weren't disappointed. Oh, I knew I could sing. "Becky," my mama would say, "you've got a volume and sweetness to your voice that's a gift from the angels!"

And I knew for a fact, even if I messed my life up every other which way, I could really sing, starting back when I began stumping and preaching with my mama and daddy. That was the truth for certain, and I felt pretty confident on that score. Well, the men weren't too disappointed on the other hand, either. Especially when you considered the pathetic, weathered faces of so many of the wives who doggedly accompanied their mates to the show.

I glanced down at my suds-covered body. Though nearing thirty, I still presented a pretty good figure, as they used to say. Yeah, the audience had been all right tonight.

The stage crew was a different matter, though. Those smart-mouth college kids who thought they knew everything. They laughed at Stan and the others. And it hurt when they snickered at my cheesy dress, as one of them had called it, and at my songs.

"Hopelessly sentimental and mushy," the kid with the long hair said as he snickered.

I had seen the signs and billboards as we had driven through the streets at dusk—the state's cultural center, the hub. Signs congratulating themselves on their achievements. Big deal! I sipped the sherry, snuggled under the suds, and swished the water around. I had seen the real big time: Chicago, Dallas, even New York City—well, once anyway—and I knew the people in this town had nothing to feel so smug about!

"Now, Becky," I spoke softly to myself. I'd always liked the way words seemed to echo in the bathroom. "Girl, it isn't worth getting riled over."

I could hear my mama's voice, clear as a bell on Easter morning: "Angry thoughts are evil thoughts, honey. They get you nowhere."

I yawned and dropped the paper on the floor and set the empty glass on top of it. I kept rubbing my body with the washcloth with slow, caressing movements—soaping, rinsing, rinsing again and again, almost symbolically. Wiping off the caked-on makeup, the stale tobacco smoke, the hundred and one smells and dirt of a crowd till I felt almost purified—at least from the dirt that was skin-deep.

But that inner sense of uncleanliness, there was no getting around that. No washing that away. I yawned . . . so tired . . . what was it Mama would say? I could hear her voice saying, "Dressed like a harlot, rolling her big eyes and tempting those men to adultery in their minds. Going around in the company of those bad thinking, foulmouthed people, drinking . . . God only knows what the next step will be down the long, but sure road to hell and everlasting fires!"

If I could only turn my mind off. I put on my sexy nightgown, satiny pale pink, slinky. I loved the way it felt next to my body. I was so very tired . . . I could barely stay awake long enough to slide under the well worn blankets.

First, I noticed a funny taste in my mouth, but when I went to roll over and take a deep breath, it was as though someone was smothering me with a pillow. My eyes were burning and I started to cough. Fire? Fire! The whole wall was on fire!

In the dark, strange room, now filled with smoke and flames, I tried to get my bearings, fighting panic and disorientation. I groped for the doorknob and safety chain. The hot metal burned my fingers, but I managed to get the door open. All I remember after that is hearing some voices, off in a distance somewhere, and the cool feeling of the tile portico as I slid down, down. . . .

When my eyes adjusted to the light, I could make out the details of a room plainer than the motel's. It was all metal furniture and painted radiators. I could even picture the mattress—blue and white ticking—over which I was lying on coarse cotton sheets. A nurse was standing by my bed, hanging an IV on a pole, replacing one that was empty. She smiled and called attention to the doctor standing at the foot of my bed reading a chart. The doctor grinned and said matter-of-factly, "Well, I figured you'd be coming around any time now. You seemed more exhausted than anything. How do you feel, Miss Reynolds?"

I kept blinking and swallowing, reliving—how long ago was it? Two hours? Two days? My body felt so limp, like it had no bones in it. It was an effort just to take a deep breath. I could tell that there was a bandage on my knee and my fingertips were tingling and bandaged, also. Other than that, I guessed I was okay, but I couldn't get my mind together. The nurse and doctor stood there, waiting for me to say something.

I felt real embarrassed, and I just didn't know

what to say. In fact, I didn't know if I still had a voice. My voice! Could I sing? A feeling of panic crept over me again. To add to my agitated state of mind, I saw a minister walk into the room. "Am I going to die?" I asked, absolutely panic-stricken.

"No, no," the preacher replied quickly. He looked for the other two people in the room to back him up, which they did very convincingly. After a few pertinent questions, the nurse and the doctor left.

"I was calling on another patient," the visitor explained. "I'm Rev. Bob Carroll. Hear you're not from these parts. It's tough, going through any sort of illness without kin or friends. If I can call anyone for you, I'd be glad to, or you could have the staff contact me later on."

I was overwhelmed with gratefulness. Few people had shown such tender caring for me, other than my parents. "Oh, thank you," I said as I tried to grasp his hand with my bandaged fingers. "Stan Jakes, my manager. He's in room thirty-one at the motel. Was he hurt in the fire, too?"

"No, no," he quickly assured me. "Only your room and the laundry room next to it were damaged. The motel manager did mention a Mr. Jakes , but it seems he left . . . didn't even check out. I'm sorry. Is there anyone else I can call?"

I had such a lump in my throat, I couldn't respond. So I just shook my head and turned on my side. So Stan had split. He hadn't even paid me for this gig. What about my belongings? It was slowly dawning on me: I had nothing!

The clock on the wall became my enemy. Its hands hardly moved, so it seemed, as day crept into night for who knows how long! My depression was intensified by the doctor's visit one morning.

"You'll be discharged tomorrow," he said in an impersonal manner. "We really can't justify your staying with us any longer. Do you want Social Services to help you make some arrangements?"

What can they possibly do for me? Give me money I don't have? Supply me with friends, a place to lay my head? I couldn't call my parents, because they had passed away. I started making some vague promises, like—if only I could find a place to stay, Lord. . . .

"Hi! Are you up to visitors?" Rev. Carroll asked as he called from the doorway. His deep, cheery voice shattered my ponderings.

I nodded my head and mumbled, "Sure. Come on in."

A plain, middle-aged woman with a warm smile followed him to my bedside. He introduced her as his wife. She gently took my hand and said, "Bob spread the word of your dilemma and our congregation took up a collection for you." She handed me a red wallet. "We hope this'll help to get you started. And if you need a place to stay for a bit, you'd be more than welcome at our house."

These kind strangers, offering to take me in, asking nothing in return! I started crying like a baby, and it was quite a while before I could settle myself down. The couple left with a promise to pick me up the next morning.

Stan—how could he do this to me? He had sure taken advantage before, but this was too much. Jerk! I worked from city to city, barely surviving on his empty promises and shallow praises. But compliments didn't put money in the bank, at least not in my bank. Stan always seemed well-off, flashing new jewelry and suits, living high on the hilltop . . . off my talents!

I stared at my reflection in the mirror.

It was an angry, hateful face. I knew I had to get a hold on myself and not let him turn me into that shrew staring back at me. Hmmm . . . my hair had been singed on one side, so it had to be cut. I kind of liked it that way.

The next day, Rev. Carroll handed me a little bouquet of flowers from his garden while his wife put my toiletries into a bag provided by the hospital. On the-way to their home, they actually stopped at the mall. Mrs. Carroll helped to pick out several outfits for me.

The next couple of weeks passed pleasantly enough. I helped Mrs. Carroll—Alice—a lot around the house and with all her other duties. She was one dedicated lady. It sounds corny, but I enjoyed smelling food cooking, knowing I had helped prepare it. I liked the way the morning sun poured through the window, talking to the delivery boy, getting the mail. I had forgotten—was this how ordinary folks lived? I even volunteered to help Alice clean the church hall for Saturday night suppers. The other women there were very friendly. They treated me like a long-lost friend, and I really enjoyed their company. It seemed funny, talking about schools and kids and community needs. What in the world had I been doing all these years that I was so insulated from these everyday concerns?

One Friday, Alice had gone to a Ladies' Aid meeting. I opened the paper and tracked down the nightclub ads. Not too many prospects, but one sounded okay. Saturday afternoon, I borrowed the Carrolls' car—said I just wanted to take a ride. I felt a little guilty, lying like that, but I didn't think they'd understand. I needed a couple of gigs, just enough to get me back to the coast where I'd have more opportunities.

The clothes I was wearing didn't fit the image I wanted to project for the club manager. My ensemble was plain, just like my hairdo, but once I was in the car, I unbuttoned the top two buttons of the pink flowered blouse and added a pair of hoop earrings which I had gotten at the church's flea market. I still didn't feel like "a stage beauty and famous songstress."

"Okay, Becky, you're on your way," I coaxed myself to get my confidence up. "At least one fellow in this town might recognize your talent and get you going again, singing those Saturday-night blues." My audition was at three, so I bellowed in the car, singing over the static-filled radio, trying to muster courage and confidence. At the red light, a group of farmhands in the pickup truck next to me clapped and yelled, "Way to go, missy!" That little bit of applause was all I needed. I knew I'd be okay.

As I stopped in the parking lot, I rolled up the sleeves of the blouse and added some extra blush and lipstick. That's the best I can do for now. Then, without giving myself time to lose my nerve, I grabbed my purse off the front seat and headed into the club.

The place was empty, except for a man at the bar wiping glasses and another man who was sitting at the piano. After a brief introduction, where I could feel his appraising eyes studying me, he handed me a couple of song sheets and asked me to pick one. I selected a popular song with an especially nice beat to it, and he started playing the piano. I poured my heart into that song. My body swayed, and I deliberately cast smoldering looks toward the manager. I leaned against the piano with a vampy, suggestive look, using every wile and guile I knew. I needed that job!

On the way home, I kept rubbing the steering wheel and grinning with glee. "I did it, I did it!" So, he wasn't completely bowled over. But at the trial run next weekend, I could really show my stuff.

Before returning to the Carrolls', I wiped off the excess makeup, rolled down my sleeves, and buttoned my blouse again. I felt kind of dirty and deceitful, but what else could I do?

I rushed over to the church hall. I had promised to help Alice with the dinner. In fact, I was looking forward to it. The congregation members showered me with best wishes and encouragement and bits of advice on how to recover from my misfortune. Not a soul there tried to preach religion to me or get me to mend my ways. But I still felt like squirming when I thought of how kind these simple people were being to me. Part of me yearned for this wholesome lifestyle, but it was only too obvious that I didn't belong there. The image of a thistle in a flower garden crept into my mind. With supper over, everyone gathered for some singing. Before I knew it, Rev. Carroll had guided me to the piano and asked if I would lead some of the songs, seeing as how I used to sing with my preacher daddy. I blushed. I'd forgotten that I had mentioned that part of my background when I was in the hospital. Even so, after all these years, the words came back just as clear as spring water. I could feel my heart swell with joy as I sang. Something reached deep into my soul and touched nerves I'd thought long dead. The other singers' voices faded and they stood, wide-eyed and gaping, as my voice filled the hall.

"Why, Becky, God has surely given you a beautiful voice!" Rev. Carroll exclaimed. He and Alice hastily conferred on the side and then together, they approached me. They seemed very excited over the plans that they were concocting.

"Won't you please consider helping us at the revival meeting next weekend?" Rev. Bob asked. "You could be the answer to our prayers. Rev. Michael Bosley is supposed to be there, but he called today. He might have to cancel because several of his lead singers are suddenly unavailable. I'm sure he'd love to have you fill in."

"And you'd be paid, of course," Alice added. "Maybe this would help to get you on your feet again. What do you say, Becky?"

This was a fine pickle to be in, I did owe these people a deep debt of gratitude, and I couldn't live with myself if I didn't repay them for all their kindnesses in some way. But I had to get on with my own life. This morning, I had no prospects for work and now, two jobs on the same Saturday night. Not fair. But, who ever said life is fair?

I gave an evasive answer, which they interpreted as a yes, and I just didn't have the heart to set them right. Oh, well, the sermons always came first and the singing last. I'd go to the club for a couple of hours and then hit the revival, at least for a part of it.

As I showered late that night I thought, *Wouldn't*

GOD'S GREATEST GIFT

Mama smile now to see me singing at a revival? But it's only a onetime thing and the nightclub gig could get my career on the track again. Oh, but what if some folks at the revival meeting recognize Rita Reynolds? Why, they'll laugh me right out of town! I caught a glimpse of myself in the mirror as I dried off. "Not much chance of that," I said aloud. After the new hairstyle and these weeks of clean living, I hardly recognized myself. I liked this new person.

That Saturday night, the nightclub was packed. It looked as though every farmhand in the county had wandered in with his wife or the other woman. They'd come in to do some serious drinking and semiserious listening. It had been a particularly hot week and the cool, dark bar and grill, its air-conditioning pumping, was real inviting.

I wasn't scheduled to start singing until eight, but I got there at seven. I stood in the parking lot, staring at the glittering neon lights that couldn't mask the sleazy appearance of the bar. But I was okay, so I told myself, as I walked into the smoke-filled hallway.

"Help you, girlie?" a rough voice shot at me.

He scared me, and, just like a dumb kid, I turned and fled back outside. I was old, for heaven's sake. Old and experienced. But suddenly, I didn't feel that way.

Maybe it was the clothes. That was the problem. What could I expect, still wearing the flat shoes and prim dress of a small-town miss. I'd very carefully wrapped my new beaded dress and spike-heeled shoes in the pretty printed shopping bag. *Once I change into my new clothes, I'll feel more like myself,* I promised myself. Sure, once I had on that

20

slinky dress, the heels that gave a sway to my walk, and the dangling earrings now tucked in the red wallet, I would feel more like me.

I shifted the bag and reached up to pat my hair. I'd teased it—not great, but it would have to do. I clutched the shopping bag tightly.

"Go on, Becky, girl. Go in and change into who you really are. Darn feet . . . move!" I coaxed myself.

A late model pickup roared past and skidded into a parking place a few feet away. Several bits of gravel bit into my shins and my unwilling feet finally moved, but a yard farther from the door, not nearer.

"Now, Becky," I lectured, "you have to do what you have to do. Who do you think you are, anyhow? Do you want to live in a small town, sing hymns, and work at dumb jobs the rest of your life? Or do you want to be someone in show business again?"

At that point, I honestly couldn't answer that question.

I put the shopping bag down on the gravel and pulled the red wallet from my pocket. I could feel the bulge of the rhinestone earrings through the red vinyl. It couldn't be much past seven-fifteen. I glanced over to the inn then back to the car. Where did I really belong? Well, for starters, I was here, so this must have been what I really wanted.

Oh, what the heck! Taking a deep, exasperated breath and gritting my teeth so hard that my jaws ached, I walked briskly into the dark hallway then stood, letting my eyes get accustomed to the dimness. The smell of smoke irritated my eyes and made my stomach feel queasy. That had never happened before. Was somebody trying to tell me something?

Well, it was too late to turn back now. The manager saw me as he was passing through the hall and motioned for me to follow him to the ladies' lounge—if it could be called that.

"I guess you want to change," he said with cheerfulness in his voice, but his appraising stare seemed to indicate that he hoped I would. "Be careful where you leave your things," he admonished. "The clientele that frequents our establishment isn't known for their honesty. See you by the piano in ten minutes." He pushed open the door for me and as I walked by, he said, "Break a leg, kid!"

I appreciated his help. It was always a good feeling to go into a strange place and see someone you know—even someone you might have just met a short while ago. I felt a little better about my decision as I looked at myself in the mirror and began to apply some heavier eye shadow. My hairdo did look becoming—far more natural than my old one. And my body, well, it was difficult to explain even to myself, but somehow, it did seem cleaner, healthier. Maybe it was all those sunlight hours I had been exposed to, and three meals a day. I toned down the shadow and applied some blush—not too much, just enough for my complexion to withstand the harsh realities of the spotlights.

The walls were paper thin between the men's and the ladies' rooms. It would have been impossible not to hear everything that was going on in there. It seemed like a regiment must have invaded the place when a group of rowdy guys tramped into the adjoining area.

"C'mon," one of the guys was urging, "you've got to get out of this stupor you've been in. No girl's worth all that."

I started to clip on my earring and grinned as I pictured the lovesick beau over there, who had probably been trying to drown his sorrows in a bucket of suds.

Although I imagined a tall, lanky lad, the next voice I heard was that of an older man, his speech slurred and almost incoherent. He must have started banging his fist on the wall, and I thought he was going to punch a hole in the paneling, just to the right of the mirror.

"I swear." He moaned. "I didn't know what I was doing. But the bookies were breathing down my neck, and I needed the money real bad. She never knew about the insurance I carried on her."

A chill came over me, just as sure as if someone had poured a tub of ice cubes all around me. My hand froze on the earring and I couldn't seem to let go. "Stan!" I hissed. "Stan Jakes!" What was he doing here? Was that me he was talking about? It never dawned on me that the fire in the motel had been deliberately set! I had pictured someone falling asleep with a cigarette, and had no reason to question it further. True, he never did try to find out how I was, all those terrible days I was in the hospital.

"Oh," Stan said as he cried, "I know she's scarred for life. That's why she ain't working anywhere. I made a mess out of the whole thing."

"Get a hold of yourself," one of the other men replied. "She wasn't anything worth worrying about anyway. Just a whistle-stopping has-been."

Slowly, I came out of my catatonic pose, reached up once again, and took the earring off. As if in a daze, I reached for a tissue and wiped most of the eye shadow and blush off my moist skin. Although my chin trembled, I didn't cry. No, I had been through my share of hurt and humiliation, and I could handle this one, too, but this was by far the worst assortment of memories. "Aw, Rita," Stan had often begged, "you know you have no family to speak of, and these guys are lonely. They want to hear a warm voice on Christmas, and Easter, and every other holiday." I would sing all-year round, but I didn't get vacations, bonuses, or raises like the people I sang for—all I had gotten was a "song and dance" . . . and a fire in a motel room!

I slumped into the plastic-covered chair propped against the wall, trying to collect my thoughts, trying to decide what to do. Sure, I could call the police, but would they believe me, considering the type of people I had always associated with and my background?

"You lie down with dogs," my mama had always preached, "and you'll get up with fleas!"

"Well, Mama," I whispered, "tonight I'm going to make you very happy." Slowly rising and returning to the sink, I took off the other earring and laid it with its mate. I clutched the bag in my hand and walked down the hall, forcing one shaking leg in front of the other.

"Rita!" The manager was calling into the lounge. Hearing no answer, he bellowed, "Where is that broad?"

I walked out to the parking lot, feeling like I was caught in a twilight zone. Full of disillusionment, I started mumbling to myself. "So Stan thought I was disfigured. Apparently, he is suffering far more mentally than I did physically. Let him go on wondering forever. Let him feel all those pangs of his misguided conscience."

Talk about Saturday-night blues! My psyche sure hit some low curves, but suddenly I heard my Mama's words: "Becky, when the Lord shuts a door, somewhere He opens a window."

I now knew what I was meant to do. I enjoyed being able to socialize with all those women and knowing that they liked me just because I'm me, Becky. I liked not being pinched and slapped on the backside, living like a mole, coming out only when the sun went down! The more I talked to myself, I could feel a glow warming all about me. My steps became brisk and I was almost running by the time I got to the car.

What time is it? I wondered, trying to see my watch in the dimness of the dome light. Eight-thirty! The revival meeting had started already, but I knew it would go on well into the night. I raced over the bumpy roads to the outskirts of town, and then drove up and down the rows of cars parked in the newly mown field, found a place at the far end of the meadow, and raced back to the main tent.

Rev. Bob Carroll was standing in back of the stage, talking with another man. When he saw me, the worry on his face vanished and he broke into a warm, relieved smile. "Thank goodness," he declared. "I thought something bad happened to you."

It almost did, I thought, *but I'm going to be okay now.*

Well, that was three years ago. Becky Reynolds did sing that night, and the next. The feeling in my songs showed that I had been there, at the bottom of the mountain, and it gave hope to all those people who packed the tent. My name became well-known in town, and young couples started asking me to sing at their weddings. I sang in churches of all denominations.

What is meant to be, will happen. That New Year's Day, I sang at a large party held in the convention center of the state capitol, and I've been spinning in a whirlwind ever since.

I feel like I've come whole circle, and my life is now full and rich, especially since meeting Peter Klawson. He's the stage director on a nationwide gospel program where I just signed a contract. In between all our commitments, we're now making arrangements for our wedding.

And Stan? Well, I did contact the police and told them about the conversation I overheard. They told me it was hearsay, and that they hadn't found any evidence to suggest that the fire was suspicious. I didn't really believe that, but what more could I do—look for Stan? I think he already got what he deserved: He's still looking in the back streets of the major cities in which we'd toured, hoping to find Rita Reynolds singing the blues on a Saturday night.

THE END

THE LITTLE GIRL WITH THE BIG DREAM

Standing in the parking lot of the doctor's office, I clutched my baby daughter to my breast as I cried. I felt as if the doctor's news had knocked the breath from me, and I knew that if I didn't get into the car soon, I might faint. I somehow fumbled the door open and, as I gently sat my daughter in her car seat, I whispered, "I'm so sorry, Mindy. I'm so very sorry." I couldn't stop my tears.

My daughter had been born with a heart defect that had required numerous hospitalizations and, at the age of six months, surgery.

Those first six months seemed an endless merry-go-round of doctor appointments and sleepless nights.

Yet, along the way, I was sustained by the belief that once she made it through surgery, all would be well for her. Unfortunately, it was only the beginning of her problems.

The procedure went smoothly enough and, by early evening, Mindy was sleeping peacefully in her hospital crib. I sat in a chair at her bedside, watching her sleep, and found myself dozing. I awakened with a start when one of her many monitors began beeping. People came running in, and I was asked to leave the room.

I reentered the room tentatively, and watched the various nurses and therapists working on my daughter. I was unable to believe that the pale little form choking and gasping was my daughter. I groped my way back to the chair, and tried to stay out of the way.

I sat by her side hour after hour, silently praying that she would live. It appeared that she was being swallowed up by all of the monitors and wires and needles. A tube protruded from her chest, a grotesque appendage, draining the fluid that had pooled around her heart. The white of her tiny face merged with the white of the sheet, punctuated only by her sunken eyes and the grayish blue of her lips. Her breath escaped her lips in short, anguished gasps. She was fighting for her life.

My heart was gripped in a fist of pain so unbearable that I could not speak or move; I could only, wincingly, stare at the helpless body that had so recently been a part of my own body, so recently been cradled and comforted in my womb. And I sat by her bedside, willing her to live, telling her over and over that I would make it all better, if only she would hang on.

As the days went by, her condition gradually improved, and I could see the life return to her eyes. Eventually, I was allowed to take her home. I sat by her crib that night watching her sleep, and allowed myself the sigh of relief that I had held back for so long.

THE LITTLE GIRL WITH THE BIG DREAM

The months following Mindy's surgery were months of alternating encouragement and despair. My husband left us a month after the surgery, unable to face the mounting medical bills and the constant care that Mindy required. I knew that her life was in my hands, and I prayed daily that I would have the strength to give her what she needed from me, both emotionally, and physically. I put my bitterness over my marriage aside, and concentrated on making Mindy well. And, at first, it seemed as if I was succeeding.

Though still very small, her color was good, as was her appetite, and the seemingly constant incidents of illness that had plagued her the first six months of her life had tapered off considerably. Her eyes were bright and alert, and she smiled and cooed whenever I held her or talked to her. As time went on, however, I began to realize that her development was at a standstill. At the age of one year, still unable to roll over or sit up, she was, for all intents and purposes, still a newborn.

Her doctors were as confused and disturbed by this as I. They searched for any possible reasons for her delayed development and had every type of specialist examine and test her. I began to feel as if the purpose of my life was to sit in waiting rooms, listening to medical jargon that I really could not absorb or understand. My mind was on some kind of automatic pilot, just waiting for someone to find out what was wrong with Mindy and somehow fix it. Over and over, I relayed the details of her illnesses, of the problems that she'd had after surgery. Finally, after many weeks of testing and uncertainty, I was called into the doctor's office for a consultation. I entered the office that morning totally unprepared to hear the news that I would be told. Their final diagnosis: My beautiful Mindy was, for whatever reason, profoundly retarded.

The strong faith for her complete recovery that I had shrouded myself in was suddenly stripped from me as if by some unseen and cruel hand. For the first time in my daughter's short life, my optimism disintegrated, and I broke down and cried. I held her to me, stroking her soft back, and wept for the injustice of her life, wept for the abrupt end of hopeful expectations, and wept for the two of us and the reality that we had to face together.

The doctors were unable to calm me that day, nor was the psychologist that they sent in to see me. After what seemed like hours, I finally convinced them that I could drive home, and I staggered blindly to the parking lot. "I'm so sorry, Mindy. I'm so very sorry," I told her as I carried her to the car.

I don't remember sleeping at all that night, my mind and heart were so full of anguish, guilt, and grief. I couldn't understand how this had happened, or why. I wondered over and over again if I could have done something differently, somehow prevented this. I paced the dark house, my mind reeling. I was unable to comprehend that this beautiful child was as they said she was. I was unable to digest the finality of the diagnosis. My mind, my heart, would not accept the brutality of their words. And, as night turned to morning, my grief turned to disbelief.

After all, the doctors really had no concrete proof that my daughter was retarded, only test results that were, at best, inconclusive. The doctors did not spend every day with Mindy, did not see the way that her bright eyes followed my every move, could not know her sensitivity, how she reacted to my voice, my moods. I failed to comprehend how they could have expected her to develop normally after the trauma that her tiny body had been through. I felt as if she had never been given a chance to prove herself. I knew, with the conviction of my soul, that there was a bright and active mind behind those eyes, and that it would be up to me to instill in Mindy the determination and courage to overcome the label that had been so clinically conferred upon her. And I knew that I needed help to do it.

Fortunately, one of the many people who had tested Mindy had mentioned to me that she had once worked at a local school for neurologically disabled infants and children. I called them the morning following the diagnosis, and took Mindy in for an initial consultation the following week. I realized immediately upon meeting the staff, that these extraordinary people were optimists, that they believed in the children in their care. And I knew that if anyone could work a miracle in Mindy's life, these were the people to do it.

The basic philosophy of the school was simple, really. The teachers believed that, through hard work and constant positive reinforcement, these children, whose problems ranged from Down's syndrome to cerebral palsy to severe brain damage, could learn and do much more than had previously been thought. The staff concentrated on helping the parents to help their children and, though some of their methods appeared harsh, the love that they felt for their students was obvious from the start.

THE LITTLE GIRL WITH THE BIG DREAM

Mindy started off by going to physical therapy twice a week. The therapist taught me exercises to help Mindy with on a daily basis to help strengthen her terribly weak muscles. Often, Mindy would cry during these sessions, as her seldom-used muscles were flexed and stretched. It was all I could do to keep on with the exercises when I knew that they caused her pain, yet I realized that they were essential if she was ever going to show any improvement.

As weeks went by, I began to see changes in her. She would offer some resistance if I pushed my hand against the sole of her foot, and could lift her head from the floor and look around her. Soon, she was able to push herself up onto her arms, and then I could see in her eyes a yearning to pull herself forward. Then, one day after we returned home from therapy, she suddenly and arduously began dragging herself across the floor on her elbows. I soon realized that mobility had opened up the world for her. She became so active, so curious, dragging herself from room to room in the house, examining everything that she could get her hands on. She began to show an interest in playing with toys, and I would often lie on my stomach and roll a small ball to her. She would scream with delight. Soon after, she began crawling on hands and knees, then sitting up, and the therapist felt that it was time to work on the skills essential to walking.

Mindy's legs were terribly weak, as they had been drawn up to her chest for the entire first year of her life.

The therapist designed a series of exercises that would gradually build muscle strength in her thighs and lower legs. One important exercise, which seemed particularly painful, required Mindy to hold the therapist's hands and walk across the floor on her knees. Mindy literally screamed in pain during these sessions, and often I would cry myself, feeling the pain in my own heart. But when she finished each pass across the room, the therapist and I would clap for her and tell her how well she had done. The exercise, however painful, was effective. Soon, she was able to support some weight on her legs, and seemed amazed the first time I pulled her to her feet, with my hands supporting her beneath her arms. I guess she'd never realized what her legs were for.

A major stumbling block to teaching Mindy to walk was the fact that she had no idea whatsoever of how to pull herself up to furniture. I knew that most babies learned this for themselves, and circled every table in their houses, but Mindy did not, at the time, possess the necessary problem-solving skills to figure this skill out on her own. The therapist decided that we would simply have to teach her to do it, and I spent many hours sitting on the floor with her, placing her hands on the edge of the coffee table, tucking one knee underneath her, and urging her to push up with her other foot. She tried over and over for weeks, but always fell or became entangled in her own legs. She would howl for a moment in frustration, then try again. Often, I would become equally frustrated with the realization that I could not instill in her, simply as a matter of will, the ability to accomplish such a seemingly simple task.

One afternoon, I became particularly discouraged, and threw myself down on the couch after Mindy had cried for several minutes over her failure.

THE LITTLE GIRL WITH THE BIG DREAM

She looked at me for a moment, and a particularly determined look came over her face. She crawled to the table, reached for the edge, and struggled to a standing position. She looked stunned for a moment as she stood on her feet for the first time, then let go of the table's edge to applaud herself and immediately fell. But she knew then that she could do it, and practiced her new skill for hours until, finally, I carried my exhausted little athlete to her bed.

As the weeks went by, Mindy's legs strengthened more and more, but she still did not seem to have the balance to take independent steps. One morning, when I took her to therapy. The therapist told me he had a surprise for us. He had ordered for Mindy a miniature metal walker, the type often used by elderly people to give them extra support. She could hold onto it to give her balance as she practiced her steps. The walker had wheels on it, so that she did not have to move it with each step, but rather could just push it in front of her. We stood her up to it, and she was soon pushing it around the therapy room, with a smile that stretched from ear to ear.

I was thrilled. I took the walker home, and Mindy pushed it up and down the hallway, going faster and faster until she'd trip or run into the wall, then she'd be up and walking again. I was tickled one morning to see that she had put my car keys in the rubber grip on one handle of the walker and was imitating car sounds as she raced up and down the hallway.

The therapist gradually weaned her from the walker, and replaced it with a dish towel, stretched from my hand to hers. The dish towel gave her a little extra support and confidence, without being the crutch that the walker or my hand would have been. After a time, she seemed to enjoy this new form of transportation even more than using the walker and, though we received our share of strange looks walking through the mall with the dish towel stretched between us, the method worked. One day the therapist told me to walk across the room with her, and he quietly reached between us and cut the dish towel in two with large scissors.

Mindy kept walking alone. She was startled when she realized, three or four steps later, that she no longer had any support at the end of the towel, and promptly fell. But, a few minutes later, she got to her feet and walked again. I coaxed her to walk around the school with me, showing the other therapists and teachers what she could do.

In the interim, Mindy had been placed in a classroom with three other children of comparable skill levels. The purpose of the class was to teach the children social and group skills, as well as to work on small motor and self-help skills. Each morning started with song time, followed by games and learning activities, and concluded with snack time. It became apparent immediately that, after spending so much time as the center of my world, it was difficult for Mindy to adapt to a group situation. For the first several sessions in class, she refused to sit still and constantly tried to climb into my lap as I sat behind her, backing her up. The teacher instructed me to forcibly hold her still in her place on the floor and, if she started to cry and fuss, to turn her away from the rest of the class and totally ignore her until she would sit quietly, at which time she would be rewarded verbally and with hugs.

During snack time, Mindy was required to nod her head when asked if she wanted her snack. If she didn't nod, her snack was withheld. Often, I think from sheer stubbornness, she would refuse to nod, then sit and scream as the rest of the class ate their treats. I realized that withholding the treat was a means of forcing Mindy to communicate her needs and, though it was difficult to ignore her tantrums, I knew that communication was the most essential tool that Mindy would need in her life.

Mindy seemed unable to learn language, as other children did, just from listening to those around her and, at the age of two, had not begun to talk at all. She was placed in speech therapy, and a home program that was designed for her to teach her the rudiments of speech.

It was a painstaking process, and there were times when my patience was taxed to the limit. Everywhere I went, I heard children chattering in their high little voices, some of them who appeared to be no older than Mindy, speaking in full sentences. And I would look at my silent little girl, struggling so hard to learn a single sound, and wonder if I would ever hear her chatter like the children that surrounded us.

As the months went on, however, she gradually mastered a few simple words and, after about a year, Mindy had a vocabulary of several words that she had learned through this memorization technique. She knew, for example, that saying "want food" at snack time would get her a treat, or "want baby" would get her favorite doll from the shelf. I was so proud of her accomplishments, but at the same time, I began to worry that Mindy was only responding with mechanical words that meant nothing to her; she was only repeating some sound that got her a reward. I was afraid that she was incapable of spontaneous speech, and that this was as far as she would ever get in expressing her needs. There were times when all of the work, all of the hope, seemed almost futile.

But I refused to give up, and just kept talking to her as if she understood every word that I said. I would take her to the store and push her up and down the aisles, naming everything that we passed. I would drive her around in the car, telling her about the trees and the sky and the buildings, hoping, hoping that somehow my words were getting through, that somewhere in her mind the concept of language was taking root.

One afternoon, I was preparing a grocery list and, as usual, rattling on to Mindy as I did it. "We'll get milk and bread and lunch meat and paper towels. Can you think of anything else that we need?"

Mindy looked up at me, and I will never forget the struggle that I saw going on behind her eyes. "P-p-p-," she sputtered, her eyes squinting as if in intense concentration.

"Tell me what you want, Mindy! Tell me what you want!"

"P-p-p-peanut butta!" She spat the words out, and then grinned at her accomplishment.

"Yes, Mindy, oh yes! Peanut butter! We'll buy peanut butter! Oh, my sweet, precious baby, you said peanut butter!" I grabbed her and danced around the room with her, laughing and crying and repeating those words that seemed so miraculous. I knew then, somehow knew, that all the hard work was going to pay off, that the puzzle pieces would all fall into place for her. I knew that our victory had finally begun.

My Mindy is seven years old now, an amazing seven years old, a triumphant seven years old. After four years in special schooling, followed by private kindergarten, then public kindergarten, she's ready for a big step. Mindy is starting first grade this year, right along with her friends in the neighborhood.

Although IQ tests place her intelligence at only one point above intellectually handicapped, prompting so-called "experts" to suggest that she should be kept out of public school, she does miraculously well. She can read simple stories, writes many words independently, and shows marked strengths in math and art. Her teachers find her delightful, and laugh at the idea of taking her out of public school. Her ability to persevere, combined with her willingness to always try, have carried her over one hurdle after another, until her performance in school is nearly at the top of her class. People meeting her for the first time have difficulty believing that she has ever had anything wrong with her, and are shocked when I tell them of her struggles.

The psychologists who test her now can't quite figure out how or why she does so well, but it is no mystery to me. My Mindy is a fighter and, though the fight will probably continue for the rest of her life, it is a fight that I know she will win.   THE END

A MIRACLE CHILD

Tommy has Down's syndrome. He came into our lives when he was seven. At that time, my four children ranged in age from four to sixteen; we had been sharing our big old country home with foster children. A friend who teaches in special education came to me one day, very upset, to tell me a bit about Tommy and to say that the welfare department was arranging to send him to a state home for the mentally disabled. She begged me to give Tommy a chance in our home. "You'll love him," she assured me. "He's a little sweetheart."

I contacted Tommy's caseworker, and she was glad to let him come for a weekend trial visit, but she was pessimistic about the outcome, warning me, "He's been in seven foster homes in six years. He's violent and destructive—tears up clothes, sheets, furniture. His speech is nothing but gibberish. He eats with his hands—he's a little animal."

As you could expect, I immediately had second thoughts about taking on such a task, but I had already promised my friend that I would give Tommy a chance. I needn't have worried. The worst behavior we saw was when my second son, "Big" Tom, entered the dining room just before dinner and found Tommy sitting in the middle of the table, helping himself to the mashed potatoes—with both hands. Big Tom picked up the little boy and put him on the floor. Tommy threw himself down and began kicking, flailing, and screaming. It took us a moment or two to decipher his words—"Him a hard guy!"

As we stood there watching that tantrum, unable to keep from laughing at the words, it struck me that both women were right. He was a little animal, but he was a real sweetheart, too.

He sang and danced for us—a little showoff clown—passed out hugs and kisses by the bushels, and fell asleep on my husband's lap as we all watched television. When his visit was over on Sunday evening, my husband stood waiting to take him back to his foster home. Tommy put on his ragged, too-small coat, then leaned into a corner and cried, his heart broken. And that settled that. No one in our family could have led him to the door after watching that scene.

Our children didn't wait for the usual family counsel session to express their opinions about a new child joining us. They picked him up, hung up his coat, and began unpacking his paper bag of clothes. My husband pulled out his handkerchief, mumbling that he must be catching a cold. I had a good case of the sniffles, too, as I called the caseworker to tell her Tommy was staying.

So that is how, under the wrong circumstances and for all the wrong reasons, we invited a lifetime child into our family. But I really doubt that we would have behaved any differently if we had taken the time to be better informed as to what we were getting ourselves into. Tommy had already stolen our hearts. Since that night, there have been many, many times when I have known frustration, failure, turmoil, and tears, but I have never been sorry that we let Tommy into our lives.

As I hurriedly began educating myself about Down's syndrome, I read something that we were already discovering for ourselves. Down's children, if well treated, are happy, affectionate, and eager to please and win praise. They are gregarious and full of fun, and able to completely charm you forever.

I began learning something about Tommy's background, too. He was one of eight children. His mother was a slender, still pretty woman who was doing the very best she could under extremely hard circumstances. Babies with Down's syndrome are often frail, prone to sudden, desperate infections. When Tommy was not yet a year old, his mother had twins. I think it was about then that she realized she couldn't cope with him. She must have suffered greatly because of that decision. She had agreed to stay out of Tommy's life and give him a chance to forget her when she saw how her infrequent visits upset him. But, once in a while, I would see her waiting near Tommy's school bus stop, where he couldn't see her. She just wanted to catch a glimpse of him, see how he was growing, and assure herself that he was all right.

During his first months with us, Tommy was often watchful, as if wary of the reactions his behavior would bring. He had a terror of dark rooms and closed doors, which made bedtime a dread for both of us. I dressed him in heavily padded training pants and plastic pants at night, but he would often get up in the morning naked, and the search would be on for his missing, wet, well-hidden clothing. We began to understand his behavior when an older boy came to live with us for a few months. He and Tommy had shared Tommy's last foster home; the boy told horror tales of Tommy being locked in his room at eight every night, let out at eight in the morning, then severely punished when he wet his bed. As my anger at that rose, I couldn't resist the very immature thought: Good for you, Tommy! If I had been in the same situation I might have done the same thing!

We discovered Tommy did not know how to play. If I sent him outside for some fresh air and exercise, I would soon find him diligently sweeping the gravel drive, or simply standing still, twirling a little stick and talking secretively to the gate. But as summer arrived, the other children's wild laughing play gradually lured Tommy into the delightful world of country fun. Soon, he was insisting upon being tackled in football, and having his turn with the baseball bat. He wasn't about to put it down until he hit the ball, and that never happened unless he had help. He demanded to be "it" in the twilight games of hide-and-seek. The other children dreaded that because he usually forgot what game they were playing and, seeing himself apparently alone in the dark yard, he would wander into the house and watch television. He left brothers and sisters scattered all over the yard, crouching in their hiding places.

In the noisy, rowdy family volleyball games, he

would stake out his claim to a little piece of earth, smack in the middle of all the leaping, kicking legs; and from then on, he moved only to jump and cheer and clap his pudgy hands. Towering athletic brothers and father, agile sisters, wiry little brother, a panting, out-of-shape mother, and assorted aunts, uncles, and cousins—alone or united, were not enough of a threat to frighten him from his claim to that little square of grass.

He had a healthy terror of the little pony in the corral, and began screaming at the mere suggestion that he ride it. But the motorcycle was something else. My daughter, Kelly, and her foster sister, Jenna, had invented a wild game where one drove the little cycle and the other rode as a passenger, wearing a blindfold. As I saw it, the object of the game was to strike terror in a mother's heart. As they saw it, the object was to be able to identify their location blindfolded, as they went roaring, skidding, and careening around the four acres. Through dizzying swoops, circles, and cutbacks, the grass disappearing, the dust rising, and the gravel flying, the passenger would shriek with exhilaration and yell: "The well house. Garage. Orchard. Garden!"

Tommy wanted to ride. Blindfolded. And he wanted it loudly. Sometimes, he planted himself in the path of the motorcycle so there could be no question of them seeing that he wanted a ride. Every time he rode it ended the same way—with Tommy throwing a tantrum while the girls complained, "Well, Mom, he won't hold on!" That was because he was too busy. He would throw his head back, laughing wildly, wave his arms, and immediately lose his balance. Scrapes, bumps, and thumps never dampened his enthusiasm. He was always ready and eager the next time he heard the motorcycle start.

We soon identified his three main passions in life—eating, coloring, and cleaning house. His eating habits astounded even our family full of growing, active boys. His books and crayons littered our world. But his housecleaning terrified us. In one swift move, he broke all of us of the messy Sunday-morning habit of leaving our slippers lying about as we hurried off to church. It was three months before we found them behind the old piano.

The way Tommy looked at it, things had to be put away—in, under, behind—it didn't matter to him where, just somewhere where they couldn't be seen. His favorite target of the cleaning sprees was the kitchen counter—car keys, purses, coats, homework, gym clothes, baseball shoes left when the kids thundered into the house after school and headed for the refrigerator. His cleaning caused an incredible amount of turmoil and noise, especially when things were missed a minute before the bus was due in the morning. It did no good to ask Tommy where anything was. By the time it was missed, he had forgotten. But we learned. The hard way. Either we put our things away or, heaven help us, Tommy would.

It wasn't long, either, until something else became evident. He knew how to pass the buck. When that dreaded but familiar question would ring through the house—"All right, who did it?"—Tommy always had the answer: "Joey did." To that, my six-year-old's little boy's complexion would redden and he would bluster in astonishment.

Joey, the baby of the family at six, suddenly found his place usurped forever by Tommy, a lifetime child. Joey had to share his bedroom and the family's attention with this sometimes demanding, odd little boy. I needn't have worried. It was several months before I discovered that Joey got up every night with Tommy to lead him through the dark, bewildering house to the bathroom. He would remove the child's bulky nightwear, wait, then dress him, and put him back to bed. It was a remarkable thing for a sleepy little first grader to do every night.

During those first months, the children studied Tommy in fascination—a seven-year-old in a chubby four-year-old body playing and eating like a two-year-old. The question came, born of their curiosity, pity, and love: "Why does God let children like him to be born?" It was an impossible question to answer, of course. Who can know the mind of God? It was years before I had one answer as I watched my children grow into generous, loving, understanding, compassionate people because of the gentle influence of their little brother.

I grew up with a severely retarded aunt and to me it was a normal, if painful, fact of life. Tommy was the first of his kind to venture much into the public eye in our little town. The school he attended was new, and "different" children lived secluded, protected lives. Tommy and I and a succession of short-term foster babies spent a lot of time following my children in their after-school sports and activities. As the students got to know Tommy, their curiosity and any possible prejudices they harbored soon turned to tolerance. They had to change—

Tommy insisted. There were no strangers in his life. Each person he met was a new friend to greet with a happy hello, a handshake, and a funny little bow—and possibly a hug and a kiss if it was a pretty girl. And he never forgot a name.

Once the children understood that Tommy was more like them than he was different, they usually became good friends. In fact, he became the most popular little boy in town, certainly the best known. Boys and girls went out of their way to say hello and shake his hand; and they would call to him from the bleachers at games. The cheerleaders soon considered it good luck to exchange pregame hand-slaps with Tommy.

His heart overflowed with the joy of living. He simply could not walk down a street properly. He would stop to gaze at a window display, and then have to run to catch up to me. Deciding running was fun, he would go on to the corner, twirling his arms like propellers, laughing wildly, looking for all the world like a teddy bear set into motion by some special magic.

His childish joy with life both delighted and embarrassed my children, depending on where we were. They were entering an age where conformity of clothes and behavior were extremely important to their happiness. But there was no way on earth—or in heaven—that any of us could impress upon Tommy our needs for dignity and anonymity. It was as if he wanted to climb to a great height and cry out, "Look at me, world! I'm alive!"

But if his behavior embarrassed my children at times, they were not about to tolerate others making rude comments or teasing Tommy. One day in the park, I became aware of my children congregating around the bottom of a slide where a boy who was old enough to know better was tormenting Tommy. As I hurried toward them, the boy yelled, "I don't care! He's stupid!"

Kelly, my shy little daughter, shoved him. My oldest son, Jim, yelled, "He can't help it! He was born that way! What's your excuse?"

The children wondered how much of this hurt Tommy understood. Did he realize he was sometimes the object of laughter and ridicule? He must have sensed something was wrong. I saw a vague change in his eyes, but he was easily persuaded to forgive because what he craved more than anything else, was to be wanted and involved in living.

Tommy had a very low IQ. Today, at twenty-two, he still measures in the four-year-old range. We'd read books that defined Down's syndrome children as having "a degree of mental development confined to low levels." My mind shrank from such cold, clinical words because they did not show Tommy working doggedly in a daily struggle with hands that did not want to hold a pencil and a mind that did not want to remember the letters that make up simple words. He worked for two long years before he was able to print his first name and a row of numbers from one to ten—a feat many three-year-olds are capable of. Those cold words don't show the stubborn determination that pushed him through those endless days, weeks, and months of defeat before he reached that first great victory.

His childhood was made up of long years of struggles and defeats. He was twelve before he finally mastered first-grade math with the aid of toothpicks to count. It was about a year later, after I had long given up hope, when he suddenly made a fantastic mental jump and began to read. A vivid memory will stay with me of that Christmas, with the children sitting in a circle on the carpet, their tears running as they listened to him read a Dr. Seuss book.

And there were the three years of patient daily struggle with Big Tom's help before Tommy finally mastered the trick of tying his shoes. Looking back, my heart aches and my tears start again, thinking of both of them—my son, so endlessly patient but so determined, and Tommy, so willing and open, to try one more time, even after those three long, long years of daily failure.

Kelly became his other mother, helping and teaching in all the motherly ways things such as bathing, watching out for him on the school bus, teaching him to button and zip, guiding him through those long struggles with math and printing, reminding him to brush his teeth and take his medicine.

If the basic skills Tommy needed loomed in his path like huge mountains, a few things came easily. He always loved to sing and dance. His singing was atrocious, but his dancing always a magical delight. He was able to improvise very well. That clumsy, contrary body became suddenly graceful, almost lithe, as he interpreted the music.

He couldn't tap his foot in time to music, but he could do intricate games of clapping his hands. I watched him one sunny afternoon as he directed a baseball bleacher full of teenage girls in one of his games. It would not do for all the girls to make the same motions. That was too easy. Each row had to come in on Tommy's cue, like a singing round. He worked himself into a frenzy before their laughter made him realize they were deliberately throwing the beat to see him stomp his foot, wave his hands, and then give the motions again. He shook a tubby little finger at them and walked away, a picture of dejection. It worked, of course, and they called him back and gave him a perfect performance.

When Tommy was in his early teens, tragedy struck our family. My husband turned forty; and as sometimes happens, to men at that age, he found a younger woman. When he left us, the pain was like the death of a loved one. It was a death, in a way, because the man we had known was gone from us for good. It was then, as I sat in the ruins of my marriage, that I had to make a decision about Tommy. I had to go to work. I could not see any way to keep him. His school hours meant that he would leave the house for his bus after I was at work; he would be alone in the house for at least two hours every afternoon. Jim was away, in his first year at college. Big Tom and Kelly were in high school and Joey was in his first year of junior high. All three of them were very involved in after-school sports.

Even if I could resolve that major problem, what would happen when Tommy was older and stronger and I was older and weaker? Maybe it would be wiser and kinder to send him to the state home.

I finally made the hard decision. When Jim came home for a weekend, we sat around the dining-room table and I told the children that Tommy was going to the state home. They were so angry!

Even as they suffered through their own pain and grief, their objections were fierce, and they each expressed their pet concerns for Tommy. Who would zip his coat? Who would cut his meat? "They" wouldn't get his medication right—Tommy was epileptic. He wouldn't get the right kind of food, or have neat clothes, or a good school. He would forget how to read and add. He would hate it! It was Joey who gave voice to the protest that was behind all their worries: "He's our brother!" That both shamed me and put my heart at peace for the first time in a month. If the child had been born to me, the agonizing debate I had put myself through would never have occurred.

My children wanted Tommy to have the best chance at life on the "outside." They wanted him to be happy. Most of all, they wanted him to be with us. I had always loved my children, but it was then that I realized how much I liked them. They had become very special people.

So we began, my five children and I, to try to piece our lives back together. I found a job and began the day-to-day struggle of trying to exist on what a woman can earn while dealing with all the problems of a house, car, and the complicated transportation problems that arise with children living miles from town. Between us, though, we found ways to deal with Tommy's school schedule; he was put on a crash course to learn the basics of caring for himself—learning to tell time, learning the responsibility to getting himself outside to meet the bus. We discovered that, just like all of us, Tommy could grow and mature through tribulation.

Joey is in his last year of college now. The three older children have gone to college and begun their adult lives. Kelly and Tom have recently married;

and Jim is making plans to take that step soon. When they were gone, Tommy and I spent a long, lonely winter in that big old house in the country. Then, I sold it and bought a little cottage in town.

Two years ago, I remarried, having the great luck and joy to find a man who not only loves me dearly, but has taken Tommy into his home and heart as if he was his own. We recently moved to the East Coast, where Tommy is waiting to enter a sheltered workshop. He will be able to have a useful, productive life as an adult there. We hope someday he will be mature enough to be able to enjoy the fellowship of living in a group home.

At twenty-two, his main passions in life are still eating and coloring. Thank goodness he has lost his mania for cleaning the house! But he has become a pack rat, laying claim to anything lying around for too long that catches his fancy. At least we know where our missing things will be—in his room.

He misses his brothers and sisters, especially Kelly. She became enormously important in his life when I went to work. He writes to them, still gripping his pencil much as a first grader would, and printing the words carefully. The fact that he can think a thing through, and translate his thoughts to paper in an understandable form, is a major triumph in my eyes, bordering on the miraculous.

Everything that most of us take for granted in our lives is either impossible for Tommy or done only with great concentration after years of heartbreaking struggle and defeat. Not one of his skills—from dressing himself to acceptable table manners to writing a letter—has come easily. He cannot leave the house alone because he could never find his way back; and I doubt that he could, under the stress of being lost, remember his address so that anyone could help him. He can only carry on conversations with people outside the family if I am there to help in translating, because his speech is still very poor, thickened and mangled by an abnormally high palate and poor hearing. He has had two major reconstruction surgeries on his left middle ear, but he is nearly deaf on that side and is prone to infections.

He cannot deal with money. It takes enormous concentration for him to identify coins; and if given a choice he would always prefer twenty pennies to one piece of paper money. He will always have trouble manipulating his hands. Cutting up his food is hard for him. My husband introduced us to fishing and our first time out Tommy caught seven trout. He loves it! We have to bait his hook for him, but he is quite happy to sit in the boat or on the bank all day long, with or without bait, waiting for the thrill of that next strike.

I will soon be forty-nine, but I no longer have that fear of what will become of Tommy when my husband and I are gone. I know my children and their spouses would welcome him into their homes.

Big Tom's first child was born a year ago—a tiny, beautiful girl who looks out at the world with a happy smile and trusting, reaching arms. She has Down's syndrome. It hurts. Oh, how it hurts. But our passage through this new grief is made so much easier because of Tommy in our lives. Yes, we are all too aware of what that sweet little baby has ahead of her—the lifelong struggle to perform the simplest of tasks we all take for granted. But we are aware, too, of the simple, good, happy things that can be hers, and of what she can give to us.

I've read about Indian tribes who looked upon special needs children as special messengers from God. I understand that. You cannot look into Tommy's happy face, or gaze at that sweet baby's serenity, without experiencing a greater awareness of God's presence in your life. They stir us, make us reach down into our souls until we find the best part of us; and we emerge from the experience as better people. It is both humbling and exalting, a rich reminder of us to treasure God's greatest gift to us—life.   THE END

FIRST DAY
OF SCHOOL

Dear Steven,

This morning when I woke up, the early sunlight was turning the white bedroom walls to gold. But I didn't think of how beautiful it was. My first thought was one of fear. *Dear God*, I thought, *today is Steven's day, and I'm so afraid!*

You know how I love to lie in bed mornings, but today my fear made me leave your sleeping dad and walk to the window. *Maybe*, I thought, *there'll be an excuse to keep Steven home—a strong wind blowing, or storm clouds on the horizon.* But when I looked outside, Steven, the sky was blue and the soft colors of the sunrise filtered through puffy, white clouds. I knew there was no way I could possibly keep you safe at home.

To ease some of this terrible fear in me, I am writing you this letter. I may never show it to you, Steven, but I need to write it. I've written you letters before, you know, when you were in the hospital.

You were born there—just over six years ago—on

a day much like this one. You came into the world just before the sun rose. We'd gone to the hospital the night before, when the contractions began. Until then, everything had gone as expected.

Because we'd gone through your sister Joanne's birth four years before, Dad and I weren't nervous about your arrival. My overnight bag had been packed for a week with things I knew I'd need: nightgown, books, and a toothbrush.

Also in that bag were the tiny, new baby things that would clothe you when we brought you home. Your Nana Kate had sewn them for you. "Sure," she'd often said, "I could buy them—but why deny myself the pleasure? My grandchildren are special. They're going to get the best."

You know Nana, Steven. She was almost more excited than I was about your birth. I'll bet she was sitting right next to the phone that night because when Dad called her, the phone didn't even ring twice. "I'll be right over," Nana said. "How is Stephanie doing, Adam?"

Your dad laughed. "Everything is great, Mama," he told her. It was true—I felt wonderful! Joanne woke up when we kissed her good-bye, and mumbled that we were to bring home a "cuddly sister or brother." Nana said the same thing.

"Will it be Steven or Beth, Stephanie?" she teased as she hugged me.

I told her it would be Steven. I had known, you see, since the first time I felt you move inside me.

Dad drove carefully to the hospital. There seemed no reason to hurry. Everything was calm inside the hospital, too. Not until right before the delivery was there a problem. I, felt Dr. Riley, our pediatrician, stiffen. "Hold it," I heard him say.

"What's wrong?" I asked—gasped, really, because just then pain gripped me. Dr. Riley didn't say anything. "Is something wrong?" I persisted.

"Nothing, nothing, Stephanie—" But then he turned to the nurse beside him. "I've lost the baby's heartbeat. Let's get going—stat!"

Things moved fast! I was given an injection, and all I remember from that point is a blend of images and pain, of fierce lights that shone into my face, and Dr. Riley's voice saying, "Here it comes."

"My baby!" I tried to say, but my tongue wouldn't move or obey me. "My baby!" I tried again, and a nurse bent over me.

"It's okay, Mrs. Laurel. It's all over. You have a son."

I wanted to hold you in my arms, but they whisked you away and gave me another shot. I drifted off to sleep and I woke up a short while later to find your dad sitting next to me. "Adam?" I whispered. "The baby?"

He bent over me. "How do you feel, Stephanie?" he asked. I didn't answer—I wanted to know about you. "The baby's fine," he said. He paused a moment and repeated, "He's just fine."

I knew then that you weren't fine at all! I struggled to sit up, but your dad gently pushed me down. "Lie still, honey," he said. I begged him to tell me what was wrong. "He's okay," he said then. "He has a little problem with his heart."

Your dad looked really pale, Steven. I learned later that he had been awake for many hours, worrying about you and wondering what to tell me. Finally, he decided to tell me the truth. You were born with a massive heart defect, which required immediate surgery. A pediatric cardiologist had been called in, and he was examining you. "He'll be in to talk to us soon," your dad said. There was misery in his eyes, but he tried to look cheerful for my sake.

All we could do was wait and cling to each other. *Why?* I kept thinking. *Why is this happening to us?* I asked that question when Dr. Carter, the cardiologist, came in with Dr. Riley.

"One child in about five hundred is born with this disorder," he told us. There was sympathy in his eyes, but he was direct and matter-of-fact. "Sometimes we can put off surgery—wait to repair the damage. In Steven's case, we can't."

"You mean you're going to operate on him now?" I cried. Dr. Carter nodded, saying that you'd be moved to a bigger hospital, where they were better equipped for such an operation. "Can't you wait even a few days?" I pleaded. "He was just born!"

"Stephanie," Dr. Riley said softly, "it has to be done now. Otherwise, Steven doesn't have a chance." He patted my arm. "He's a feisty little guy. He'll make it."

When the doctors left, your dad and I just looked at each other, unable to speak. Finally, your dad said, "You hear about things like this happening, but you never think it can happen to you. It's supposed to happen to other people's kids, not your own." I leaned my head against his shoulder, and he said, "Stephanie, I think we both should go and see our boy and wish him well."

I nodded, knowing that this might be the first and last chance I'd have to see you.

FIRST DAY OF SCHOOL

Steven, you were so tiny! Watching you through the glass of the special unit where you'd been placed, away from the other babies, I fought back tears. "Good luck, Steven," I said. "Your dad and I love you."

That was the first time I saw you, Steven. The next was shortly after the operation. Oh, Steven, I thought I'd faint when I saw you through the glass window in the pediatric cardiology unit. Your chest was a network of bandage-covered incisions, your tiny heels raw from punctures for blood tests. I really cried, but Dr. Carter said he was pleased with the results.

"This boy is a fighter," he told your dad and me. He said that you'd undergone surgery, which had virtually saved your life, but that another operation would be necessary to correct your heart defect.

My mind reeled at the thought of more surgery. "When?" your dad asked, his lips set tightly.

"When he's older," Dr. Carter said, "we'll be able to do more work on him. For now—this is it." As he spoke, I looked at you—all hurt, bandaged, and raw. Your eyes were wide-open, and you were looking at me. There was no fear or pain in your eyes. Do you know, Steven, that even then I drew strength from looking at you?

You grew strong, too, Steven. You healed well, almost as if your will was stronger than your frail body. The nurses adored you. "Our darling," they called you, or "Little Steven." They would wait for me to come each day and tell me bits of good news. "Stephanie, do you know he's gained a full ounce?" or "Stephanie, he's so strong! Feel how hard he can grasp your finger!"

59

I was allowed to hold you and hug you gently. Wearing a special coat and mask, I whispered into your ear that we were all waiting for you. Joanne couldn't understand why you weren't home yet. She kept asking us, "Where's my little brother? Why haven't you brought him home?"

But if Joanne was worried when you were in the hospital, she was even more so when you came home. She took one look at you and her eyes opened wide. "Mom, what's wrong with him?" she gasped.

"You know, honey," your dad explained gently. "He's got a problem with his heart."

Joanne knew that. But she hadn't expected to see you looking so weak. "Is he okay?" she kept asking. We tried to reassure her, but her fears wouldn't leave her.

I had many fears, too. Before we took you home from the hospital, Dr. Riley gave us instructions. "Don't let him cry for very long," he warned. "Remember that he's had extensive surgery." Every time you cried, I jumped. So did Dad and Nana— when she was with us.

We didn't realize what all this was doing to Joanne until she came running inside one day, headed for her room, and slammed the door.

Nana looked at me. "I'll go see what's wrong," she offered. When she returned a few minutes later, she said, "Stephanie, go talk to her. She's had a fight with her friend Nicole. It seems that Nicole told her that Steven would grow up crippled because of his heart. Joanne's crying her eyes out."

I tried to comfort your sister, but the word "crippled" had worried me, too. After that, I watched you even more closely, Steven. Day and night, my ears were tuned to hear you cry, move—anything! Sometimes at night I'd wake from a deep sleep, run to your room, and bend over your crib just to hear you breathe. I had to reassure myself that you were alive! One time, Dad caught me at it. He came into the room while I was bending over your crib.

"Stephanie," he asked, "what's the matter? Is he sick?" I shook my head. "It's after two in the morning!" he then exclaimed. "You're going to make yourself sick, Stephanie."

"I thought I heard him—"

Your dad's voice was stern. "I know you heard him! I've seen you listening, Stephanie. Whatever you're doing—whether you're eating, talking to Joanne, or being with me, you're listening for Steven's cry."

I became angry, too. "You know very well why I run!" I choked on the words. "If he cries, it may hurt his heart!"

Your dad put his arms around me and drew me close to him. "Stephanie, I love that boy as much as you do. But we have to try to live normally—not just for our sakes, but for his, too! Your running whenever Steven moves has made us all jumpy. Poor Joanne looks lost and worn out. And as for Steven—"

There was a soft sound in the crib, and we saw that you were awake. Your eyes were wide-open, and you were watching us in an interested way. "Remember what Dr. Riley said about him?" your dad reminded me. "He's a fighter. Let him fight for himself, Stephanie. Don't hold him so tightly that you squeeze the fight out of him!" Then he began to chuckle. "Steven thinks so, too. See? He's grinning at us!"

And you were, Steven. Your smile had sunlight in it.

I tried to leave you alone a little bit more after that. It wasn't easy. I let you cry when I knew you were just fussing, even though each cry tore at my heart. When you could crawl, I forced myself to let you get your own toys, and I told Joanne to do the same.

She was proud of you, Steven. "Mom, Steven's crawling a lot better than Kyle," she'd tell me. Kyle was Nicole's baby brother—the girl who told Joanne you'd be crippled for life.

Sometimes I wished that you had less spirit—that you weren't so anxious to taste life. Even though your body tired more quickly than other babies', you were just as curious and always poking into things. Soon, you were toddling around with Kyle and playing—sometimes a little roughly.

Kyle's mother worried about you. "Honestly, Stephanie, how can you stand watching them?" she'd ask me. Whenever Kyle pushed you, she warned him, "Cut that out! Don't you know Steven's delicate?"

Everyone seemed to know that except you. But sometimes your determination wasn't enough. When you were three years old, a cold turned into pneumonia, and you were hustled back to the hospital. Your dad and I resumed our vigil as you again fought for life. Day passed into night without my even knowing. Dad went back and forth from the hospital to the house, but I stayed with you. He brought back messages from Joanne and Nana, and I wrote short notes to you. "Steven, we're all cheering for you. Joanne, Nana, Dad, and I love you so much. Steven, hang in there. You're a fighter, honey, and we know you can beat this."

You did, and you came home to us thin and frail, but determined to go on with the business of walking, playing, and eating as if you were completely normal. We tried to let you alone, but we all watched you carefully. Again, at night, I went to your room to listen to you breathe. How I prayed that you would keep on breathing—that you'd wake up the next morning.

I guess I was waiting for the next crisis to happen. But when it did, I was unprepared. You didn't get sick. You just announced on your fourth birthday that you wanted a bicycle. "Kyle's getting one," you said. "With training wheels. Can I have one, too?" Your eyes shone with excitement.

Your dad and I looked at each other. I remember thinking: Now what? Before this, you'd been happy to play at home with Joanne and your good friend, Kyle. But a bicycle?

"I don't know—" I began, and your dad added quickly, "You aren't big enough for a bike, champ!"

"I am so!" you exclaimed. Pulling yourself up as tall as you could, you said, "I'm almost as big as Kyle. Can't I have one, please?"

After you left the room, your dad said, "First, let's check with the doctor. Maybe it will be okay. A bike is a special thing to a boy."

But the doctor didn't agree. "Riding would put pressure on Steven's heart," he said. So that was that.

I watched your face when you saw Kyle's new bicycle. I expected you to cry, but you didn't.

FIRST DAY OF SCHOOL

Instead, you took to walking beside Kyle as he rode his new bike on the sidewalk. You walked slowly, which Kyle understood, and I didn't worry—not until one day when Joanne burst in with the news. "Mom! Did you know?" she asked. "Steven is riding Kyle's bike—he learned how! Come see!"

I'll never forget that moment, Steven. I raced out on the porch expecting to see you pale and gasping for breath. Instead, there you were, riding proudly on Kyle's bicycle! And the training wheels were off!

"Mom, I did it!" you shouted at me, and there was such triumph on your face that I couldn't scold you. We compromised after that. We bought you a bike with a special attachment that made pedaling easier. You and Kyle began to take short rides together. "Kyle's my best friend," you announced one day. "We made a promise. We're going to go to kindergarten together. We're going to ride the big bus together, too!"

Your eyes shone, but my heart sank. We lived half a mile from the school bus stop. How would you manage such a long walk each morning? I asked Dr. Riley, and he shook his head. "I don't advise it," he said. "Steven isn't strong enough yet."

It was a bad year for you. Before you could start kindergarten, you became ill and went back into the hospital. You were in and out of the hospital a lot that year. Kyle, bless him, sent you pictures of school, and little notes. I wrote you letters, too, full of news to make you laugh. You were learning to write, too, and once you sent me a note: "Hi, Mom. The nurse is helping me to write this. Love, your son, Steven."

We hoped that the doctors would authorize corrective surgery for you that year—surgery which would allow you to lead a more active life. But they still felt you weren't ready.

After your stay at the hospital, you returned home to recuperate. Eventually, you attended kindergarten part-time. I drove you to school each day and picked you up two hours later. You were bright and eager, and you worked hard until the teacher enthusiastically promoted you to first grade. "Mom," you told me, "next year I'm going to go on the school bus."

I said nothing, remembering the doctor's words. Nana agreed. "Let him have his dream," she said. "A year is a long time. Perhaps he'll get stronger." Joanne and Dad were optimistic, too. But, Steven, I kept on being afraid for you—afraid you wouldn't be strong enough to go to school, afraid of your terrible disappointment if you couldn't.

The months passed, and I registered you for the first grade. As Nana had predicted, you were stronger, but you still tired easily. Even riding your special bike was difficult at times. So when you asked me, "This year, can I ride to school on the bus?" I had to say no.

"Steven, I don't think so. But I can drive you, and—"

"Mom, it's not the same! I want to go on the bus with Kyle and the other kids!" You didn't say it, but I knew you were thinking: I want to be like other kids!

Your dad suggested we ask the doctor again. To my surprise, Dr. Riley didn't veto the idea. "If he walks slowly, it might be all right," he said. "Steven's older this year—stronger. He's going to need strength and self-confidence when it's time for

the corrective surgery we've been waiting to do."
Dr. Riley smiled at me. "Steven is a smart young
boy. He has a good idea of his strengths and weak-
nesses. Perhaps this time we should see just how
much he can do."

Your dad agreed with the doctor. Nana was still
worried, but she knew you should be given the
chance to be like other kids.

"If you don't, he'll be so upset it might hurt him
more than if you let him go," she pointed out. "You
could make him leave the house earlier and let
Joanne walk him slowly to the bus stop. Watch him
for a while and see how it works."

I knew Nana was right. Then, something happened that we hadn't counted on. A woman from
the office of the superintendent of schools called to
tell me that Steven would be picked up at home by
a special bus.

"The special bus services all handicapped children in our school system," she explained. "I just
wanted to make arrangements with you to make
sure Steven was scheduled on this bus route."

I was relieved, but slightly hesitant. "Steven wanted to ride the regular bus," I told her.

She sounded shocked. "Oh, no, Mrs. Laurel!" she
said. "We couldn't take the responsibility for someone in Steven's condition! With his heart problem . .
." Her words trailed off.

I thanked her and hung up. Now I wouldn't have
to worry about you not being able to walk to the regular bus stop! I didn't tell you right away. I put it off,
hoping for a good time to break the news. But you
found out on your own.

One late afternoon, I was finished with all my

housework and was watching a TV news show. You were out on the porch with Kyle, and I thought nothing of it when you came in and slammed the door behind you. *They've had a spat,* I thought. But you went straight to your room and closed the door—something you never did. "Steven?" I called, but there was no answer.

Just then, Joanne hurried over. "Mom, Steven's crying in his room," she reported. "What's wrong with him?"

Oh, no! I thought. *Is he sick? Is he in pain?* I hurried to your room and opened the door. You were huddled on your bed, crying. "Steven!" I gasped. But before I could ask what the matter was, you glared at me.

"Why didn't you tell me?" you cried. "Why didn't you tell me I had to ride the crippled bus?"

I winced at the cruel words. "Who told you that?"

"Some of the guys," you muttered and turned away, so I wouldn't see you cry, but I heard the catch in your voice. "I'm a handicap," he whispered. "That's what I am."

I wanted to say, "Steven, it's going to be all right," but the words didn't come. I bent to touch you, but you moved away. I left and went back to turn off the TV, feeling very alone in the sudden silence.

Until now, I thought, you never knew you were handicapped. You felt you could do things as well as anyone else. I remembered how you'd taught yourself to ride Kyle's bike. Now, you turned your face to the wall and wept.

For what seemed an eternity, you didn't want to do anything. You were too tired to play with Kyle, or ride your bike, you said. I took you to the doctor, but physically nothing was wrong.

As the first day of school approached, you became even more silent. Many afternoons, I felt tempted to call the superintendent of schools to ask him to reconsider letting you ride the regular bus. Other times, I told myself that he was right—you had to come to terms with your medical problem.

Then, one afternoon, I was listening to a radio talk show. The guest was a woman who headed a local group called PACCT—Parents and Cardiac Children Together. The group's goal was to aid parents of children with cardiac problems. PACCT had just started in our city, but the woman said there were many PACCT groups in larger cities.

"Many children are born with severe cardiac defects," she said. "That's a fact of life. Our group helps us live with the fact."

The show encouraged calls from its listeners. I was on the phone instantly. I didn't talk to the local chairwoman, but I learned the address of PACCT's office. When I telephoned for an appointment, I was invited to a meeting of PACCT parents in the area.

I had several misgivings before Dad and I went to the meeting; I shouldn't have had any. We met several parents who had kids like you, Steven, and sharing problems and solutions helped more than I can tell you! One woman had even had the same problem that we were dealing with now—the problem with the school bus!

"I knew my Sandy wanted to be like other kids more than anything else in the world," she told us. "She'd cry herself to sleep because she had to be driven to school each day."

She went on to explain that she'd taken her

daughter to meet both the superintendent and the principal of her new school. She'd also received written permission from her doctor for her daughter to ride the regular bus. "I worry each day Sandy walks to school, but it's worth it," she told me. "It's made her stronger and happier!" She paused. "It's worth trying, Stephanie."

After a lot of soul-searching, Dad and I decided to take this advice. I had a long talk with Dr. Riley, who wrote a letter to the superintendent of schools. Then I went to see the principal of your school. I took you with me, Steven, remember? You and Mr. Ross told elephant jokes to each other! I also told him not to worry about your health. "People feel that a child with heart problems might keel over dead," I said. "That won't happen—I've finally realized that. If Steven gets sick, it will happen gradually."

I don't know if what I said convinced Mr. Ross; maybe you won him over. He laughed at your eagerness. "If we had more students like Steven, we'd be one happy school," he said. Then he added that he would recommend that you be allowed to ride the regular bus.

You were full of joy, Steven, weren't you? "I'm going to go on the real bus!" you yelled when you saw your sister, Joanne. Later, Kyle came tearing in and you jabbered and laughed like your old self.

But I was still afraid. I'm afraid now, too. Last night, when Dad and I tucked you in, I saw the new sneakers by your bed—ready for their first walk to the school bus. My throat tightened with tears. I'm afraid not just for the walk, Steven. I'm afraid for the years ahead. Will you always have to walk more slowly than anyone else? How many times will you grieve over being "different"? As I kissed you, I said a prayer: *God, please let me be doing the right thing!*

All night I thought about you, Steven, and now it's morning. Soon it will be time to wake you. I'm still hoping I'm doing the right thing. Suppose you try this walk and you can't do it? How will you feel then?

But I think I know the answer to that. For someone like you, it's better to try and fail than never to try. Right from your first hour on earth, you had to try. You always were—always will be—a fighter. And me? I'll never stop worrying about you or being afraid for you. But like your dad said to me when you were a baby, I have to step back.

Soon I'll fix you a big breakfast. Then I will wave good-bye as you and Joanne leave the house. Even though I'll want to, I won't follow you to the bus stop. I'll watch you in my mind. The trees will shade your way, sunlight will make your path golden. You'll kick a stone and send it spinning. You'll laugh your happy little-boy laugh. When you get to the bus stop and you will—the yellow school bus will carry you away to school!

So—for now and always—I love you my beautiful, strong son.   THE END

ONE DAY MY PRINCE WILL COME

"I understand your predicament, Heather," he said in a low, hollow voice. "But if the baby's born before final exams, who will record my grades? I should interview for a new girl now. Nobody would take the job if she knew it was only for a few weeks."

Nobody would take it if she knew what a jerk you are, either, I thought bitterly. Besides handling his students' records, I typed articles the professor submitted to historical magazines. He was a poor speller, and no scholarly publication would buy Dr. Drew's work if I didn't correct his grammar and overblown style. But he took my skills for granted. Just like he assumed that since I was divorced and pregnant, I considered it a privilege to accept his tiny paycheck. The last few months had been torture, working in his windowless office that reeked of cigars. I'd been counting the days till my last one at the end of the semester.

I sighed and turned the key; my old car sputtered before settling into a rumbling roar. With a final angry thought of Dr. Drew, I backed out of the parking space. There was a loud crunch. I was thrown against the wheel and in a panic, I stared into my mirror. *Of all the cars in this lot, I hit an expensive-looking foreign job!* I thought.

I swallowed hard. Then I shifted into drive and floored the gas pedal. I knew it was wrong—I knew I should stay and take my licks from the owner. But how could I pay for his fancy fender when I couldn't afford a muffler from the discount store? With my heart hammering, I raced toward the exit. Suddenly, two guys were swearing loudly as they jumped in front of my car. I jammed on the brakes. One was tall and terribly handsome, while the other was stockier. He pounded on my window. "What do you think you're doing?" he hollered. "That's my car back there—the one with the bashed-in fender. I saw you hit me. Get her license number and call the cops, Morgan."

The good-looking man ran back to the car. I rolled down my window, fully expecting the shorter man to strangle me, mad as he looked. "I-I'm sorry," I whispered, "but I just lost my job and I was upset—"

"You leave the scene and then expect me to fall for your tearful story? Tell it to the judge, sweetheart." He pounded the roof of my car and whirled around to look at his. "You're blocking traffic. Pull into that spot you just left. And don't try anything stupid."

Carefully, I inched back toward the building. Everything was happening in slow motion, like a nightmare I couldn't wake up from. All I could think was: *Why me? Why did this all come down on my shoulders?*

ONE DAY MY PRINCE WILL COME

My car chugged to a stop and died in the parking space. Several customers had come out of the restaurant, but I was too embarrassed to look for Dr. Drew. He probably wouldn't help me anyway. I saw the red-and-blue flash of a campus patrol car. Wrapping my sweater tighter against the raw March wind, I walked over to where the fancy car owner was ranting at the policeman.

The officer studied me while he listened to the guy's story. Then he walked to the front end of the dented car.

"Yes, Mr. Bramley, she did smack into you. But that doesn't change the fact that you parked by a fire hydrant, does it?" the officer said.

Bramley's jaw dropped. "Don't tell me—you're going to let her off and give me a ticket?" His gaze fell accusingly on my bulging stomach, as though he thought I was getting preferential treatment because of it.

"I'll need both of your driver's licenses," the patrolman replied. "Meanwhile you two can discuss whose insurance company will cover the damage. You have every right to press charges, Mr. Bramley. Either way, you'll pay for parking illegally. Had you not been here she couldn't have hit you. Right?"

The officer's attitude wasn't helping my case. The man beside me glared at me with icy eyes, his jaw hardening. Bramley was a rich college kid, judging by his designer jeans and cashmere sweater, and he would've been cute if he'd turned his glare down a notch or two. He yanked a pad from his pocket and thrust a pen at me. "Do you have insurance?" he asked.

"Y-yes, of course. It's illegal to drive without it," I stammered.

"You call leaving the scene legal? Hope you're not too attached to that clunker—you may have to sell it to afford the premium hike after you buy me a new fender. You picked a rotten time for this, sweetheart." He frowned impatiently. "Well, go on—give me your name, number, and insurance company."

I could understand his anger, because I had been wrong. And I'd hurt his pride by putting a nasty dent in his car. But his attitude irked me. "Maybe I should take your name, too. In case the baby or I were injured when we were thrown into the steering wheel. Owning a midget sports car doesn't give you the right to park illegally."

His eyes froze over and he scribbled the information on another slip of paper. We exchanged names; he read mine and snorted. "Miss McVeagh?"

"It's Mrs. McVeagh."

"Good. Maybe your old man will keep you off the streets now. Pregnant as you are, you probably had the seat back too far to reach the brake."

Anger heated my cheeks. The officer was coming back with our licenses, so I knew better than to sound off. "I'm sorry about your car," I said coldly. "I hope we can settle this soon because I have enough to worry about without listening to your insults, Mr. Bramley."

"See you in court, sweetheart," he jeered.

It was a wonder I got to Mrs. Campbell's boardinghouse without hitting someone else, upset as I was. I lumbered up the stairs to my room. Once inside, I rolled onto the bed, tightening myself into a ball around the baby. I was shaking all over, from nerves and because my landlady didn't keep the upstairs very warm.

It had been the worst morning I could remember, first losing my job, and then hitting a loudmouthed rich kid's car. Seth Bramley, the paper had said. Even his name sounded wealthy—and vaguely familiar. His family was probably connected to the university, which meant my name would be swinging on the faculty grapevine by tomorrow. I'd probably never get another job in this town. I wondered if Seth had seen through my bravado about being married; I wouldn't have mentioned that outdated fact except it made me look like a more solid citizen, considering my condition. Not that it mattered. Johnny McVeagh taught me that keeping up appearances is a losing proposition.

I met Johnny last fall and fell for his handsome looks immediately—which was easy for a college senior to do when her math tutor bent the rules to ask her out. We complemented each other perfectly: he helped me pass a required algebra class, and I edited and typed his research papers for his graduate-course work.

"The professor thought this report read like a novel," he said when he received an A on the first one I helped him with. "Looks like I just hired a ghostwriter. What do you say?"

His easy drawl seduced me as quickly as the sexy smile he wore. "I don't intend to write under somebody else's name all my life," I teased. "Someday I'll have a real novel out."

Those are sweet dreams to anybody who writes. Almost as sweet as the kiss he was giving me, which slowly turned into our first time making love. I fell in love with Johnny. He was handsome, intelligent, and studying to be a computer-software designer. And he was interested in my ambitions, too. Not like the guys I knew who cut morning classes but never missed a party. Neither of us was as smart as we thought, though; toward the end of September I knew I was pregnant.

I was in tears when I told him. But the way Johnny handled it made me love him even more.

"Don't worry, honey," he whispered as he held me that night. "We'll make it. By the time we graduate we'll have our careers mapped out and a family, too. Nobody else I know can say that."

Nobody I knew wanted to say that, but I was too troubled to realize it. Since Johnny's folks were divorced, we wore our wedding rings to my parents' house for Thanksgiving. They gave us an even bigger surprise by asking us to leave before dinner.

"If you want to waste your whole life on some Romeo, I'm not paying for it," my dad said as he held the door open. "How can anybody so intelligent be dumb enough to get herself in trouble her senior year? And don't come home again until you can apologize to your mother."

I looked at Mom. Her trembling lips told me I'd disappointed her, but she still loved me. She'd never go against what Dad said, though. Johnny and I returned to the apartment for sandwiches and so many endless, silent nights. We'd counted on their tuition money to get us through our second semester, because Johnny's tutorial salary was barely enough to cover our rent and food. I'd been working for Dr. Drew since school started, but that was only twenty hours a week at minimum wage.

Neither man was thrilled with the way morning

sickness stole my energy, but Johnny gave up on me first. He walked to the computer lab to take his semester exam and literally disappeared. His friends swore he took his test; they thought he went for a drink afterward, but from there on they all drew a blank. I heard from a California lawyer after the holidays. Johnny wanted a divorce. The lawyer wouldn't reveal Johnny's address or circumstance, except to say it was a no-fault arrangement, with no alimony. I couldn't afford to fight it, so I let him go. When I pawned my wedding ring, I discovered it was as phony as his love had been.

That left me at Dr. Drew's mercy for the second semester. I was divorced, pregnant, and broke—a victim of a three-month marriage that shattered my life. It was too late for an abortion, and too late to crawl back to my folks in time to finish my education. By working as many hours as I could, I was able to afford a couple of meals a day and a room in Mrs. Campbell's boardinghouse. But not for much longer—the landlady had a rule about no pets or kids. She'd been eyeballing my stomach lately.

That left me with Johnny's rumbling clunker, and a small checking account I'd been smart enough to keep in my own name. I was saving that money for the baby's doctor fees, so I was hardly able to buy Seth Bramley a new fender. He was probably right—I would have to sell the car when the next insurance notice came. With all the problems I'd had lately, I wondered how I'd faced up to Seth. I guess his rudeness and the fact that he'd been ticketed made me bolder than usual.

Would he take me to court? If he did, he wouldn't win much. Maybe being broke had its advantages.

The thought helped me drift off into a much-needed nap.

I was jolted awake by pounding on my door. "Heather, you've got a phone call," Mrs. Campbell said. "Don't tie up the line. Five minutes."

Struggling, I sat up. The carpet on the stairs was worn and slick, so by the time I eased down them my caller was impatient. "Mrs. McVeagh? Do you always keep people waiting?" It was Seth.

"It took my answering service awhile to reach me," I replied tersely. I kept my voice low, watching the landlady load the dishwasher. "What do you want now, Mr. Bramley?" I asked him.

There was a cheerless laugh. "I was going to let the insurance companies handle the situation. Until I discovered that you're not only careless and sneaky, Mrs. McVeagh, but you're a liar, too. Your policy was canceled for nonpayment."

I felt like someone had kicked me in the stomach. "I didn't know," I gasped. "Please believe me—my husband walked out—he must've let it expire—" I turned so Mrs. Campbell couldn't see my tears. "I didn't intend to worm out of this. Really. What—what do I do now?" I asked.

He was quiet for a moment. "The replacement parts I need will run me eight-hundred dollars. I don't want to go to court any more than you do—I'm leaving town next week. If you can meet me with the money—cash—before Sunday night, I'll consider it settled. Otherwise I'll have to turn it over to my attorney. And don't think that baby'll win you any sympathy in court."

I swallowed hard. Raising eight-hundred dollars over the weekend was impossible, but with the baby due in two months, I couldn't drag this thing through court, either. Mrs. Campbell cleared her throat impatiently.

"Okay—Sunday then. Where do I meet you?" I asked.

Seth gave me his address, and we set three o'clock as the time. I hung up, trembling so badly I wondered how I'd make it back to my room.

"More man problems, Heather?" My landlady's voice was casual, but it had a suspicious edge.

"Isn't that all men are good for? Problems?" I felt like she and everyone else was against me. They wanted me out of the way before my checks bounced or my baby interrupted their comfortable lives.

When I got to my room I slid into the rocker, hugging my unborn child. "What are we going to do?" I murmured as I swayed forward and back. I gazed at my swollen belly as though it were a crystal ball. But the answer would only be found in the black-and-white of my bankbook. With Dr. Drew's latest check, I had six-hundred-and-fifty dollars to my name. If I gave it all to Seth Bramley, I'd have nothing for food or rent till my last check arrived in two weeks—not to mention money for the baby's delivery.

I went to the bank Saturday morning to close out my account. I'd thought about skipping out like Johnny had, but how far would I get with six-hundred dollars and seven months of maternity weighing me down? I stared at the crisp bills and kept twenty back; I had to have money for food, even if my rent was late. It was horrible knowing that everything I had was worth less than a fender on Seth

Bramley's sports car.

When my car coughed up his driveway Sunday afternoon, I was still short almost two-hundred dollars and an explanation. I looked at the three-storey brick house with its manicured lawn, and my spirits sank even lower. People who lived like this, even if they just rented the third-floor apartment, as Seth did, didn't want to be bothered with small change like me. I sighed and slowly climbed the back stairs.

When the door swung open, I got quite a shock—the place was a mess! The carpet was littered with scraps of paper and clothes were strewn everywhere. A half-eaten sandwich had died on the coffee table days ago. The air smelled foul—like old sweat and dirty socks. I was afraid to look into the kitchen.

Seth grinned sheepishly. Then he resumed his impatient scowl. "I wasn't sure you'd show up. But this saves us both a lot of hassles." He took the envelope from my hand. "Yeah. But I—"

"Hey, you're short, sweetheart. There's only six-hundred dollars here."

My cheeks flamed as I glared at him. "You think I can't count? I may be divorced, pregnant, and broke, but I'm not stupid. And I'm not your sweetheart."

That shut him up, but only for a moment.

"I won't let you rip me off—"

"You'll probably never go hungry because the sandwich machine ate your last quarter, either," I said, my eyes narrowing. "I bet your parents pay your rent and tuition, and you probably hire somebody to shovel out this sty so you can impress your dates after you wine and dine them. You and your fancy sports car—" I turned abruptly. Angry tears were streaking down my cheeks.

"I gave you next week's rent as it is," I went on. "Mrs. Campbell will probably boot me out when she hears I'm losing my job on top of paying her late. That's all I've got. I'll send you the rest when I can."

The silence was almost as stifling as the smell of the dirty clothes. Seth's eyes bored into my back. "When's the baby due?" he asked quietly.

My shoulders went limp. "In the middle of May."

"Less than two months, huh?" He sighed and came around in front of me. "Mrs. McVeagh, I—"

"Knock it off. My name's Heather."

His eyes widened. He controlled his temper, though. "I'm starting courses at a business school upstate tomorrow. It's sort of a sudden decision, and I'll have to forfeit my damage deposit here, obviously." He looked around the messy room and then back at me. "That's two-hundred bucks. If you would be willing to clean this place up, I'd get my deposit back and we'd be even."

I glanced cautiously toward the kitchen.

"There's nothing contagious here. It's mostly surface dirt, honest."

I blinked, looking into calm eyes and a face that was cute in its natural way. And he actually had a sense of humor. "Sounds like that's my only choice. What's the catch?" I asked.

Seth stuck his hands in his jeans pockets. "I can't get blood out of a turnip. This way it's settled fair and square." A whimpering noise came from the direction of the bedroom. Seth kept studying me. "Do you like dogs, Heather?" he finally asked.

"I guess so. Why?"

He gestured for me to follow him to the other room, kicking a T-shirt out of our path. Sprawled across one pillow of his unmade bed was a golden retriever dog. "This is Lucky," he said as he sat beside her. "I had her spayed Thursday and she's still a little sore."

"Poor girl," I crooned, smiling when her ears perked up.

Seth looked at me with an odd expression on his face. "Like I said, this move came up suddenly or I wouldn't have bought her in the first place. I can't take her to my new apartment, and the couple downstairs works full-time. The landlord doesn't want her, so I guess I'll have to drop her off at the pound."

My face fell. "You can't find her a home?"

"I haven't got the time. Unless you'd want to stay here with her while I run an ad." He stroked the dog. "My rent's paid through May. There's no sense showing her till she's on her feet again; meanwhile, you could feed her and clean the apartment. I'll call the ad in to the paper, but then, it'd be a lot of trouble for you."

"No, it wouldn't," I piped up.

Seth grinned like I'd played right into his hands. "You'll do it? I'd much rather see her go to a good home than the pound. You could walk her after your classes."

"I—I quit school."

He shrugged. "So you'll just have the apartment and Lucky to look after. Shall I tell my landlord that's our deal?"

A grateful smile spread across my face. Then I sobered. "What about the rent? I could never repay you for the month I'd be living here."

"That's your dog-sitting fee. Better say yes before I change my mind."

"All right, I'll do it. But I still don't believe this is happening. There's got to be a catch."

"Look around you and tell me you won't earn it," he said with a chuckle. Then he, too, must've remembered why I came here. "But don't get too attached to the arrangement. The dog has to go, and you'll need another place before the baby's born. I'm allergic to kids."

So I moved in. When I plopped down on Seth's couch Monday afternoon, I doubted it was such a good idea. His stuff was everywhere—I wondered what he'd taken to his new place—and after six hours of Dr. Drew I was in no mood to clean. He'd paraded two girls through his office today, applicants for my job. His false smile left no doubt that he'd gladly let me quit early.

But I needed the cash, just like I needed Seth's messy apartment till I could find someplace else. Mrs. Campbell hadn't shed any tears when I packed, either. Nobody wanted a twenty-two year old failure hanging around, mooching every chance she could. That's what they seemed to think, anyway.

Lucky was gazing at me with big eyes. She hopped up beside me, ignoring the clutter on the couch. "Well, girl, it's just you and me. And baby makes three," I mumbled, stroking her coat. "We'll open the windows before we take your walk. Maybe it'll smell better when we get back."

It didn't, but the exercise perked me up. I fixed a sandwich from food that looked reasonably recent in the fridge. Then I picked up the clothes, and sorted them into piles. I didn't have the energy to trot back and forth from the basement, so Lucky and I went downstairs for the evening, dropping huge garbage sacks of smelly clothes ahead of us.

Nobody else was there. When I'd loaded all four machines, I picked up an old magazine and sprawled in a lawn chair with my feet up on another one. It felt good to let it all hang out, but then I noticed a man in the doorway.

"You're Seth's temporary housekeeper?"

I straightened up, tugging self-consciously at my maternity top. Then my mouth fell open. It was the good-looking man who'd been at the scene of the crime. "I didn't expect to see you again."

"I own the building," he said with a casual shrug. "I'm Ash Morgan, your new landlord."

I shook his hand, amazed that a guy his age owned such a large, well-maintained house. "I'm Heather McVeagh. I—I hope it's alright that I moved in. It must look sort of shady to you, but I promise—"

Ash laughed and pulled up another chair. "This is a college town—anything's possible when it comes to tenant combinations. And your work's cut out for you. Seth's my best friend, but he's the biggest slob I know." His eyes lingered on me. "He says you paid up, and saved Lucky from the pound. It looks like you handled the situation a lot more gracefully than Seth did last Friday."

Coming from a man with a voice that flowed like hot syrup, his words were the nicest I'd heard in months. I couldn't help thinking he should be sipping cocktails in a ritzy bar, wearing a tux—and talking to a girl much skinnier than I, and certainly not pregnant. "He had a right to be mad. I didn't watch where I was going."

"Still, his temper didn't solve anything. He had other problems on his mind and he took them out on you." The washer creaked and stopped spinning. Ash stood up. "Don't be a stranger, Heather. Leave the laundry down here. I'll bring it up later, so you won't strain yourself on the stairs."

He later commented about my progress in the war on filth when he dropped off the laundry.

I went to bed with Ash Morgan's gorgeous face on my mind—knowing, of course, that his smiles wouldn't lead anywhere. I was so taken with him that I wasn't particularly curious about Seth Bramley's problems. But I found out about them firsthand the following Thursday night.

I was sacking up trash, finally able to say the place looked presentable. When I lifted the first bag out onto the landing, I knew better than to carry it any further. I called Ash to help me.

After he carted the trash to the curb, he ran the sweeper for me. Then he flashed me one of his wonderful smiles. "Do pregnant woman like to eat pizza?" he asked. "I haven't had dinner yet, and I hate to eat alone."

Knowing how many other girls would've fought for the chance to join him, I called the nearest place that delivered. We talked on the couch while we waited. I could forget about despicable Dr. Drew and all my other problems when I heard his creamy-rich voice. And while we ate, it was like he forgot about my shape and was interested in me.

"What were you doing before Johnny led you on?" he asked, focusing his sparkling eyes on me.

"I was a senior, majoring in English and hoping to be a big-name writer someday. I gave up my dreams when I found out I was pregnant," I added, patting my belly.

Ash smiled kindly. "You never know when you might be able to follow your ambitions again. I was your typical ninety-eight-pound weakling who dreamed of being a movie star when I was a kid. Now I'm a model. In fact, I'm leaving for some jobs in New York next week."

My mouth dropped open. It made perfect sense that a man so good looking and immaculately groomed would end up modeling. What didn't make sense was that he was spending his time with me. "Pardon me while I stare," I said, chuckling. "You do fashion shows and ads? Like a cover boy?"

"You guessed it." Ash's eyes twinkled. "Looks glamorous, but the work's a bore sometimes. There're a lot of plastic people in my business, so self-absorbed they can't talk about anything except how much iron they pump or how many women they—well—"

He chuckled and guided another slice of the steaming pizza onto my plate. "It's so nice to meet a woman like you, Heather. Sure, you've got problems, but you stand up to them. You don't let them get you down."

Lost in his gaze, I held my breath, hoping he'd let me swallow before he kissed me. Then somebody pounded on the door and barged in before we could move.

A middle-aged woman in a crisp, gray suit stared accusingly at us. "So it's true," she said in a venomous voice. "There's a tramp in my son's apartment, leeching off him. And entertaining another man while he's away."

Ash stood up. "Let's get the facts straight before we blow this out of perspective, Ruth. First, let me introduce Mrs. Heather McVeagh. Heather, this is Seth's mother."

I nodded, wrapping a protective arm around the baby. Lucky moved closer to my leg.

The woman was unimpressed. "Why are you letting her stay here, Ash, when you know Seth won't be back? She's living on his rent—my money, really—and I want her out. What is this, some sleazy way for you to profit from Seth's leaving town?"

The heat rose in Ash's face. His words were clipped. "You must've heard about the fender bender and traced Heather through faculty gossip. The lady's paid up, Mrs. Bramley. And she's saved Seth his damage deposit by shoveling out his mess. The lease and utility agreements have been changed to her name, and she's several months ahead on rent. Since Seth is gone, what's the point of harassing us? We were only talking over dinner."

Knowing better than to ask questions, I stared at our intruder. Mrs. Bramley's eyes probed my middle; she snorted in disgust. "If I find out that anything you've said isn't true, Ash Morgan, I'll have the city council rescind your multiple-family zoning. Count on it."

I winced when the door slammed. Ash sank down on the couch, running his fingers through his hair. "At times like these, a rugged-looking pose comes in handy," he said with a nervous laugh.

I scowled. "How can you make jokes? She'll check around and know you lied."

"Nope. I told her nothing but the truth." He leaned his head on the back of the couch, looking at me. "You weren't supposed to know all that stuff, Heather. So if Seth comes back for some underwear, act dumb. Okay?"

"But I didn't pay—"

"Sure you did. That cash you gave Seth is now in my account. Your rent is paid. He gave it to me and changed the lease. He said he had enough saved up to buy his fender without your money." Ash smiled and took my hand. "Keep these details to yourself. The university grapevine must be in full swing for Ruth to storm over here so soon. She's head of the education department; her husband, Philip, is in music history. They kicked their oldest son out for marrying a girl after he got her pregnant. So much for a guy doing the honorable thing, huh? Guess she doesn't want Seth following in his big brother's footsteps."

I shook my head. "I don't get it. Did Seth know he was leaving town before I hit his car?"

Ash chuckled and reached for the pizza. "It's another of her crusades. She and Philip envisioned Seth as an attorney. They said they'd pay for law school, but refused to recognize his manual skills— the guy's an ace mechanic. When he wanted an advanced degree in business, so he could manage his own chain of shops, they branded him a perpetual student. They refused to foot the bill. Seth struck back by quitting school here and enrolling in a business college up north. The Bramley family is full of ups and downs."

I leaned back to let all this information sink in. Then Ash gave me another slice of pizza. I took a bite, gazing at Ash while I chewed. His eyes gazed at me; his lips parted to reveal even, white teeth. And then he was kissing me, moaning low in his throat before pulling away sooner than I wanted him to.

"Ash, I—"

"That didn't happen, all right?" he whispered. "Before I get carried away, I've got a favor to ask."

I looked at him, waiting.

"I'm leaving Monday morning, and I was wondering if you'd manage the building while I'm gone. Seth always did. It just involves calling somebody if something goes wrong. Can you handle that?" he asked.

"Yeah," I murmured.

"Thanks, Heather." He gave me another light kiss and left.

I had such a crush on Ash it didn't faze me to collect my last paycheck on Friday. It was silly to stare out my windows, listening for his car all weekend. But at least when I dreamed about Ash, who'd kissed me and defended my honor, I wasn't fretting about being lonely and broke. I saw Ash on Monday before he left for New York on business, when he gave me a list of repairmen and his keys. No kisses, but the visit fueled my fantasies the whole week he was gone.

Sunday night I went to bed still hearing his mellow voice, seeing his handsome face before we kissed, and remembering the feeling of holding each other close. In the middle of the night my eyes flew open. Was that click real or had I been dreaming? I pulled the sheet closer, wondering why Lucky wasn't curled up beside me or barking. I must've imagined the noise.

Then I stiffened. That was definitely the front door opening and closing. My heart skipped a beat and then pounded wildly. *Who's here? Why didn't he knock? Better pretend I'm asleep and hope he takes what he's after instead of hurting me.* I squeezed my eyes shut and held my breath. Footsteps approached the bedroom.

Heavy, irregular breathing paused at the door. I opened my eyelids enough to see a man's shape in the darkness. But he wasn't casing the dresser or the closet—he was shuffling toward the bed. The moment he dived for the other side I hit the floor. And screamed.

The guy grunted; his arm flopped over my pillow. "Not to worry, sweetheart. It's only me."

I clutched at my sheet, still shaking. It was Seth!

He belched. There was a strong odor of alcohol.

I snatched my pillow and went out to the couch, nearly tripping over Lucky in the doorway. She'd recognized her owner before he'd unlocked the door, and had gone back to sleep. But it took me a long time to drift off.

I woke up to a stubble-faced, hung-over Seth Bramley, who was watching me from his seat on the floor. Tired as I was, I almost ordered him out of the apartment. But he wore such a pathetic expression.

"About last night—" he mumbled, rubbing his red eyes. "I got off to a bad start. Can we talk about it over breakfast? My treat?"

I pulled the afghan over my body, grimacing at his wrinkled clothes. "Can I get you some coffee?"

He tried to smile. "Some coffee would help, if it's not too much trouble."

ONE DAY MY PRINCE WILL COME

It's Monday morning—why isn't he in class? I wondered as I made the coffee. Seth didn't appear to be up for any questions when he came out of the bathroom, though. It took all his concentration to keep his towel wrapped around him as he reached for his mug. By the time I'd showered and dressed, my guest had come back to life. He smiled, escorting me down to a bottle-green convertible.

"A new car?" I asked as he opened my door.

"A new fender," he teased lightly. "Thought I'd give her a fresh coat of paint while I was replacing it."

He drove up to a diner outside of town, where we chatted over waffles. Seth seemed relaxed—not a bit like the hotheaded snob I'd first met. After breakfast he offered me a ride through the countryside. We drove around curves, laughing, with the breeze blowing through our hair. It was a beautiful spring day, and for the first time since my divorce I felt alive—really happy and having fun. He pulled into a little park and killed the engine.

"It's great to see you smile, Heather," he said, looking across at me. "I haven't given you much reason to do that, and I'm sorry I've been such a jerk. I hope things'll fall into place now."

Seth leaned back in his seat, continuing in a thoughtful tone. "I was mad at my folks when I met you, peeved that they'd pay for their dreams but not for mine. I don't want to be a lawyer! I'm a mechanic. I was certain an advanced degree in business would help me set up a chain of automotive shops. And, as you probably noticed, I flew off the handle before I thought about what I was doing. Quitting school wasn't the right answer, but it helped me see that a business degree wasn't, either. Are you following this?" he asked.

I nodded, noting the intensity in his eyes.

"I'm back at the shop where I used to work during the summer. My old boss gave me a chance to fix up the car, and then offered me full-time work. I took it, because I've got a shot at being the foreman before the summer's over." Seth smiled and reached for my hand. "I owe you for this, Heather. Your speech about how I never had to support myself woke me up. I don't need that fancy degree—no matter who pays for it—and I decided it was time to stand up to my parents and live life my way." His hand was warm, slightly calloused, but tender, as it squeezed mine.

"What about your degree from the university? It's a shame to waste it so close to graduation."

"Yeah. That's why I got today off—so I could talk to my professors about finishing the work. There was a special lady I wanted to see, too."

I stared at him. "I—I'm not sure I understand, Seth."

"Of course you don't. Because as usual, I'm forging blindly ahead." He lifted my hand to his lips, placing delicate kisses on my fingertips. "Heather, I—I was hoping we could see more of each other because, well—you see things so clearly, and you don't take any crap. That's not a romantic thing to say, but I respect that in a woman. Do you understand? Can you believe I really like you after the crude remarks I made when we met?"

"Maybe if you explained why you came stumbling in last night—"

"Another bad move." Seth shook his head. "I got

sidetracked when Ash asked me in for a drink, and one kept leading to another. Sounds like his trip to New York was one big party. Why couldn't I have been born with his face?" He chuckled, and then looked at me for a long time. "You like him, don't you? Why, you're blushing!"

"Well, he is a nice guy," I stammered. My face got two shades redder. "I mean, he helped me carry the trash out of your apartment. And he was sympathetic about me losing my job with Dr. Drew."

"What'd you do for that old guy?" he asked.

"Secretarial stuff. And I edited his historical articles before he submitted them to magazines."

"I'd bet that's where my mom heard you were living at my place. He's in her bridge club. Ash told me about her surprise visit." A sad smile settled on Seth's face. "He also told me about how you didn't knuckle under to her, and about your writing. I should've known he'd do this—he gets women without even trying. Now I feel like a real idiot, talking to you this way."

"Seth, that's not true—"

He started the car, wearing a hurt expression. "We might as well head back. Ash probably told you so much about my family history that you'll never be interested in me. Some guys have all the luck."

On the way home I tried to think of something positive to say. "Oh, I haven't gotten any calls about Lucky."

"I'd better run that ad. I was hoping we could keep her." He pulled into the driveway, staring ruefully ahead.

"Do you want me to move, since you're back in town?"

"Nope. A deal's a deal. I've got a bunk above the garage. By the way, the apartment looks terrific. Thanks."

Talk about feeling two inches tall. "Seth, this isn't fair. I'll get my old room back and have Ash refund your rent. I—" He shot me another wounded look. "Sorry. He told me you paid ahead and changed the lease. That's the biggest break I've gotten in months, and I feel terrible about—"

"It's something I wanted to do for you," he answered quietly. "Come on, let me help you up those stairs. There's no sense in dragging this out."

It was a silent climb to the third floor, made more tense because a vase of red roses was waiting beside the door. I tried not to act overly eager as I opened the card.

"They're from Ash, aren't they?"

"Yeah. Seth, I'm sorry—"

"Why? You certainly deserve flowers, after all the bad times you've had lately. No hard feelings, right?" He kissed me softly on the cheek. As his sneakers thumped mournfully down the steps, I sensed I'd ruined a friendship before it'd even gotten started.

The little card said to come downstairs. After I set the roses inside, I knocked on Ash's door. He was wearing a silk shirt that set off his eyes, and a suave smile.

"Hey, babe! Any problems while I was gone?" he asked.

"No. The roses are beautiful."

"Just a little something for your time. I have another proposition for you. How was Seth? He drank so much last night, I'm surprised he's walking today."

I looked away, slightly annoyed by his tone. Maybe he hadn't come down from being in New York yet.

"Not that it matters. How would you like to be my housekeeper, Heather? I'll be traveling a lot these next few months, and it'd be nice to come home to a clean place and a pretty woman—I mean, I'd pay you, too." His smile was devilish.

"You'd want to share your apartment with a baby?"

"You're keeping it?" he asked. Then the phone rang. Ash strode over to answer it. He grinned and turned his back. "Sure, doll. You know I'll be there," he crooned into the receiver. "We'll meet at my place around three. Wear that slinky little—"

I didn't stay to hear about what she would wear. As I slipped out, I kicked myself for not anticipating this. Of course, he had a place in New York, with any number of housekeepers. And if he thought I'd give up my baby to play maid and lover for him here, he didn't know me very well. I went up the stairs, sorry that I'd been so infatuated with Ash that I hadn't taken Seth more seriously.

I hadn't been taking myself seriously, either. Here I was, more than eight months along with no future plans beyond my apartment lease. I'd drifted into one bad situation after another—a doomed marriage, a thankless job, a playboy who assumed I'd love to clean his house for him. What happened to the educated woman who'd planned to write? How was I going to support myself—and my baby?

I plopped down on the couch, stroking Lucky's silky ears. Seth's words about standing up to problems and living life your own way came back to me.

He was a far better example of that than I. If only I'd acted more interested—he'd done so much for me—he probably would've helped me through the lean times ahead. Seth wasn't coming back, though. Men don't risk wounding their egos for a woman twice. So it was up to me to get my act together. After losing out on two men in one day, I wasn't sure I could handle that.

All I could do on Monday morning was wallow on the couch. I was in no condition to look for a job. Everything hurt—my back, my legs, and my feet. My thoughts throbbed through my head. Looks like my next trip will be to the welfare office. I let out a loud, pitiful groan.

"Heather, are you all right?"

I jumped a foot. Squinting toward the silhouette at the screen door, I struggled onto my elbows.

"Don't get up. I'll let myself in—if that's okay."

"You must be hard up for company, Seth. I wasn't exactly Miss Congeniality the other day."

He smiled and came over to sit on the floor. "I needed some more clothes. And I decided you deserved another chance. I didn't want you to think I'd give up without a fight."

His sly grin made me smile. "I thought you'd be up to your axles in grease by this time. What's going on?"

"I took the afternoon off to see you. I do have some news, but it can wait." He leaned over the couch, studying me with serious eyes. "Are you sure you're all right? You look pale, honey."

"It comes with being tired and pregnant. In case you hadn't noticed."

Seth smiled, glancing at the bulge, which rose

beside him. "Still pretty, though. You have such delicate skin, long lashes." He touched my face with gentle fingertips. Moments later his breath was warm on my face as he kissed my forehead. "Does that make you feel any better?" he whispered.

I nodded, my eyes still closed.

"Heather, I meant what I said about admiring the way you face up and fight back. You're too good to be part of Ash's harem. What's wrong?"

My eyes flew open and I breathed in sharply. Then I relaxed. "Nothing, I think."

Seth looked at the hand resting on my stomach and covered it with his own. "May I? I-I've never touched an insider before."

I smiled, pressing his palm to the spot where a tiny foot was beating against me.

His face filled with awe. "Oh, Heather—"

I doubled over, a spasm gripping my midsection like a pair of electric hands. My body was covered with sweat; I could hardly breathe.

"I think we'd better get you to the hospital."

"I think you're right," I said.

Thank goodness Seth was calm. He called my doctor. Then he practically carried me down the stairs and ran back for my suitcase. Once at the hospital, he helped me answer the admittance questions—by that time I could barely talk, the contractions were so strong. The last thing I remember before being wheeled to the delivery room was Seth's voice: "Hang on, Heather. I'll be here for you."

It was five hours before my little girl arrived. I heard her cry, and then fell back in a heap of exhaustion. When I came around I was in a regular room. The air smelled heavenly sweet, and when I focused I saw a bouquet of roses on the nightstand. Red ones, yellow ones, and pink ones. There must've been more than a dozen.

"I didn't know which color you liked best, so I got some of each," Seth said.

I turned to see him sitting in the armchair. He was cradling a tiny pink bundle against his chest as though he'd held hundreds of babies. "You're doing a fine job for somebody who's supposedly allergic to those. I'm surprised they trusted you with her."

He chuckled, his eyes twinkling. "I've got a niece, remember? I told the nurse I was the baby's father. I didn't think that it would matter. Want to hold her?"

"In a minute. It's fun watching you." I gazed at him, the muscled mechanic charming the newborn with smiles and feather-soft kisses. My baby. She's finally here. "Seth, you—you don't have to do this. Ash told me what a crisis your older brother caused and how your parents kicked him—"

"He forgot to tell you they're living happily ever after now, eating Mom's chicken every Sunday, didn't he?" Seth said. "By the way, Mom called yesterday to congratulate me on my new job. She'll handle this, eventually."

"But I feel terrible, knowing you sleep on a grimy little cot while I'm at your place—"

"So invite me to live in your apartment." He chuckled when my eyes widened. "I'd rather see you stay there alone and think about your options, though. Until you're back on your feet, or ready for me to pay your bills."

I scowled. He was sounding snobbish again. "I have a job offer. I don't intend to be your charity case," I lied.

"Good. I'm not looking for one." He moved to the side of the bed, still holding the baby. "I want a wife, Heather," he said softly. "A woman who follows her dreams and makes them come true. A woman whose love is so strong she keeps a child she could've given away. I'll give you all the time you need—and my heart, if you want it. If not, well, I can't say I didn't try."

Tears stung the corners of my eyes. I'd been wrong about Seth risking his ego again. He was offering me love like a blank check, for as much as I wanted whether or not I'd pay it back. He didn't spout pretty words or flash flirtatious smiles—he simply wanted to take care of me. I'd never met a man like that, so I figured I'd better play straight with him. "About that job—I turned Ash's housekeeping offer down. So I don't have anything lined up after all."

"That's even better. I may have a chance with you yet." A smile played at his lips as he placed the baby in my arms.

I lead a busy life these days, caring for little Noelle and working in the evenings when Seth comes home to watch her. It's not terribly creative—proofreading and doing secretarial chores for the campus press.

I also anticipate a friendly relationship with the Bramleys. When they saw Noelle, they found all sorts of toys and clothes in their attic, just waiting for another little granddaughter. I've written to my parents about Seth, and the baby, too, hoping they'll want to see us someday. Until then, Seth and I do the best we can. We've never been happier—loving each other and working toward the dreams we share. For us, that's what life's all about!   THE END

WHEN OUR LOVE WAS PRECIOUS AND NEW

The year I was seventeen, I was smug enough to think I had my future all planned. One last year of high school, then teachers' college, and after that, I'd teach in an elementary school until the right man came along. I didn't know just who that "right man" would be. But even though I couldn't see his face, I knew he would be handsome and successful, and we would settle down happily and raise a family.

I wasn't in any rush for these things to happen. I was content to take it one step at a time, confident that all my plans would work out. For the present, I was happy to go to school, to help Mom around the house, to help Dad with the work of running our Montana ranch, to ride my buckskin mare, Shere, and to have an occasional date with Alan Marshall or some other boy.

I had known Alan all my life, but there wasn't anything serious between us—at least not as far as I was concerned. Oh, he was nice enough, and I knew some of my girlfriends envied me for having a guy like Alan at my beck and call, but there just didn't seem to be any spark there. He was my friend, almost like a brother, but I just couldn't work up a romantic interest in him.

I can hardly believe how naive I was then. There are so many things that can happen to a person to cause a change in plans. In my case, what happened was that I met Jase Alden. Just about everyone in our little town knew about Jase Alden, but few people actually knew him, including me, even though he lived on the ranch next to ours.

Jase was two or three years older than me, and he'd come to live on his Uncle Joe's ranch when he was about twelve. Nobody was sure what had happened to his parents, but rumor had it that they had abandoned him and he had been passed around from one foster home to another, finally ending up with his Uncle Joe.

"Something should be done about it. Joe Alden is no fit person to raise a child," the people around here said. But nobody really wanted to get involved, so Jase remained where he was, his uncle continuing to drink himself into a stupor regularly, and Jase was holding himself aloof from the people who looked down on his uncle.

My dad and most of the other ranchers thought it was a shame that a good ranch like the Alden place was allowed to go to ruin, as they could remember when it had been a productive ranch, before Joe Alden's wife had died and he'd started drinking heavily. As Jase grew older, he took over most of the work and did the best he could, but it was apparently a losing battle, with his uncle drinking up all the profits. Some of the folks wondered why Jase didn't strike out on his own, but I think he stayed because the ranch was the only real home he'd ever known, and also because of some misguided loyalty to his uncle.

Because of the difference in our ages, I hadn't seen much of Jase until I started high school. He was almost ready for junior high when he moved here, and I was a little fourth grader, so I had only an occasional glimpse of him. Although he took part in the games and sports on the school playground, I sensed even then that he was an outsider, not one of the kids who "belonged." I was too young, of course, to understand that the hungry look in his eyes was as much a longing for acceptance and respect as it was a real physical hunger.

By the time I reached high school, Jase had grown tall, and the years of doing man's work had given him a lithe, muscular build. There was no denying he was handsome, but he was known to be a loner. He did just enough schoolwork to keep out of serious trouble, and was the despair of his teachers, who didn't seem to be able to get him interested in studying. His independent attitude often got him into trouble, and I think he was sometimes blamed for others' misdeeds because he was too proud to say anything in his defense.

One incident that stands out in my memory is when I was a sophomore and I went to the drama club tryouts in the auditorium. Jase wasn't in the drama club—I had the feeling that he wouldn't have been caught dead taking part in an extracurricular activity—but was merely taking a shortcut through the auditorium when Mrs. Marvin, the club's adviser, spotted him. No doubt picturing what a striking leading man Jase would make, with his dark good looks and deep voice, she called from the stage, "Jase, I'd like you to come up and read for the leading role."

He stopped and looked up, surprised. We all sort of held our breaths, wondering if he'd refuse. He hesitated, as if weighing it in his mind. Then, with a shrug, he mounted the steps and took the script Mrs. Marvin held out.

"Start from this speech," she directed. Jase took a few seconds to find his place and scan the lines. When he began to read, a hush fell over the auditorium. It was a dramatic speech, full of passion, and he put just the right amount of emotion into his reading to make us feel the anguish of the character in the play. By the time he was finished, we were all spellbound. Wordlessly, he handed the script back to Mrs. Marvin, left the stage, and continued on his way. I heard later that he'd been offered the leading role, but had turned it down.

Jase didn't even come to his own graduation. Maybe it was because he knew there would be no one of his own there to be proud of him.

After Jase finished high school, I had a brief glimpse of him now and then in town or when I was out helping Dad around the ranch, but for the most part I was scarcely aware he existed. I had a lot of things to keep me busy, and Jase Alden was the furthest thing from my mind.

At least that was the case until that day in late winter when I was a senior. It was one of those rare days that come along like a precious gift after a long, dreary winter. Although it was too early for spring and the calendar said we still had a few weeks left of winter, this one day was as warm and sunny as April or May—a perfect jewel of a day, with promises of spring and a teasing scent in the air.

Fortunately, it was Saturday, and I knew exactly how I wanted to spend my day. It was my little sister Patty's turn to help Mom in the house so, after doing my outdoor chores, I packed a lunch and a few necessities, saddled Shere, and we were on our way.

Shere was as restless as I was after a long winter. I held her to a walk for the first mile or so, then let her have her head, glorying in the feel of her powerful muscles beneath me as she flew across the fields, exhausting her pent-up energy. I lost track of time as we raced along, but finally realized she was becoming overheated, and I knew that too long a run the first time out wasn't good for her. Reluctantly, I started to rein her in, and that's when it happened, the incident that changed the course of my whole life.

Normally, Shere was a perfect lady and would never have dreamed of misbehaving. However, the weather was obviously having the same effect on her that it was on me, and she shied to one side and gave a high-spirited buck. Usually that wouldn't have bothered me. Shere and I had won a few ribbons in local horse shows and I had even done a little barrel racing, so I wasn't exactly a beginner. But I guess she just caught me off guard. The next thing I knew, I was on the ground, looking ruefully at Shere's retreating tail. I was too angry to notice the dull, aching throb in my left ankle as I called futilely, "Shere, you come back here!" She slowed down just long enough to give her head a playful toss, then galloped on.

I hadn't realized how close I had ridden to the boundary line between our ranch and the Alden place until the beat-up old pickup truck that I recognized as Jase Alden's rattled toward me and shuddered to a stop. The rolls of barbed wire and tools in the back told me he had been out mending fences.

"Are you hurt?" Jase sounded really worried as he jumped down from the truck.

"No, just mad. And embarrassed."

"Here, let me help you up," he offered.

Gratefully, I accepted his outstretched hand as I gingerly got to my feet. Brushing myself off, I shifted my weight from my right to my left foot, and then cried out as a sharp, stabbing pain shot through my ankle. I started to sink back to the ground. Jase caught me as I fell, easily scooping me up.

I'd been too angry at Shere to feel uncomfortable about being out in the middle of nowhere with someone I hardly knew. Suddenly, though, I became aware of Jase as a man, and a darned good-looking one at that. All at once, the pain in my ankle took second place to the delightful sensation of being held as if I was as light as a feather. Jase's shirt was open at the neck and I could smell his clean, outdoorsy scent. Just for a second, I leaned my cheek against his chest and shut my eyes.

"Feeling a little faint?" he asked. There was real concern in his voice as he looked down at me.

I was tempted to nod weakly, just so he'd go on holding me, but it really wasn't in me to play the helpless female. "I think I can stand on my ankle now," I said. "You can put me down."

"Not here. The ground's a little damp." He carried

me up a small rise and deposited me gently on a patch of new, soft grass where I could lean comfortably against a tree trunk. Then, he dropped down beside me. Carefully removing my boot, he examined the injured joint with strong but gentle fingers.

"I don't think anything's broken," he said, "but it'll be pretty sore. You'd better stay off it for a while." He took a large, clean handkerchief from his back pocket and deftly wrapped it around my ankle, which was now beginning to swell.

"Better?"

I twisted my foot experimentally and nodded.

"Want me to catch your horse?" he asked.

"No, she'll come back when she runs out of steam." Suddenly, it occurred to me to be embarrassed about my predicament, and also about submitting so willingly to the ministrations of someone I hardly knew. "Thanks for coming to my rescue, but I'll be fine now," I said. "You don't have to stay here with me."

"I wouldn't think of leaving you out here alone when you're injured." Then, that closed look came over his face, the look I used to see in school. "Unless you want me to go."

"Oh, no, I don't want you to leave," I protested, appalled that he might have misunderstood. "I mean, I just don't want to keep you from your work. I can see you've been mending fences, and I've helped my dad enough to know what a never-ending job that is."

That closed look vanished and he smiled. "To tell you the truth, I was getting tired of working and was just thinking of taking a break," he said. "I've got my lunch in the truck. How about sharing it with me while you rest your ankle?"

"Oh, but I couldn't take your lunch," I told him. "Anyway, I brought along my own in my saddle-bag—if that beast ever comes back with it." In the distance, I could see Shere starting to slow down as she made a wide circle.

"That's okay, I brought plenty. Anyway, you don't look as if you'd eat much," Jase teased, eyeing me.

"You might be surprised!" I said. "I've been told I eat like a lumberjack. Dad says he never saw any-one who could eat so much and stay so skinny."

"I'll take the chance." He laughed.

As Jase walked over to the truck, I admired his tall, lithe form. *Why have I never noticed him before?* I wondered.

By the time he returned with the lunch and was seated next to me, generously dividing his sand-wiches, Shere had come back and was apologeti-cally ambling up to me.

"Go away," I muttered. "I'm mad at you."

She took this as an invitation to begin nuzzling my hair. I pushed her away, but she was determined to make up. Jase took an apple from his lunch sack and held it out to her.

"She doesn't deserve that, you know," I said. "She's been bad and now you're spoiling her. But as long as she's here, you might as well grab my saddlebag before she decides to take off again."

He retrieved the bag while Shere munched con-tentedly on her apple, and I offered him part of my lunch. When he protested, I said, "Go ahead. Take it. It's the least I can do after you shared your food with both me and Shere." I handed him half of my ham sandwich and a foil-wrapped package of cookies. He looked skeptical as he undid the foil and held up a green-frosted cookie in the shape of a Christmas tree.

"Oh, those are left over from Christmas," I explained. "Mom and Patty and I always make cookies at Christmastime, and we usually get carried away and make too many. Then we have to freeze some, so we have Christmas cookies at the strangest times."

For just a second, something passed over his face, and I had a glimpse of that lost, lonely, twelve-year-old boy with the hunger in his eyes. I realized that probably nobody had ever baked Christmas cookies or decorated a tree for him, and I felt a sudden rush of thankfulness for my own warm, loving family.

To cover the awkward moment, I went on pulling fruit and potato chips out of the bag, spreading all my goodies between us. "Go ahead and help yourself," I urged. "I see I packed too much."

My saddlebag still wasn't empty, and Jase picked it up. "I guess you weren't kidding when you said you eat like a lumberjack."

"That's not food," I said, laughing. I reached in the bag and pulled out a slim volume of poetry. "I had planned to ride out to a quiet spot and spend an hour or two reading, but I guess Shere had other plans. The book was a Christmas present from my sister Patty and I haven't had a chance to really sit down and enjoy it."

Jase thumbed through the book until he came to a certain poem. "Are you familiar with this one?" he asked. At my look of surprise, he said, almost shyly,

"It's one of my favorites."

The look that passed between us was one of two friends enjoying a shared interest. Delighted at this discovery, I showed him one of my favorite poems from the book.

Suddenly, we were interrupted by Shere pushing her head between us. She had been grazing nearby, but had apparently decided it was time to get moving again.

"Go away. I'm still mad at you," I scolded. I tried to push her away, but she refused to budge. "Well, so much for broadening our literary horizons," I said, closing the book with a resigned sigh. I looked at my watch and was surprised to see we'd been sitting there for over an hour.

"I guess I'd better be going," I added, suddenly shy. "I've kept you from your work long enough." I started packing my saddlebag so I'd have something to do with my hands.

"I've enjoyed it." Jase smiled at me in a way that made my heart lurch crazily. *This is ridiculous,* I told myself. *I had always been considered so levelheaded, and here I was, getting all breathless over a guy I barely knew, and one who had a faintly unsavory reputation at that—although I realized it was mostly undeserved.*

Jase helped me to my feet and I put my weight on my ankle experimentally. It was only slightly sore now and I managed to mount Shere with just a little help. Jase held the reins with one hand while with the other he helped me arrange the saddlebag.

"Well, thanks for coming to my rescue. I don't know what I'd have done if you hadn't come along," I told him.

He looked embarrassed, but pleased. "Be careful on the way back," he warned. "There might not be anyone around to pick you up."

I held out my hand and he put both of his around it in a gesture that was more a caress than a handshake. As I rode off, I looked back once and saw him standing there watching me. I raised my arm in a final farewell wave, which he returned. Shere tossed her head restlessly, anxious to be on her way.

The next day the weather turned cold again, and we had another week of icy rain and bone-rattling winds, as though winter was making one last-ditch stand. School was closed for three days because the building's heating system had broken down, and I prowled about the house restlessly.

"What in the world is wrong with you, Ronnie?" Mom asked. "You're as jumpy as a cat."

"Yeah, you sure are jittery lately," Patty said, looking up from her drawing. Patty was always painting or sketching. As long as she had her art supplies she was happy anywhere.

"I guess it's just the weather. I hate being cooped up in the house like this," I said. I had debated telling my folks about my chance meeting with Jase, but decided against it. It would just worry them. Besides, I didn't want to make a big thing about it. It probably wasn't important to him, anyway.

That cold, wintry week was finally over, but the skies were still gray and the ground was soggy. It was another week before the sun came out and things began to dry up. On the first fairly decent Saturday, I saddled Shere, telling my folks I was going to take her out for some exercise.

Shere seemed somewhat subdued, not as frisky as she'd been on our last ride, and we moved along at a sedate trot. Resolutely, I kept away from the area where I'd met Jase, determined not to go looking for him. We rode through the valley, and then along a trail that eventually took us to the fence line, which we followed for a while.

I was just about to turn and go back the other way when we came to a break in the fence. I could see a small grove of firs on the other side, and I guided Shere in that direction, intending to make a quick exploration and then go back. But as I came closer, I could make out a shape through the trees. Curious, I skirted the firs and discovered a small cabin on the other side, half hidden by branches. Many of the ranches in the area had such cabins, which had been used, in the past, for various purposes, but most had fallen into disrepair. Our own ranch had one that my cousins and I had turned into a playhouse when we were children.

This cabin, however, didn't have that closed, neglected look that most of them had. The windows seemed to be clean, and the surrounding area was free of brush and fallen branches. I dismounted and let Shere's reins trail on the ground so she wouldn't run off. I was filled with a sense of excitement, as if I was on the verge of an interesting discovery, as I cautiously approached the cabin and peeked in a window.

I thought I must be dreaming! Instead of the cobwebs, dust, and broken remnants of furniture I'd expected to see, the interior was clean and had a lived-in, cared-for look. In one corner, there were two chairs and a small wooden table covered with a

112

checkered cloth. Along one wall was an old sofa with a blanket thrown over it, and next to it was a comfortable-looking rocking chair. There were several colorful throw rugs on the floor, including a large one in front of the stone fireplace, and bookshelves were filled with books. Another shelf above the chipped sink and rusty old pump held plates and cups.

Hurrying around to the front, I put my hand on the old-fashioned latch and was delighted when the door opened easily. I was so charmed to find this cozy little cabin hidden away in the trees that I wasn't even aware of trespassing as I stepped inside. Someone was obviously living here, but I couldn't imagine who, or why anyone would live way out here. Of course, tramps occasionally took shelter in places like this, but no tramp would go to this much trouble. Why, there were even some framed pictures on the walls.

"What do you think of it?" The deep, rich voice behind me startled me.

I whirled around to see Jase Alden smiling down at me. Behind him, I could see his horse grazing near Shere, and I realized I must have been so engrossed in my discovery that I hadn't even heard him ride up.

"Welcome to my humble home," he said.

"This place is yours?" I asked.

"Well, sort of. It's just a little place I've fixed up for when I want to be by myself."

"And here I am trespassing. I'm so sorry," I apologized. "I'll go right away."

"No, please don't go. You're the first visitor I've had, except for a curious animal or two. Stay and have some coffee."

He seemed so eager that I let him take my arm and escort me to the table. I was too surprised to argue, and besides, if I'd been completely honest with myself, I'd have admitted that I wanted to know more about this interesting half-stranger.

Jase filled a battered metal coffeepot with water from the pump, and started a pot of coffee brewing on the old wood stove, then took some cookies from a can and arranged them on a plate.

When everything was ready, I took a sip of the coffee, which tasted surprisingly good. "How long have you been using this cabin?" I asked.

"About a year. I discovered it one day and I decided to clean it up and put some of my things here."

"Do you sleep here, too?" I asked.

"No, not usually. I just like to come here when things get a little rough back at the house." His face took on that closed look I had seen before.

I felt a sudden rush of compassion as I realized how dreary life must be with his Uncle Joe—how desperately lonely Jase must be. Impulsively, I put a hand over his in a sympathetic gesture and was rewarded with a smile so genuine and tender it almost brought tears to my eyes.

To cover what might have become an awkward moment, I picked up my coffee cup and walked over to the bookshelves. "Oh, you have some books that I've read!" I exclaimed. I could see that most of the books were well worn, and I had the feeling that they had been painstakingly collected from second-hand stores and garage sales.

We spent two hours in the cabin, talking and laughing. When I finally left, I no longer felt shy with

Jase, and he invited me to come back anytime. I was tempted to take him up on his offer the very next day, but I restrained myself, not wanting to appear too eager.

But when I ran across a book a few days later that I thought Jase would enjoy, I decided that would be a legitimate reason to visit him. The book was on a bargain table at a local discount store, for practically nothing, so I snapped it up, intending to drop it off at the cabin as soon as possible. I tried to tell myself I just wanted to repay Jase for his kindness when I'd injured my ankle, but deep down I knew that Jase was beginning to become a special person to me.

I felt a sense of pleasant anticipation as Shere and I headed out toward the cabin the following Saturday. During the past week I had thought of all kinds of little incidents that I wanted to share with Jase, funny little things that I was sure he'd enjoy. *Is this what falling in love is like?* I wondered. This was the first time I'd put it into words, but looking back later, I realized that I'd fallen in love that day Jase had picked me up and carried me so tenderly.

But I came back to earth with a, thud when I found the cabin empty. I don't know why it hadn't occurred to me that he might not be there. After all, he had a ranch to run. I considered taking the book back home and bringing it another time, but that really would look like I was chasing him. There was no reason for not leaving it right then. I didn't want to just barge into Jase's cabin when he wasn't there, so I looked around for a safe place to leave the book. Just outside the door was a snug wooden box with a tight-fitting cover. Investigating, I saw that Jase used it for storing fireplace wood. So I put the book inside the box, knowing he'd find it the next time he brought in wood. I felt strangely lost and empty as I rode home.

A few days later, I convinced myself that I should stop by the cabin to make sure Jase had found the book. *After all,* I told myself, *it wouldn't be good for it to lie around in that wood box very long.*

The cabin was deserted when I rode up, but my heart skipped a beat when I opened the wood box and found a piece of folded paper.

Thanks, the note read. *Stop by soon so I can thank you in person. I'll be working out near here Friday afternoon.*

It was such a little thing, but I was happier than if I'd just received an invitation to the prom. I saved the note in a little box that I used for special keepsakes—one with a small key, since Patty liked to poke around my things, the way thirteen-year-old sisters sometimes do.

It seemed that Friday would never come, and several times that week, I found Mom looking at me curiously when she had to repeat something two or three times to get my attention.

I jumped off the school bus Friday afternoon, and ran into the house just long enough to toss my books on the bed and change into my jeans. "Going riding," I called over my shoulder to Mom as I headed out to saddle Shere. Soon, we were racing across the fields, my hair blowing around my face in the spring breeze.

Before I could knock on the cabin door, it opened—as if Jase had been waiting for me. "I was afraid you wouldn't come," he said huskily, drawing me inside. His nearness had an unsettling effect on me, and I could feel my heart begin to pound. Then suddenly, surprisingly, I was in his arms and he was kissing me tenderly. And what was even more surprising was that I was returning his kiss. It seemed so right. I felt that I wanted to stay right there forever, with Jase's arms around me. But he broke away at last, as if guarding against letting things go too far. He led me to the sofa and then took both of my hands in his.

"I love you," he said, looking directly into my eyes. "I know I'm rushing you, but I've been waiting all my life for someone to love—waiting for you."

I could hardly believe it. This gentle, wonderful man loved me! And I loved him back, with all my heart.

We talked out our feelings for a long time that day. Jase wanted to go immediately to my parents and tell them how we felt about each other, but I convinced him to wait.

"Are you ashamed to tell them about us?" he asked.

"Oh, no, Jase," I protested, afraid I'd hurt him. "They'll love and respect you as much as I do when they get to know you."

I knew that was true. They would understand that he wasn't to blame for his uncle's failings. My dad was a fair man. I had overheard him talking with other ranchers, and I knew they had a grudging admiration for the way Jase had tried to run the ranch single-handedly. No, it wasn't shame that kept me from wanting others to know about us. It was just that our love was so new and beautiful that I wanted to keep it as our own special secret for a while longer, and Jase reluctantly agreed.

"I just don't want to share you with anyone yet," I said.

That was the beginning of a strange, beautiful time. I felt as if I was two separate people. One of me went to school, helped Mom and Dad, occasionally argued with Patty, and put Alan off when he asked me to go out with him.

"But we haven't had a date since right after Christmas. Are you mad at me about something?" he asked.

"Oh, Alan, of course not," I replied. I hated hurting him. He'd been a friend for most of my life. Mom and Dad liked Alan and were wondering, too, why I wasn't seeing him. Dad mentioned a few times that he hadn't seen Alan around much lately, and Mom asked once if we'd had a fight. Patty was downright mad at me. At thirteen, she had sort of a crush on Alan and couldn't understand why anyone wouldn't want him for a boyfriend.

I really was sorry to see our friendship come to an end. I knew that Alan would be going away soon. He had been offered a job with his brother-in-law's construction company and would be leaving for Denver shortly after graduation. Colorado was a long way from Montana and I would be sorry to see him go. I felt as if a chapter in my life was closing.

The other me lived for my moments with Jase, carefully keeping this part of my life a secret. I had always been in the habit of taking long, solitary rides on Shere, so my family didn't seem to notice anything unusual. A few times, I thought I heard hoof beats behind me as I rode out to meet Jase, but when I looked around, I never saw anything except trees and hills. I decided it must be an echo, or maybe one of Dad's hired hands on another part of the ranch. Sound carried in strange ways out there in the open.

Day by day, my love for Jase deepened. I was shocked by my response to his very touch, and relieved that he had more self-control than I did.

That is, until that afternoon, shortly before graduation, when we were surprised by a sudden thunderstorm. It was a school holiday so I had ridden out to meet Jase, and we'd been strolling through the trees, talking about our future, and just enjoying being together. Then, without warning, the sky darkened and a few tentative raindrops fell. Jase looked at the black, threatening clouds.

"Maybe we'd better head for the barn," he said. "We're too far away from the cabin."

Before we were halfway there, the rain started coming down in earnest, accompanied by flashes of lightning and deep rumbles of thunder. Jase grabbed my hand and, heads down, we ran the last few yards to shelter. Once inside, we collapsed on the sweet hay. "You're shivering," Jase said, pulling me close and putting his arms around me protectively. He brushed a gentle kiss across my forehead. Then his lips found mine, tenderly at first, then with an urgency that startled me.

Shivers of delight raced through me, and I was shocked at my eager response. The loud rumble of thunder seemed to echo the pounding of our hearts as we were caught up in our desire. Jase gently eased me down on the hay again and my body melted against his. . . .

Afterward, I lay in the haven of his love as we listened to the rain, which had now abated and was falling gently on the roof. Jase traced his finger along the line of my cheek. "I want to talk to your folks right away," he said, rising up on one elbow. "I can't go on sneaking around to meet you. It's not honorable. Besides, I want to marry you as soon as possible after you graduate."

I knew he was right—we couldn't continue meeting in secret. I had told him of my plans for college, but now I realized I had to make a choice, and I knew what that choice would be. As much as I wanted to become a teacher, I wanted Jase more, and I didn't want to wait four years to be his wife.

When we parted, I told him I would meet him at the cabin at noon the next day, and together, we would go talk to my folks. I knew it would be a shock to them—they weren't even aware I was seeing Jase. But I was sure they'd realize how decent and honorable he was when they came to know him.

The next morning, while we made breakfast, Mom and Patty both looked at me strangely as I went around the kitchen humming.

"You're certainly cheerful today," Mom commented.

"Why shouldn't I be? Look what a beautiful day it is," I said.

At breakfast, Dad said, "Ronnie, I need you to go into town for me this afternoon and pick up that stuff from the vet."

"When this afternoon?" I asked, trying to keep the dismay from showing on my face.

"Right after lunch. He's not open on Saturday mornings and you know I need it as soon as possible."

I started to ask why I had to be the one to go, but I knew I was the only possible choice. Dad had enough to do around the ranch that he couldn't be spared for running errands. Besides, he had a new bull being delivered that afternoon. Patty, of course, was too young to drive and Mom absolutely refused to drive the beat-up pickup except in cases of dire emergency.

"Okay, I'll go right after lunch," I said. "This morning I'd like to take Shere out for some exercise, though."

"Seems like that horse is getting a lot of exercise lately," Dad commented.

I jumped up to refill his coffee cup. "What time are they bringing the bull?" I asked, changing the subject. That gave Dad the opening he needed, and I knew he could talk about his new bull for as long as anyone would listen.

As soon as I could get away, I headed for the cabin with a note in my shirt pocket. "I have to run an errand for Dad and I can't get away at noon," I'd written. "I'll meet you at two instead. I love you." I put the note in the wood box where Jase would be sure to find it, and headed home.

At one o'clock, with the items from the vet on the seat beside me, I threaded through the usual Saturday traffic in town, thinking dreamily that I would be with Jase in less than one hour. Just as I was ready to turn onto the main highway leading to the ranch, I was rudely jolted back to reality by a grinding noise coming from under the hood and a subtle change in the feel of the steering wheel in my hands.

I eased over to the shoulder and braked to a stop. Climbing down from the cab, I opened the hood and peered in, having no idea what to look for. I guess I just thought that anything that made such a horrible noise would have to be instantly obvious.

"Having a little trouble?"

I looked up, surprised, as a man from one of the neighboring ranches strolled up to the truck. I hadn't heard him pull up behind me. "I'm not sure. It just made this awful noise and then it felt funny," I told him.

The man grinned at my description of the problem, then stuck his head under the hood and began testing wires and connections. He asked me to get in and start up the motor, and when it still made the same grinding sound, he motioned me to shut it off.

"Looks like you've got troubles," he said, slamming the hood. He rattled off a technical description of what was wrong. "Better not try to drive it. I'd give you a lift, but I've got an appointment in town. If you're still here on my way back, I'll drive you home."

"Oh, that's okay. I'll call Dad," I said. "Thanks anyway."

After he drove off, I walked down the road to the nearest phone booth and called home. We had an old flatbed truck that we used mainly for ranch work and I knew Dad could come after me in that.

"I just can't come now," Dad said, sounding harried. "The bull is being delivered in a little while and I have to be here."

"But what about the stuff from the vet? I thought you needed it this afternoon."

"I do, but I can't be in two places at once. You'll just have to stay there and wait until I can get away. I can't promise how long it'll be. If one of the hands comes back, I can send him."

I went back to the truck to wait, doing some quick calculations as I looked at my watch. I'd told Jase in my note that I'd meet him at two. Unless something happened soon, I'd never make it. I knew he'd understand when I explained later, but I could imagine his hurt feelings when I didn't show up. For all his outward independence, he was vulnerable and easily hurt, almost as if he had trouble believing anyone could really love him.

For the next two hours, I alternated between pacing restlessly up and down the road and sitting resignedly in the truck. Then, at almost three o'clock, a familiar car pulled up behind me. It was Alan Marshall. Right then, he was the most beautiful sight I'd ever seen.

"Sorry you had to sit here so long, Ronnie," he said. "I'd have come sooner if I'd known you needed help."

"How did you know I was stuck here?" I asked him.

"I just stopped by to see you, and your dad said the truck broke down and you'd been waiting since about one o'clock for someone to come and get you."

"I thought Dad would have come by now," I said. "Did his bull get there yet?"

"Yes, but they were having trouble getting him unloaded," Alan told me. "When I got there things were pretty hectic, so I figured I could be the most help by getting out of the way and coming after you."

Remembering to bring the box of items from the vet, I hurried to get into Alan's car. As we were wait-

123

ing to pull out onto the highway, a familiar truck drove past and I saw the look on Jase's face as he recognized me sitting there next to Alan. I felt a dull ache inside as I pictured him waiting for me at the cabin, wondering why I didn't come. And then to see me riding in Alan's car!

When I got home I wanted to go immediately to the cabin, even though I knew Jase wouldn't be there. At least I could leave a note to explain why I'd stood him up. But when I saw the state of affairs around our place, I could tell it would be impossible to get away without arousing suspicion. The new bull had decided to be stubborn, and Dad and one of his hired hands had finally finished getting him into his pen. I knew that even with a hired hand there, Dad would need help to get caught up on all the chores that had gone undone while he'd spent most of the afternoon dealing with a troublesome bull. And there was still the pickup to be towed home and repaired.

I pitched in and started helping with the chores, but by the time things were back to normal and dinner was over with, it was almost dark and I couldn't possibly have ridden out. I knew there was no phone at the Alden place, or I would have slipped away and called, leaving a message with Uncle Joe and hoping he would come out of his stupor long enough to deliver it to Jase.

Dad looked so tired when he finally came in from replacing the water pump that I was instantly sorry for him, and I was glad I'd stayed around to help with the chores. I kissed him on the cheek before I went up to bed, and he looked surprised and touched at the unexpected gesture of affection.

"Thanks for your help today," he said wearily. "You're a good daughter, Ronnie."

There was a lump in my throat as I recalled that this was the day I'd planned to introduce my future husband to Dad and Mom.

It wasn't until after church the next day that I finally got a chance to go back to the cabin. I looked in the wood box first and saw that my note was gone, so I knew Jase had gotten it. But there was no answer. I decided to go in and wait a while, hoping he'd show up.

The cabin had a deserted, empty feel as I entered, and I drew my jacket tighter around me to shut out the chill. I wandered around restlessly, thumbing through books without seeing the words on the pages, going to the window to look out, then pacing back and forth.

Finally, when I could stand it no longer, I found a piece of paper and a stub of pencil and wrote a short note. I was too tense to try to explain clearly why I hadn't been there to meet him yesterday, or why I was in Alan's car. After chewing nervously on the pencil for several minutes, I just wrote, "Jase, I have to talk to you. Please meet me here at four. I love you."

That was the longest afternoon of my life, even longer than the previous afternoon I'd spent sitting along the side of the road in a broken-down truck. I kept telling myself everything would be all right when I had a chance to explain to Jase what had happened. Jase loved me and would understand that I hadn't stood him up on purpose. I was filled with a sense of foreboding, as if something precious had been lost, something that could never be regained.

When I returned to the cabin at four, there was no sign of Jase. I knew he must have been there since my note was gone. *Why do we keep missing one another?* I wondered. *And why didn't he leave an answer?* That just wasn't like Jase. I knew he'd been hurt when I hadn't come yesterday, but I couldn't understand why he wasn't at least answering my notes or giving me a chance to explain.

The next evening at dinner Dad said casually, "I heard today that Jase Alden left this morning to look for work somewhere else."

I was just picking up a dish of vegetables, and my hand stopped in midair.

"It's about time he got away from here and started to make a life of his own," Mom commented. "But Joe Alden surely can't run that ranch alone."

"Down at the feed store they were saying that Jase hired Hank Murray's two boys to look after the place while he's gone."

"Where would he get the money to pay hired hands?" Mom asked. "I always thought they just barely got by over there."

"Well, I don't know, but I could run over and ask Joe Alden about their financial status," Dad teased. Then, more seriously, he said, "I got the idea he made some kind of deal to pay them when he has a steady paycheck coming in."

"Are you going to hold that bowl of carrots all night?" Patty asked me impatiently. "The rest of us want some too, you know."

"What? Oh, I—" Automatically, I passed the bowl to her. I had suddenly lost my appetite anyway. Somehow, I got through the rest of the meal without giving away my shock and bewilderment.

WHEN OUR LOVE WAS PRECIOUS AND NEW

The next few weeks passed in a kind of daze; I barely noticed what was going on around me. Once, a few days after Dad dropped his bombshell, I rode out to the cabin with the hope that Jase might have left a message or a word of explanation. I wasn't too surprised when he hadn't. When I entered the cabin, I saw that the furnishings were already gathering dust, and the whole place felt deserted and unused. I didn't go back again.

Then, two weeks before graduation, I was sharply jolted out of my lethargy when I began to suspect I was pregnant. I'd been raised in the country around animals, and had even assisted in a birthing or two, so sex wasn't a taboo subject around our house. I knew there was no mistaking my symptoms. I felt even worse at the thought of what this would do to my parents, never mind what it would do to my own life.

One evening, I felt I had to be alone for a while, so I went out to brush Shere. The evening chores had already been done, so I knew I wasn't likely to be disturbed. In the privacy of the cool, quiet barn, I leaned my cheek against Shere's smooth side and let the hot, scalding tears flow. I'd been holding them in for so long as I went through final exams and graduation rehearsals, pretending to be the carefree graduate. Now, I sobbed out my heartbreak, my utter despair. How could Jase have lied to me and pretended to love me? How could I have been so completely taken in?

"Hey, are you in here?" a male voice called.

I froze, holding my breath. "Anybody here?"

I wiped my eyes on the back of my hand, and swallowed back the tears. "Over here, Alan," I said.

127

He walked over casually, hands in his pockets. "I just came by to see if you want to go to the senior picnic with me. Your mom said you were out here."

I kept my face averted as I busily brushed burrs out of Shere's tail. "Oh, I'm not sure I'm going to the picnic," I said. "Things have been so hectic lately I may just skip it."

"But nobody skips the senior picnic—" he began. Then he caught sight of my red eyes. "Hey, what's wrong?"

"It's nothing. I'm just a little sad over graduation and everything," I explained lamely.

Alan stood there in silence while he thought this over. Then, slowly and resolutely, he took his hands from his pockets, took the brush from me, led me out of the stall, and sat me down on a bale of hay. "I know it's something more than just graduation jitters. Want to tell me about it?" When I didn't answer, he said, "We've been friends most of our lives, right?"

I nodded.

"And what are friends for if you can't tell them your troubles?"

I turned away. I couldn't unload this on him.

"I've been noticing a change in you lately, sadness." Alan said. "I've got a good strong shoulder to cry on."

He was so dear and so dependable. Suddenly, his arm was around me and I was sobbing against him as he patted my shoulder comfortingly. "Oh, Alan," I wailed, "I'm pregnant!" I hadn't meant to blurt it out like that, but I'd been keeping my feelings under control for so long that it seemed they finally had to come out.

The patting stopped just for a second, and then started up again. I lost track of time as Alan held me like that, but finally I felt all cried out.

"Want to tell me who he is?" Alan asked. "Maybe I could go beat him up or something."

I knew he was trying to make me smile, and I managed a weak, watery grin.

"Is he going to marry you?" he persisted.

I shook my head.

"Are you sure?"

"Positive. He's out of my life forever," I said.

Alan gave a slow whistle, as if acknowledging the seriousness of the problem. "What are you going to do?"

"I don't know," I replied miserably.

He continued to hold me, and after a long silence, he said, "You could marry me."

"Oh, Alan, I couldn't do that to you. You deserve something better," I protested.

With one arm still around my shoulder, he put his other hand under my chin and tilted my face up to his. "You know I've always loved you. And if you don't love me in return—well, I can live with that if you just like me a little. Please let me do this for you." That started me crying again, although I'd thought there were no tears left.

We talked for a long time, and in the end I agreed to marry Alan, resolving to myself to be the best wife in the world to him. I knew I wouldn't have to worry about him being a good husband—it just wasn't in him to be anything but kind and gentle. I made up my mind to do everything possible to repay him for this sacrifice he was making for me.

My parents were delighted with the news of our

marriage plans. If they'd noticed my preoccupied air the last few months, they just seemed to think Alan and I had had a lovers' quarrel and then had finally made up. We were married a week after graduation, and two weeks later, we left for Denver. Mom cried as we left and Dad gravely shook Alan's hand and said, "I know you'll take good care of our little girl."

My little son was born less than eight months after Alan and I were married. I'd told my folks that the baby was due a month later, so I'm sure they were hurt and disappointed when he came "early." But when Alan called them from the hospital, Mom immediately hopped on a plane to come out and help me, and as soon as she set eyes on her grandson, all was forgiven.

Mike was an adorable, happy baby, and Alan became his true father in every way except biologically. In fact, watching the two of them together, I sometimes forgot that Alan hadn't really fathered him. Another surprising thing that happened was that I fell in love with my husband. At first, I thought it was just gratitude because he was so kind and thoughtful, but by the time our first anniversary rolled around, I realized that I really loved Alan. Our marriage was blissfully happy.

When Mike was almost two, I answered the door one day to find Alan's brother-in-law standing there, looking uncomfortable. Even before he said, "There's been an accident," I had a feeling of foreboding, and I knew something terrible had happened. The only consolation I had later was that Alan's death had been quick and painless, and that Alan had known, before he died, how much I loved him.

WHEN OUR LOVE WAS PRECIOUS AND NEW

After the funeral, Mom and Dad wanted me to come back home to live, but I was no longer a little girl and I knew I had to take the responsibility of providing for myself and my child. I received a generous insurance settlement, but I realized it wouldn't support us forever, so I used it to complete my interrupted education. It was a long haul, trying to go to college and look after my son, too, but eventually I received my teaching degree. Mike and I celebrated with a trip to Disneyland, which just about blew my carefully planned budget, before I settled down to full-time teaching.

I had been teaching for about three years when Dad—my strong, vigorous dad who'd never been sick in his life—died of a heart attack. Mom was devastated, and I knew that now I'd have to move back home and help her run the ranch. Mike was delighted that we were moving back, but he was as sad as I was that Grandpa would no longer be there. He'd adored his tall, good-looking grandfather, and on our visits home he had trailed after him like a shadow.

Although Dad's death left a desolate, empty spot in all our lives, I slipped back into ranch life as easily as if I'd never been away. Mom, still young and attractive, threw herself into the work of the ranch as therapy for her grief, and together, with the help of a couple of hired hands, we managed to keep things going. Even Mike, now going on ten, was a big help.

Patty lived in town now but visited regularly. She had gone to art school and then had worked as an artist for a year or so. Now her whole life centered around her husband and two children, and her art training was put to use only for such projects as making posters for the PTA or designing a cover for the cookbook the ladies of the church were putting out.

During my visits home over the years, Mom and Patty had kept me up to date on all the local gossip, including what was going on around the Alden place. It seemed that Jase had found a good job and had worked hard and saved his money so that when he returned after his Uncle Joe died, he had enough to fix up the ranch and buy some new stock and equipment. Without the old man around to drink up the profits, Jase had finally gotten the place to make money. He had a couple of hired hands now, but still did a lot of the work himself and was well on the way to becoming a respected member of the community. Apparently, he was still a loner, and despite the efforts of many a matchmaking mother, managed to elude all the marriageable young women in the vicinity.

I hadn't set eyes on him in all those years until one day when Patty and I were in town shopping. We were talking along the sidewalk, laughing and chatting and not looking where we were going. Suddenly, I came up against what seemed like a brick wall and my packages went flying every which way.

My apology died on my lips as I found myself looking into the unmistakable eyes of Jase Alden! I felt the blood rush to my face and I was sure the pounding of my heart must be audible. The Jase Alden I remembered had been a tall, good-looking youth, but this man staring down at me was easily the handsomest man I'd ever seen in my entire life!

To cover my confusion, I bent to retrieve my

packages and the awkward moment passed as Jase helped me pick them up. "Thank you," I managed to croak in a hoarse whisper. He gave a curt nod and went on his way. That was all there was to it, but afterward, I noticed Patty looking at me strangely.

Mike took to ranch life so eagerly that I was a little sorry we hadn't moved back sooner. There were so many things for a boy to do that he was busy from morning until night. My horse, Shere, was still there—a little slower, a little grayer around the muzzle, but still sprightly enough for a former city boy just learning to ride—and Mike spent long hours astride her, exploring the ranch. One day, he came home and excitedly told me about his new friend Jase, whom he had just met while out riding.

"I hope you haven't been over there bothering him," I said. "And you really should call him Mr. Alden."

"But, Mom, he said I could come over any time I wanted. And he told me to call him Jase," Mike insisted.

I hated to dampen his enthusiasm. He seemed so pleased that I realized how he missed having a father figure in his life. But fear gripped me as I thought of what might happen if Jase were ever to discover that Mike was his son. What if he wanted to take him from me, just to be vindictive? *Don't be silly,* I told myself. *Why would he do that?* Besides, Mike resembled me. There was no way anyone could tell Jase was his father.

Another new interest of Mike's was fishing, and he often took Dad's fishing tackle and walked across the field to the creek. One afternoon when he was out fishing, I heard a rumble of thunder and I stepped out onto the front porch to see the sky beginning to darken. Worriedly, I scanned the horizon for a sign of Mike, but he was nowhere to be seen. I didn't want him out in the kind of storm that was coming up. I had just about decided to go looking for him when a truck pulled into the yard and Mike jumped down from the passenger seat. I didn't recognize the vehicle, but there was no mistaking the tall, authoritative figure that stepped down from the driver's side and strode up onto the porch.

"This guy belong to you?" Jase asked. "I found him walking home and thought I'd better give him a lift before he got soaked."

My first instinct was to pull Mike into the house and lock the door against what I felt was a threat. *Take it easy,* I told myself. *He's just being neighborly.*

I replied calmly, "Thanks. I hope he hasn't been making a nuisance of himself at your place."

"No. I've invited him to come over whenever he wants."

"That's very kind of you." *Why, we're like two polite strangers,* I thought. Because I couldn't think of anything to say to Jase, I turned to Mike. "Where are your fish? I thought you were going to bring us some for dinner."

"Aw, Mom, the only ones I caught were so little I threw them back so they could grow up," he replied with a sheepish grin.

I wasn't sure what it was about Mike then—maybe the lift of an eyebrow or the grin—but whatever it was, it was so like Jase that I held my breath, wondering if he'd seen it, too.

"You'd better go in and wash up," I told Mike. "You smell like fish."

As soon as he had gone in, I turned to confront Jase, whose face was now as dark as the approaching storm.

"Why didn't you tell me he was my son?" he demanded.

"No!" I exclaimed. "He's mine!" Jase towered over me threateningly as he caught my wrist in his strong hand. "You're hurting me!" I cried.

"Tell me! Is he my son?" Jase thundered.

I knew it was useless to deny it. "Yes," I admitted in defeat.

He released my arm and stood there, hands hanging at his sides. "And all these years you kept it from me. You must really hate me," he said.

Suddenly, I wanted to hurt him. "Why shouldn't I hate you?" I cried, rubbing my aching wrist. "You ran out on me!"

"I ran out on you?" he repeated incredulously. "You dumped me, and I have the proof in your own handwriting. I saved it just to remind myself never to trust a woman again."

What in the world was he talking about? In the space of a few seconds, I had gone from frightened to angry to puzzled, and now the whole scene was starting to take on a nightmarish quality, with the wind beginning to howl in earnest and the thunder crashing around us.

Just then, Mike came outside, slamming the door noisily. Simultaneously, Patty's car pulled into the yard and parked next to the truck.

"We'll finish this discussion later," Jase promised threateningly, before driving off with a squeal of tires.

"What was he doing here?" Patty asked curiously, herding her children up the steps.

"Oh, he just gave Mike a lift home. Come in and I'll put the coffee on. It's been lonesome out here, with Mom gone," I said. Mom was spending a few weeks visiting her aunt in the next county, leaving Mike and me on our own.

"I thought you'd be ready for some adult company by now," Patty said.

After Mike and his cousins had gone off to play and Patty and I were seated at the kitchen table, she stirred her coffee thoughtfully.

"Something on your mind?" I asked.

"Yes—no—well, there is. Sis, there's something I have to tell you—something I should have told you a long time ago."

Patty was obviously upset, and I became more and more curious. "Okay, I'm listening."

"You and Jase Alden had something going on once, didn't you?" she began. "Back when you were in high school."

"How did you know that?" I blurted out.

"I saw the two of you together once, so after that, I followed you a few times," she admitted.

I let my mind drift back to those long-ago days, and suddenly I realized that Patty's words explained the hoof beats I'd sometimes heard. But I still didn't understand why that should cause her to be so upset now, or even why she'd brought it up after all these years.

"And?" I prompted.

"Well, I knew you used to meet at that old cabin, and you left messages for each other in the wood box," she said. "Oh, Ronnie, those last two notes you left him, I—I took them." She was almost in tears.

I was afraid if I showed any emotion, she might be afraid to tell me the rest of it. I patted her hand reassuringly. "Tell me about it," I said.

"It was that day Dad got the new bull—the day the pickup broke down. I followed you to the cabin when you left that note saying that you'd meet Jase at two instead of noon. I replaced it with a different note, one that I wrote."

"I see. And what did this other note say?" I was surprised that I was taking this so calmly.

"It said that you didn't want to see him anymore, that you realized the two of you weren't right for each other and that you were breaking off your relationship. I signed your name to it. I don't know where I got all that stuff, but I was only thirteen."

"But he surely would have known it wasn't my handwriting," I said.

"I'm an artist, you know," she said quietly. "It wasn't hard to copy your writing. And then the next day, I followed you again and took that note, too."

My thoughts were coming so fast I could barely sort them out, but a lot of things were beginning to fall into place. "But why, Patty?" I asked. "I don't understand why you did it."

"I guess because I was half in love with Alan—in a little-girl way—and I couldn't stand to see you ignoring him. I thought you'd pay some attention to him if Jase was out of the way. And it worked, didn't it?"

I took a sip of my coffee. "Yes, I guess it did. But why did you just now decide to tell me?"

"When I first did it and then Jase went away, I was

proud of myself for getting you and Alan together," she explained. "But then as I grew older and got a little sense, I began to wonder if I'd really done the right thing or if I'd just messed things up for you. You were married to Alan then, so I couldn't say anything. But it's been on my conscience for a long time. And now that you're back, you'll be running into Jase more and more, so I had to tell you."

When I didn't say anything for a long time, she asked warily, "Are you mad at me?"

"No, I'm not mad at you," I said. "I'm glad you told me." I got up and gave her a reassuring hug.

"Do you think there's a chance the two of you could get back together?" she asked.

"I doubt it." *We've both been hurt too badly,* I thought, but I didn't say it. There was no sense in making Patty feel any worse. What had happened was over and done with now, and the past couldn't be changed.

Patty left soon after that, taking Mike along to spend a few days in town visiting his cousins.

For the next few days, I felt completely drained emotionally, after the scene with Jase and then Patty's confession. I cried a little over what Jase and I had once had and then lost, and over the hurt we'd caused each other, but I was too empty to do much except wander around the house listlessly. With Mom and Mike both gone, the house was too quiet, and I found myself thinking of things that were better left forgotten. Every time I heard a car go by, I was afraid it was Jase coming to claim his son. Mike was the most important person in the world to me and I was prepared to fight to keep him, but I knew I would be no match for Jase if he was determined

138

to have his way.

One day, when I could no longer stand the silence and my own thoughts, I saddled Shere and we went for a long, leisurely ride, exploring forgotten corners of the ranch. When we finally ended up near the cabin, I started to turn the other way, and then changed my mind.

Might as well get rid of the ghosts once and for all, I thought.

The interior of the cabin was thick with dust and one window was broken. The floor near the broken window was littered with dead leaves, and there was an odor of decay about the whole place. I surveyed the wreckage, thinking how similar it was to the wreckage of the love Jase and I had once shared. So much for sentimental journeys, I said to myself, wrinkling my nose in distaste.

When I turned to leave, the cabin suddenly darkened as a tall figure filled the doorframe. Jase stepped through the door and I panicked. I had to get out of there. As I brushed past him, it was as if an electric current was shooting through my body.

"We had something pretty good between us once, didn't we?" he asked.

His words brought me to a halt. "That was a long time ago. It's all over now," I said quietly.

"It doesn't have to be. We could start over," he said.

"No, Jase, it wouldn't work. Too much has happened," I told him. "Anyway, you'd never believe that I really loved you—that I didn't dump you, as you put it."

"Why don't you try me?" he challenged.

"Oh, Jase," I said wearily, "what do you want from

me? And why are you here?"

"I wanted to talk to you, and I just had a feeling I'd find you here. Did you know your sister came to see me yesterday?"

"No!" I cried, surprised. "Why did she do that?"

"She said she had to clear her conscience and try to atone for what she'd done as a silly kid." He raised one eyebrow. "I honestly don't think she'll feel that she's been forgiven until you and I get back together."

I couldn't tell if he was serious or being sarcastic. "I wish you had some idea of how hurt I was when you ran out on me," I said. "I couldn't stand to go through that again."

"How do you think I felt?" he asked.

"But you weren't the one who was pregnant!" I shot back, then instantly wished I could take my words back.

Something in Jase's face changed. "Then you admit Mike is my son." It was a statement, not a question.

"Yes," I answered. "Oh, Jase, don't take him away from me. He's everything in the world to me."

His face softened. "I wouldn't take him from you. I thought maybe—maybe we could share him."

"That wouldn't work," I said, shaking my head. I knew I couldn't have regular contact with Jase if being near him could send me into this kind of turmoil.

I honestly don't think he realized the effect his presence had on me. "I know you've been hurt, but don't forget that I have been, too," he reminded me, mistaking my meaning. "How do you think I felt that day when you didn't show up—when there was only that note saying it was over between us?"

"But you know now that I didn't write it," I protested.

"Yes, I know now, but I didn't until yesterday. For over ten years, I've lived with that hurt," he said.

"But I did leave a note that day, and another the next day. So at least you know now that I loved you." I turned to leave, not knowing what else to say.

"Don't go," he said.

What happened next is confused in my mind, but somehow I was in his arms and I had feeling of coming home, of being where I was always meant to be. All of the hurts and agonies of the past had been explained away, and now Jase and I were free to admit we still cared, still needed and wanted each other. We weren't the uncertain, suspicious boy and girl we'd been ten years ago. We were adults now, ready to commit ourselves to a man and woman's deep love.

Jase and I are married now, and Mike calls him Dad. We haven't explained to him yet that Jase is really his father, but I think, somehow, he senses it. When the time comes, I want Mike to be able to love Jase, his father, without losing the love he feels for Alan—who was also truly a father to him.

For now, though, what's "legal" doesn't really matter. What counts is being together, being a family—being blessed with love.   THE END

THE PRECIOUS BABY

I was working on my sketch of Rachel and Ted when the phone rang. I picked up the receiver with my free hand, tucked it under my chin, and went on working. "Hi, Julia," my friend Mary said. "Busy?"

"Just fiddling with my sketch of the kids," I replied. My friend Mary Sturbridge knew all about the sketching class I'd taken up after my twins started first grade. "Are you at work?"

"Yes," Mary said. Her voice was subdued, worried. "I have a big problem, Julia. I was hoping you could help me."

I put down the sketch. In all the fifteen years I'd known Mary, she'd never sounded this serious. "What's the matter?" I asked.

"Julia, it's one of my kids. A baby."

I smiled in relief. Mary was a social worker, and she had plenty of children who became dear to her. People talk about social workers developing hard shells for their own protection, but Mary had never managed to do so. She was always calling me to tell me about "her children."

As if she'd read my thoughts, Mary said, "It's not the usual sob story, Julia. Yvonne's no ordinary baby." She took a deep breath. "She's just weeks old, and she's going to die. She's going to die within a month or so."

Suddenly, it seemed very still in my kitchen. It was as if someone had switched off the bright sunlight that shone through my kitchen window. "I'm sorry, Mary," I said softly. "I wish there was something I could do—"

"There is," Mary interrupted. "Julia, promise me you won't say yes or no before talking it over with Russell. I want you to take Yvonne."

My first impulse was to cry, "Yes!" But then, almost immediately, I felt a sense of panic. How could I possibly take a baby into my house—a baby who was going to die? I wasn't equipped to deal with sick babies. And anyway, it had been years since Rachel and Ted were babies.

"Promise me you'll talk with Russell," Mary said. "Julia, I know I'm asking for a lot, but Yvonne has so little time left and no one is willing to take her. There aren't enough good foster homes to start with, and with a baby like Yvonne—"

"What's wrong with her?" I asked.

Everything, it seemed, was wrong with Yvonne. She had multiple birth defects, was blind, and had episodes of cyanosis where she couldn't breathe and turned blue.

"She was born to a young girl, an unmarried girl," Mary said. "She was going to be adopted, but when the adoptive parents learned what was wrong with her, they backed off."

She added that the doctors were convinced that
Yvonne couldn't live for more than a few weeks—a
few months at best. "If no one takes her, she'll be
left in Lincoln Hospital where she is now," Mary told
me. "They'll take good care of her there, but it won't
be the same as if she were in a home. She only has
a few weeks, for heaven's sake.

"I thought about you and Russell because you've
always struck me as such wonderful parents. I used
to watch the two of you with Ted and Rachel—" She
broke off, laughing. "I don't mean to twist your arm,
Julia. Just talk it over with Russell and call me,
okay?"

After I'd hung up the phone, I looked at the sketch
I'd been working on. Then I went upstairs and down
the hall to the rooms where Ted and Rachel slept.
Ted's room was a colorful mess of toys, football
pennants, and athletic gear. Rachel's was feminine
and neat, with a carefully printed sign reading,
"Home is Love." Rachel had made it last year in
kindergarten.

"I can't," I whispered out loud. "Mary can't blame
me if I refuse to do this. Yvonne's not my flesh and
blood. It would be hard enough with my own child .
. ." My voice trailed off and I caught myself wondering where I had put Rachel's baby clothes, and
where we had stored the bassinet, the stroller, and
the plastic tub I had bathed the babies in. "No," I
told myself loudly, as if the loudness could stop my
thoughts. "She's dying. How can we take care of a
dying baby?"

I didn't say anything to Russell when he first got
home that evening, nor did I mention Mary's call
during supper. Later, however, when the kids were

playing an after-dinner game, I took two cups of coffee down to Russell's workshop in the basement. Russell liked to fix things and putter around down there, and he enjoyed a cup of coffee while he "messed around." When he saw me, though, he smiled at me and asked, "Want to talk?"

"How did you know?" Russell's smile always warmed and relaxed me, but at that point nothing could ease the worry and trouble I felt.

"You were fifty miles away during dinner," he told me. "You handed me the gravy instead of the salt, and you didn't hear the kids when they asked you questions." He put down the coffee and drew me into his arms. "What's wrong, Julia?"

I told him, then, about Mary's call. Russell didn't interrupt, and when I'd finished he just stood there quietly, his arms still around me. "What do you want to do?" he finally asked.

"I don't know, that's the problem! My first reaction was to say yes. It's so awful for a baby to die in a hospital, unwanted by anyone! But, Russell, it would mean so much adjustment all around. The kids would have to share the house with a baby—a baby who is sick, dying. And we wouldn't be free to pick up and go anyplace any more. We'd be tied down. And there's my life, too. The kids are off at school now, and I have my sketching class and I was going to look for a part-time job."

Russell frowned. "I know all that," he said. "But that's not what's bothering you the most. It's the dying part, isn't it?" I nodded. "It bothers me, too," he said then. "You and I can handle someone's dying, but the kids—do we have the right to expose them to that kind of thing?"

146

THE PRECIOUS BABY

We talked it over for a while, but nothing seemed to really fall into place. Neither Russell nor I was convinced that we should take Yvonne, and yet neither of us could bear to come right out and say no. Finally, we decided to sound the kids out on our taking in a "very sick" baby. After all, this was their home. It was their decision, too.

We weren't prepared for their quick response. Ted, the practical one, said, "Will she sleep in a bed or in a crib? I can sleep in a sleeping bag and Yvonne could have my bed till you could get a crib."

Rachel, the quiet one, pressed her cheek against my shoulder. "How sick is she?" she wanted to know. When I said very sick, Rachel looked concerned. "But, Mom, shouldn't we bring her home right away, then?" she asked.

Even then, we weren't convinced. After talking it over between us, Russell and I decided that we should see Yvonne before deciding one way or another. I called Mary the next morning and arranged for Russell and me to see her that afternoon.

On our way to Lincoln Hospital, I was so nervous I kept breaking out in a cold sweat. Inside the hospital, I clung to Russell's hand. "Don't worry, Julia," he kept saying, in a way that made me sure he was worried himself. "If we don't want to do this, we can back out, no problem. We can just walk out of here and forget it."

But there was no way we could do that after seeing Yvonne. I don't know what we'd been expecting to see—a different-looking baby, perhaps, or a sickly-looking baby. But what we saw was a tiny, sweet infant asleep in her crib behind a glass wall. Yvonne was tinier than Rachel had been, but otherwise she looked normal.

"She looks a little like Rachel did at the same age," Russell said. He was trying to speak calmly, but there was a quiver in his voice. "What do you think, honey?"

"I think Ted had better get out his sleeping bag," I said.

Then Russell and I hugged each other and laughed, and I think we cried a little, too.

When we told Mary, she hugged us, too. "I knew it," she exclaimed. "I knew you'd take Yvonne!"

Russell and I felt good about our decision—then. But that was before we talked to Dr. Brose, who had been treating Yvonne. Dr. Brose gave us a long rundown on Yvonne's problems, and as he talked, I could feel my heart slowly sinking to my feet. With Yvonne's medical history, it was a wonder she was still alive.

"She's losing ground every day, Mrs. Williams," Dr. Brose told me. "There's no good way of trying to get around the fact that she's dying. She has severe brain damage—a rare type of condition—" He paused. "Babies like Yvonne can only be made comfortable until . . ."

He left the sentence hanging. "Until she dies," Russell murmured. I looked at him, and he stared back at me. We'd seen Yvonne. Whatever was wrong with her, there was no way we could just walk away from the hospital and pretend that she hadn't touched our lives.

"I guess—I guess we'll just have to make her comfortable," I whispered, "until she dies."

Mary made the arrangements for us to take

Yvonne home the next afternoon. The kids were overjoyed at the news, but our families and friends were shocked. My sister-in-law, Betty, was the most outspoken.

"You must be out of your minds, doing such a thing!" she cried. "Didn't you think about Ted and Rachel at all?"

Russell said we'd talked it over with them. "They want us to bring Yvonne home with us. They know how sick she is—"

"Kids that age don't know what 'sick' is," Betty said shortly. "Don't you realize what you're doing? You and Julia are adults, so you understand about death. Kids don't. When that baby dies, you'll have to deal with Rachel's and Ted's feelings, and all their questions about death!"

She paused to let that sink in, then added, "You might scar Rachel and Ted for years with such an experience. You might even scar them for life!"

We didn't know what to say. *Maybe,* I thought, *Betty is right!* And she wasn't the only one to speak out against what we were doing. My next-door neighbor, Joanne, was dead set against our bringing Yvonne home.

"Julia, I know you're doing what you think is right," Joanne told me, "but I won't feel comfortable letting my Steffie play at your house while—well, you know. Suppose the baby dies while Steffie is there? It might scare her so badly she'd have an abnormal fear of death for the rest of her life!"

I nearly called Mary right then and there and told her that we'd changed our minds. The only thing that prevented me from doing so was the memory of that tiny baby asleep in her hospital crib. I knew

Russell felt the same way, even though we didn't say much to each other about our fears. And the next day, when we drove out to get Yvonne, I felt tense and afraid. When it came time to take her in my arms for the first time, my heart was beating like a sledgehammer and my arms felt stiff and taut.

Yvonne felt so light in my arms. She didn't struggle or move around as my babies had done. She just lay there, her eyes open and unseeing. Even her crying seemed to have a different sound. I told myself that this baby was just like any other, but I couldn't believe my own words. I felt jumpy and unsure as Russell and I carried Yvonne to the car where Rachel and Ted were waiting for us.

They crowded close. "Let me see her!" Rachel exclaimed. "Oh, she's so small, Mom! Was I that small, too?"

"Pretty close," I said. I slid into the car, and Ted peered critically into Yvonne's face.

"She's kind of ugly," Ted said. "I thought babies were supposed to be cute."

"She'll get prettier when she grows up," Rachel said charitably. Then her eyes widened. "I forgot. She might not grow up, right?"

I tried to think of an answer, but I couldn't come up with one. I thought of what Betty had said, and of Joanne's words. *Are we doing something wrong and foolish?* I wondered. Yvonne could have been taken care of in the hospital. She would never have known anything was wrong or different. She'd never know that we had taken her home with us. *Why am I exposing all of us to this?* I asked myself.

I tried to think more positively. Once we'd reached home, I let Rachel help me undress the baby and bathe her tiny body. Yvonne was so tiny she was like a baby bird, and she lay quietly in the water as I washed her gently.

Later, dressed in Rachel's old baby clothes, she remained quiet as I fed her the formula Dr. Brose had given me. Then I burped her and put her in her crib.

Only later did I realize that something had been missing from the bathing and the feeding. I hadn't talked to Yvonne. To my own kids—active, squirming, eager babies—I had talked a blue streak. Cuddling and kissing them, laughing, singing, and talking, I had made bath time and bedtime active, sharing times for Rachel and Ted. Even when they were little, I thought, I used to talk to them. But why would I talk to Yvonne? She doesn't know. She doesn't understand. I doubt if she even feels anything.

I felt terribly depressed. The kids must have sensed my depression, because that evening they were really quiet, not talking much or playing with one another. The silence engulfed Russell, too. Usually, we talked over a cup of tea at the end of the day. But that day he said he was too tired even for the tea.

"Is Yvonne asleep?" was all he asked.

"Yes. Russell, were we right bringing Yvonne home? Maybe. . . ."

But he cut my words short with an impatience that wasn't like Russell. "Julia, I don't have all the answers," he said. "Let's just give it time, okay? She's already here. Let's see how it goes."

That whole night I couldn't sleep. We'd brought Yvonne's crib into our room so I could make sure she was breathing properly, and every few minutes I sat up in bed, sure that her breathing had stopped. I was up and down all night, and when I finally managed to doze off I was awakened by her feeble crying—she was awake and hungry. I fed her and put her down in the crib again. By that time, I had to get Russell and the kids off on their way.

Usually I welcomed each morning—the bustle of getting breakfast, then the long, leisurely day ahead of me. But that morning I felt caged in and afraid. I kept rushing over to Yvonne's crib to make sure she was okay. It was exhausting, and by afternoon my nerves were wire-taut. When Rachel and Ted came racing home from school, I yelled at them for making such a racket.

"Can't you see the baby's asleep?" I shouted. Then, seeing their stricken faces, I felt like crying. "I'm sorry," I said. "Mom's just tired. I guess I'm not used to having the baby around, that's all."

The kids crept away and went to play at Joanne's house. They hadn't been out of the house fifteen minutes when the phone rang.

It was Joanne. "I hear things are pretty rough around there," she said sympathetically. "Rachel came over with a long face." She paused. "Want me to give your kids supper, Julia? I bet you could do with a rest."

I thanked her, but said I could manage. Then, before Joanne could ask about Yvonne, I said good-bye and hung up the phone. Then I went and looked in on Yvonne. She was awake, her sightless eyes staring at nothing. *Oh, poor baby,* I thought, *have I done the right thing for any of us?*

The days passed, and with each day I was less

sure of myself. Everything seemed so different now that Yvonne was with us. The kids were always quiet around the baby, and went out of the house to play with their friends. When they were home, they were as argumentative and tense as were Russell and I.

I missed the fun and the laughter that had always filled our home, and I also missed my freedom. Before Yvonne had come, I'd been able to visit, shop, draw. Now I felt closed in. I dropped out of my drawing class and stopped going out because I couldn't find anyone willing to sit with Yvonne.

One afternoon, Russell suggested we visit his sister, Betty. "We can take Yvonne with us," he said.

"How can we?" I burst out. "Betty would feel uncomfortable with Yvonne around!" I didn't add that I would feel uncomfortable with the whole family staring at the "doomed baby" in my arms.

Russell frowned at me. "Julia, this isn't good," he said. "If I'd known it'd be like this, I'd never have agreed to bringing this baby here. You're uptight, and the kids aren't happy in their own home. I don't blame them; I hate coming home myself. The place is like a tomb!"

My temper flared. "If you feel like that, why don't you go to Betty's? You should be glad to get away from me for a while! Take the kids and just go!"

Russell said nothing—he just looked at me and left. But that look hurt more than anything he could have said.

After he and the kids had gone, I stood in the silent house for a long time, just thinking about what he'd said. Then I heard Yvonne starting to cry.

Wearily, I went into our bedroom and looked

down at the baby in the crib. Mechanically, I checked her. She wasn't wet. I tried to feed her, but she wasn't hungry. When I was satisfied she was okay, I put her back in the crib, only to hear her start crying again.

"What's wrong with you, baby?" I lifted her into my arms, anxiously searching her face. As I held her, the crying stopped, and the small face moved closer to my breast. One small hand, moving aimlessly, touched my finger, grabbed it, and held on.

I felt my eyes fill with hot tears. Long, long ago Rachel had cried and cried until I had picked her up and held her. And then, close to warmth and comfort and love, she had fallen asleep. *Yvonne may have a hundred and one things wrong with her,* I thought, *but somehow she knows, too. She knows when she's being held, cuddled, and cared for. And she knows she wants love.*

"You know, don't you, baby?" I whispered. The little hand continued to grip my finger tightly. "Well, now that I know you know, I'm not going to let you down." The tears slid down my cheeks as I carried Yvonne to a rocker in the family room and began to rock her. As I rocked her, I talked to her—gently, softly, soothingly, like I'd once talked to Ted and Rachel. She nuzzled closer, and as we rocked, she fell asleep.

I must have dozed off, too, because when I opened my eyes Yvonne was fast asleep against me, and it was turning dark outside. *Russell and the kids will be back soon,* I thought. And when they did get back, they were in for a surprise. I kissed Yvonne's cheek and carried her back to her crib. "Just for a little while, sweetie," I told her. Talking to

Yvonne came easily now. For some reason I felt refreshed, calm, and at peace.

When Russell and the kids got home, the house was full of lights and music and the smell of an apple pie in the oven and good stew on the stove. The music came from the stereo in the family room, where I'd moved Yvonne. On her tummy on a thick blanket, Yvonne looked as if she was listening to and enjoying the music. Ted and Rachel laughed at the sight.

"Does she like the music, Mom?" Ted asked.

"You used to love music at that age," I told him. "Yvonne seems to like it, too, don't you think?"

The kids went to lie down next to Yvonne to listen to the music with her. After awhile, they brought out a game and played next to Yvonne, talking to her often or stroking her fine hair. Russell came over to me and put his arms around me.

"I missed you at Betty's," he said.

"I know," I replied. "I missed you, too. Next time we'll all go." I drew a deep breath. "We'll go everywhere together."

Russell kissed me. It was a sweet "hello" kiss. "I'm sorry I snapped at you before," he said. "Or maybe I'm not. You've worked it out, I guess."

I had. If Yvonne had only a few short weeks to spend with us, during that time I was going to give her everything I could.

That evening, after I'd fed Yvonne, I brought her bassinet close to our dining-room table. She lay there, content, as we ate and laughed and joked. Later, when she was put to bed, Russell and the kids came to kiss her good night.

"Tomorrow," practical Ted suggested, "we

should take Yvonne for a walk. It's supposed to be warm, and it'll probably do her good. Let's take her to the park!"

We did just that. After school, we bundled up Yvonne and put her in the baby carriage. Rachel walked alongside, talking to Yvonne, telling her what a wonderful, warm day it was.

"The sun's really bright," she said. "The sky is blue, and there are fluffy white clouds up there. I wish you could see that beautiful butterfly, Yvonne, or the way Ted's chasing it. . . ."

"Julia!" I looked up and saw Joanne standing on her porch, staring at us. "Julia, is that wise?" she asked, hurrying over to us. "Bringing the—uh—baby outside? I mean, why? She doesn't know anything, does she? She can't see anything. So what good does it do?"

There was no way I could explain to Joanne how I felt—that just being with Yvonne was doing us good. Our walk, because we tried to explain everything to Yvonne, was one of the happiest walks of our lives. And later, as we all sat in the park, Ted and Rachel collected grass and wild flowers so that Yvonne could smell them and feel them tickle her hands and cheeks.

Finally, Rachel burst out, "Mom, I'd forgotten how many kinds of flowers there are till I started collecting them for Yvonne!"

There were plenty of "flowers" in the world, and Russell and I tried to give them all to Yvonne. I drew a sketch of her, which Russell said was the best thing I'd ever done. Then there was music . . . bright, sunshiny walks . . . quiet times on Sunday mornings when all five of us read the Sunday funnies in our big bed . . . laughing bath times and loving good nights. Each of these we offered Yvonne as gifts of time and love.

We started taking Yvonne to friends' homes and family gatherings—even over to Betty's house. At first, Betty wasn't too happy about this, but when she saw how matter-of-factly Rachel and Ted treated Yvonne, she changed her tune.

"After all," Betty actually said to me the second time we brought Yvonne to visit her, "it might be a good experience for your kids to be with a baby like Yvonne."

Joanne was harder to reach, but even she began to see the sweetness in Yvonne. After awhile, she and her daughter, Steffie, began to walk to the park with Ted and Rachel and me. And Joanne, too, began to talk to Yvonne, and bring her little gifts— cuddly toys and rubber animals for her bath.

Then one day, while Rachel and Ted were in the family room with Yvonne, I heard Ted's frightened gasp. "Mom!" he shouted. "Something's wrong with Yvonne! She's turning blue!"

I ran into the family room and saw Yvonne struggling for breath. We raced her to the hospital, where Dr. Brose took care of the problem. Yvonne was able to return home with us, but after that things weren't the same. It was as if we all knew instinctively that Yvonne didn't have much time left.

Soon afterward, Yvonne contracted pneumonia. "This could be it," Dr. Brose said. "She's very small, and she hasn't any resistance at all."

"No," I said. I wasn't ready to let Yvonne go—not yet. Ted felt the same way, and so did Rachel.

As for Russell, he said that Yvonne was a fighter.

"She's not going to knuckle under to any dumb pneumonia," he said to us all. "Not our Yvonne!"

Yvonne proved Russell right. After a week-long stay in the hospital, she returned home to us. When she came home this time, Joanne and Betty and our family and friends had made a huge banner that read: "Welcome home, Yvonne! You're our girl!"

It was Yvonne's first and last party, but it was a great one. Everyone came by to bring Yvonne gifts, kiss her, and wish her well. Through it all Yvonne lay quietly, seeming to sense what she couldn't see. She looked happy, peaceful, and completely at home.

After that, Yvonne began to fade quickly. She grew weaker, and she couldn't catch her breath. Her appetite failed till she was eating very little, if anything. Her crying became so weak, I could hardly hear it. Dr. Brose said that it was near the end, but Russell and I just couldn't accept it. *Live,* I'd beg her silently as I held her close. *Please, darling, live.*

The days passed, and slowly Yvonne slipped away from us. Then one day, something made us aware that Yvonne was going. It was a beautiful Saturday, with bright spring sunshine all around us. I held Yvonne in my arms and sat in the family room, with the windows open so that the warmth could touch our baby. Russell sat with me, and the kids came in often to see how Yvonne was. They talked to her, and about her.

"Remember how I thought she was pretty ugly when she came?" Ted said once, touching Yvonne's fuzzy hair. "Well, she's still kinda ugly, but I like you all the same, Yvonne."

"Remember our first walk in the park?" Rachel asked.

THE PRECIOUS BABY

I remembered—and my heart ached as I tried to let Yvonne go. It was so hard. Russell and I and the children had come to love this child only so we could lose her. As I grieved, I felt Yvonne's hand curl around my finger and hold on. It was as if she was reassuring me, comforting me, returning my love in the only way she knew how.

"Remember, Yvonne," I whispered to her. "Wherever you're going, remember us."

Around noon, Yvonne died quietly.

Russell and I packed her things—her baby clothes, blankets, toys—and drove her to Lincoln Hospital as we'd arranged earlier. The hospital would arrange for her funeral.

It was a sad time, and yet a happy time, too. The house, when we returned to it, still seemed full of Yvonne, and the kids and Russell and I spent a lot of time remembering the happy things about our baby. I guessed that we would always remember them.

It's strange. In the beginning, I was afraid to bring Yvonne into our lives because I was afraid of confronting death. The odd thing is that Yvonne didn't bring death into our family at all.

As Rachel said, "I'd forgotten how many flowers there were till I started counting them for Yvonne."

Yvonne made us stop and count the flowers. She taught all of us about life. THE END

WHO WILL GIVE THIS LITTLE GIRL A HOME?

I was sitting home, waiting for my son to come home from first grade, when the phone rang. It was my husband, Kevin. Before I could even finish saying hello, he broke in. "Honey, how would you like to legally adopt Patty?"

"What are you talking about?" I asked him. He knew how much I loved and missed Patty, and I was annoyed that he would even be questioning me about it.

"Connie, it's true, Ruth says I can take her home tonight."

As soon as I could speak, I practically screamed, "Yes, yes, yes! But how did it finally happen?"

"I'll explain everything when I get home."

"Be sure you see a lawyer to get a legal document giving us permission to bring Patty to see a doctor."

"I don't know if I can find anyone now, honey, but no matter what happens, I'm bringing Patty home to us—where she belongs."

The words sounded so wonderful, but even after

we hung up, I was afraid to really believe that in a few hours Patty and Kevin would be here with me. I had hoped and prayed for this to happen for too long now, and I didn't think I could handle any disappointments.

When my son, Donny, came home from school I told him that Patty might be coming back to be with us tonight, but I tried not to get him too excited in case something happened and Kevin wasn't able to accomplish it.

After Donny and I had a snack and watched a show on TV, Kevin called back. He told me that he had found a lawyer and the necessary papers were being prepared.

Once we hung up, I silently thanked God for helping Ruth decide to let us adopt Patty. I can still remember the first time I had seen little Patty. We were visiting my brother and his wife when their daughter Ruth came by looking for a place to stay.

Through family members I had heard that Ruth had three young kids, each by different fathers whom she had never married. Her parents were raising the oldest child, and my sister had the youngest child, who was only a year old. Ruth had her middle daughter, Patty, with her, and she told me that day that she'd never let anyone else have her.

I asked Ruth where the child was and she told me that was why she had come to see her parents. She and Patty were living in a two-bedroom shack with ten other people. She hated living there, but she had nowhere else to go—unless her parents would take them in. She was in tears as she described the way the landlord demanded all of her money and then gave her beans and potatoes to eat, while he and his wife ate steak every night. She said things had gotten even worse last night after the landlord had tried to seduce her and she had fought him off. Because of this, he was evicting her. Kevin and I felt so sorry for her, and for her little girl, Patty, that we offered to let them stay with us.

We all got into our truck, and I waited there, while Ruth, my husband, and our young son, Donny, went inside to bring out Patty and their things. Kevin and Donny made several trips, and then, finally, Ruth came out with the most pitiful-looking little girl I had ever seen.

"This is Patty," was all Ruth said as we all got into the truck.

"Hi, honey," I said, trying to get the little girl to smile, but there was no response from her.

She was very dirty and her clothes were soiled and torn, and Ruth's appearance and personal hygiene weren't much better.

The entire ride home was very uncomfortable and awkward because no matter what I tried to do, Patty remained silent, and Ruth seemed to be mad at the child.

I was never so glad to see our nice, clean home as I was that day when we drove up, and I could tell that Donny and Kevin felt the same way.

After everyone was situated, we explained how we lived and what we expected from Ruth. Her appearance was very embarrassing. The next day we made a futile attempt to sort through her boxes of clothes, but they were so dirty and old that we ended up throwing them out. It was so sad to discover that Patty didn't have any toys.

Later, we went shopping, and I bought Patty and Ruth things they needed, and, much to Patty's delight, several new toys.

As the days passed, I learned just exactly how bad a mother Ruth really was. Her daily routine was consistent. Every day she slept until noon and forced Patty to do the same. If Patty woke her up, she would take her into the bathroom, lock the door, and spank her. Patty would cry and Ruth would yell at her to shut up. Then Patty would make low, moaning, whimpering sounds.

Afterward, Ruth would bring Patty into the den and make her sit on the floor, with no toys or television as punishment. Then she'd proceed to drink coffee until she was ready to fix Patty some cereal or a sandwich. After she ate, Ruth made Patty sit on the den floor again, where she'd gaze at her surroundings with a look of fear and boredom in her eyes.

I would intervene, but Ruth would haughtily tell me to mind my own business and not interfere with the way she raised her child. Her abuse broke my heart and caused me to be extremely nervous and emotional. It was difficult to remain patient as I continually explained to her how wrong her inexcusable actions and behavior were. But I kept trying for Patty's sake, even though Ruth was so naive she couldn't comprehend and would become so angry and rebellious that she'd vent her temper and profanity at me and Patty.

Her physical and verbal abuse reduced me to constant tears, but she'd try to appease me by cleaning the house until it was spotless and acting so remorseful and appreciative that I would feel very sorry for her and forgive the horrible, unpleasant experiences, until every day became repetitious and I realized she would never adjust. All our attempts to help were futile. The only saving grace was that all of this happened while Donny was at school and Kevin was at work. By the time they came home everything was normal.

But I couldn't take it for too long, and finally Ruth said she'd leave. We all loved Patty and begged Ruth to let Patty stay with us while she made proper arrangements for the two of them. This upset her and she cried and told us how she loved all her kids and how Patty was all she had left. We suggested that she place her in a foster home, but Ruth was terrified of the idea. We couldn't convince her that it wasn't the same as adoption, so we proceeded to call several family members and ask for their help. We were informed of the many different times they had helped Ruth, and their experiences were all similar to ours. Everyone felt sorry for little Patty, but no one wanted to keep her. They thought she was mentally retarded because she couldn't speak more than a few words and was a very passive child.

Finally, because of Ruth's insistence, we left the two of them at her brother's. He lived in an abandoned house and seldom worked. My husband gave Ruth money for groceries and his office number, and asked her to call if they needed anything. She called once or twice a week to borrow money. And then, finally, the day came when she called Kevin and asked him if we wanted to adopt Patty. She explained that she'd had only two meals in two weeks. Kevin knew she'd squandered the money he had given her. He didn't hesitate to tell her that we would love to adopt Patty, and then he called me immediately. Patty was now four years old.

At last Kevin pulled into our driveway, smiling and holding up the legal papers that gave us temporary custody of Patty and permission for medical assistance.

Donny and I didn't see Patty at first because she was asleep in her booster seat. We gently woke her up, anxious to give her a big hug and kiss. She recognized me, smiled, and wrapped her arms around my neck and said, "Mama."

I told her that I was her mama and introduced her to Daddy and her brother, Donny. We were completely happy for the first time in months.

The next morning we took Patty on another shopping spree. I was shocked to discover how thin she was. The next few weeks were hectic with constant doctor appointments. Patty didn't gain weight so her doctor ran tests to rule out several things that could be wrong because Patty woke up every night sweating. Her doctor told me that he was ninety-nine percent sure that Patty had tuberculosis so he did a test. He quarantined us for forty-eight hours. Thankfully, the tests were negative. Our optometrist checked Patty's eyes and fitted her with glasses. She had a lazy eye and was almost legally blind in her left eye. I had to patch her good eye for several hours each day to force her to use her lazy eye. I showed her pictures in magazines, hoping to build up her vision. This procedure greatly upset Patty and she would cry every time.

Meanwhile, our attorney was proceeding with the adoption. We were told Ruth was given sixty days to come and claim Patty. We were interviewed by a social worker and she talked and checked Patty. I'll always be grateful for her kindness and wisdom. She was a remarkable person.

Every day I would teach Patty how to talk, feed herself, dress and undress herself, and behave. She would hold food in her mouth for hours. I thought she must remember feeling hungry and tears would slide down my cheeks. I showed her all the food in our home and carried her to the grocery store and taught her the different food groups. I would reassure her that we would always have plenty of good food to eat. Eventually she stopped.

Many nights I would cry and pour out my heartaches, fears, and frustrations to my husband. He was always so understanding, supportive, and encouraging. This motivated me to continue. I would tell Patty simple words and have her repeat them to me. She pronounced fan, pan; girl, dirt; finger, gofer; monkey would sound like gunkey. I knew I had to take her to a speech therapist. Ruth stuttered, and perhaps this affected her ability to pronounce words correctly. Sometimes I would say simple words like table, chair, sofa, and ask her to show me each item. She would look at me with a blank stare. Dear God, she doesn't know or understand what I'm talking about. What on earth had happened to this baby? Where was she kept for years to not know anything?

This scared me and I began to wonder if she was mentally slow and if I were doing more harm than good. I thought about giving up for both our sakes. The emotional and mental strain seemed unbearable. The only thing that kept me from doing so was knowing I was all she had to help teach her, and if I gave up she had no one and might never learn enough to live a normal life. She deserved this chance, this opportunity.

Although I was scared and afraid, and didn't feel qualified to do this astronomical task, I continued to teach her every day. I asked her to tell me when she was hungry. It took exactly one month to the day for Patty to come up to me and say, "Hungry, Mama."

I was so thrilled! It was the very first time she'd put two words together! I couldn't stop the tears from streaming down my face as I gave her some food. She had just given me the assurance and confidence to continue to teach her by letting me know that she was learning; she did understand.

Ruth called from California ten days before her sixty days would have been over. I was terrified that she wanted Patty back, but she assured me she would never take her from us and asked me to tell Patty how much she loved her. She said she was very happy with her new boyfriend and that they hoped to have a baby.

After counting off the next ten days, I put a big red mark on the last day! Now we were happy and relaxed and planned a celebration for our new daughter with family and friends. It was now only a matter of time and formalities with our social worker, attorneys, and judges.

Patty and I continued to work diligently for months.

Her speech improved tremendously, but she still needed help. It was time to take her to a speech therapist.

After the therapist checked Patty's ears and speech, she assured me that Patty didn't have a hearing problem or a speech impediment and to continue to teach her as I had been doing.

I was so proud of myself and especially of Patty. She deserved an award for all her hard work and accomplishments, so I took her shopping and let her choose some new toys. Then we went to her favorite place to eat. The love, happiness, and pride I felt for my daughter meant more to me than anything money could buy. We still had one more doctor's visit. I felt guilty for taking her to so many doctors, although she never complained, and I kept telling myself I was doing what's best for her.

I took her to be mentally evaluated, and once again I explained our dilemma. I was permitted to observe each test and was surprised to learn that I had already taught her everything on the test. The test results showed extremely high intelligence.

The doctor praised us and encouraged me to continue doing exactly what I'd been doing. This was another especially happy time, and I finally felt qualified to be an adequate mother for Patty. I felt very remorseful for ever thinking she was mentally slow and so thankful I didn't give up.

She certainly seemed like a different little girl. She was very intelligent with a fantastic memory and was growing taller and bigger every day.

Patty still had many obstacles to conquer. Such as her fear of water, even raindrops and beautiful white snowflakes. She was very afraid of all insects, especially flies. Her actions and words indicated she didn't feel secure. But in time, she proudly mastered each task. We praised her, and I felt our hearts would burst with pride and happiness. Our adoption became final and we enjoyed living as a happy family.

Patty's progress was amazing, except for potty training. She was over four years old, and still I constantly had to clean her, her sheets, and the carpets. I didn't understand how she could be so intelligent and memorize everything else so fast, yet not remember to go to the bathroom. Her doctor said there wasn't a medical problem.

This changed, when early one morning, I went into her room and smelled the odor.

After giving her a bath and changing her bed, I felt so weary and frustrated that I sat down on the floor and cried my heart out. Patty came over to me, put her little arms around my neck, and started crying also.

"I promise I won't do it again," she said, and from that time on, she never had another accident.

Later that night I told my husband, "If I had known, I would have sat down on the floor and cried a long time ago!" We still smile about this.

Soon Patty started kindergarten. It was imperative for her to be prepared chronologically, physically, and emotionally to adjust to the structured environment of school. Every day she learned more and more. Still, it was very difficult to hold back my tears as I waved good-bye when she proudly stepped onto the bus. The few remaining doubts and fears were totally unfounded when I saw how much she loved school and was eager to learn. She made high marks on all her subjects, and her only problem was talking too much!

Since she hadn't spoken until she was four years old, she was trying to catch up. I explained this to her teacher and she understood. She noticed Patty was a little immature for her age and suggested ways I could help her to mature. I followed her instructions and noticed an immediate improvement.

Because of our many experiences, there is a strong bond between me and Patty that can never be broken. I earned the right to be her mother, and no matter what it entails, I'll always love her and protect her. I'll always strive to give her the opportunities she so richly deserves for a happy life. So will her dad and Donny.

My sister adopted Patty's little brother, and the oldest boy still lives with his grandmother. Ruth has never married and she never calls us. I feel so very sorry for her, but I thank her with all my heart for Patty. Because so many girls want to keep their babies, I hope this story will help them to realize that tiny babies grow up to be big boys and girls. They deserve parents who can raise them properly and provide a loving home and family and give them all the opportunities they richly deserve. There are thousands of wonderful childless couples willing to wait years to adopt newborn babies. It is most unfortunate that there isn't a big demand for older children. If only more emphasis would be given to these special ones.

If you are trying to decide what's best for your baby or older child, be positive you do not make a selfish decision. Always do what's best for the child. May God bless you and help you.   THE END

THE BOY
NOBODY WANTED

For the past two years, things hadn't been looking good at Lehrer, Inc., a small machinery company. I had worked for the company for ten years and was earning pretty good money. But if the company went bankrupt, and it looked as though it might, then I'd be out of a job. So a year earlier, I had begun putting out feelers for another position.

Finally, after a year of searching, I found the job I was looking for. It meant a lot of changes in my life. And, of course, the changes were of such magnitude that I couldn't even begin to think about them without first discussing them with my wife, Yvonne.

We had bought a home in the suburbs, and we had lived there for a number of years. The house had been small. So when my twin daughters, Laura and Lauren, were eight years old, I had added on an addition, which included two bedrooms for them.

The girls had started school, and all their friends were there. And Yvonne had a part-time job—three days a week—in a bookstore.

THE BOY NOBODY WANTED

Accepting the new position meant taking a pay cut and moving to a small, quiet town just across the state line. It meant taking the girls away from all their friends and having Yvonne give up her job. It meant giving up all the things I'd worked so hard for. But, in the long run, I knew the new position was a better one, and, eventually, I'd make back the money I'd lost, plus a whole lot more.

Yvonne, the twins, and I made several trips to look over the town and the new plant. We finally decided the new job was worth all the changes that we'd have to make.

I put the house up for sale and got lucky. I had a buyer within five weeks. Then I stumbled onto a nice house with four bedrooms and a swimming pool, less than a mile from the new company.

The sale of the old house and the purchase of the new one had all taken place during the summer. The girls didn't have to miss school and they would have a chance to make some friends.

I really liked the fact that my new house was so close to my job. It allowed me the time to come home for lunch, which I did frequently.

One day, shortly after we'd gotten settled, I came home for lunch and was in the kitchen pestering my wife as she tried to fix something to eat. I was nuzzling her neck, when I happened to glance out the window toward the swimming pool.

Both girls, who were then ten years old, were swimming. A skinny, dirty-looking little boy sat at the edge of the pool with his arms wrapped around his knees. He looked to be about nine years old.

"Who's the kid?" I asked as I nodded my head toward him.

"His name is Sean Davison," Yvonne replied. "He just wandered in here today and started talking to the girls."

Yvonne put lunch on the table, then called the girls to come in to eat.

As the twins hurried into the kitchen, wrapped in beach towels, Lauren stopped and looked back at the boy. He was still sitting at the side of the pool, but had turned his head to watch the girls enter the house.

"Mom?" Lauren asked. "Can Sean eat lunch with us?"

Yvonne had a helpless, undecided look on her face. She knew I enjoyed having meals with my family, that's why I frequently came home for lunch. She really didn't know what to say, so finally she said, "That's up to Daddy. What do you think, Larry?"

I looked at the kid again. He was still looking toward the house. He was a pathetic-looking little thing. He looked as though he didn't have a friend in the world. I felt a sudden surge of pity inside my heart, so I said, "Sure."

Laura had stood next to Lauren awaiting my answer. She waved to the boy in a beckoning motion.

He jumped up and started toward the house. As he entered I saw that he was all skin and bones. His clothes were filthy and ragged. And he was as filthy as his clothing.

The girls seated themselves at the table, and the boy started to sit down at the extra place Yvonne had set.

"Just hold it a minute, buddy," I said rather

gruffly, because I couldn't remember what Yvonne had said his name was. "How about removing a few layers of that dirt? The bathroom's down the hall, second door on the right."

He winced, then looked at me wide-eyed and scared. He acted as though he thought I was going to hit him. But he hurried down the hall as I had directed.

A few minutes later, he returned. His face and hands were clean, but his neck and arms were just as filthy as before.

I just sighed. I hadn't expected the kid to take a bath. And, at least, he looked a little bit better.

He ate his meal rather timidly—eyeing me the entire time.

I didn't like the kid, and I really don't know why. He seemed polite enough, so it wasn't that. And it wasn't because he was obviously very poor. I had come from a poor family myself. I really couldn't put my finger on the reason. I just didn't like him.

When I finished my meal, I kissed Yvonne, and gave the twins a peck on their foreheads. I was about to leave, when I saw the look in the kid's eyes. It was a hungry look. But how could he be hungry? He'd just eaten.

But I guess I wasn't thinking about the fact that there are many different kinds of hunger.

I looked at the boy's hair. It was straggly and dirty, and I guessed it probably hadn't been washed in a month or more. I hated the thought of even touching him, but as I watched his eyes, I suddenly realized, he was hungry for a little of the affection that I had bestowed upon my family. I reached out and ruffled his hair. "You take it easy, old man," I said.

His eyes suddenly twinkled, and he smiled. "You too, Mr. Summit," he said.

As I drove the short distance back to work, I couldn't help but wonder what kind of parents the boy had. How could they be so apathetic about his personal cleanliness?

Then I started thinking about my own parents. I was the eldest son, second oldest child, in a family of five children. My father had been a hard worker, but had died when I was twelve years old. My mother had had a difficult time, raising us alone—she never remarried—but she did the best she could.

Many times, I can remember eating some pretty meager meals, but we'd never gone hungry. And Mom always made sure that we were clean, and that our clothes were spotless and mended.

The survivors' benefits that Mom had received from Dad's insurance included some kind of educational funds for her children. So I was permitted the opportunity to attend college.

I met Yvonne in high school, and married her soon after my third year of college. My twin daughters were born the same summer I earned my bachelor's degree and started my new job with Lehrer, Inc.

I did well at my job and was promoted faster than other employees within the company. But I'd gone as far up the ladder as I could. There was nowhere else to go. So, when the company started to have financial problems, I began looking for another job. It meant starting at the bottom of the ladder again, but there were plenty of opportunities for advancement, given time, I knew I'd do well with the new company, too.

THE BOY NOBODY WANTED

I guess I'm probably typical in that I wanted to give my children a better life than the one I'd had. So I had limited myself to two children and had tried to give them the best life that I could.

My mind returned to Sean again, and I wondered what things motivated his parents. I wondered what kinds of things they wanted for their son.

When I returned from work that night, I was a little surprised to see that the boy was still there. He'd been there all day.

When Laura asked if he could stay for supper, I said, "Don't you think he ought to go home? I'm sure his folks must be worried about his whereabouts."

"Nah," Sean said. "They don't worry about me." But I just figured that was simply a typical kid answer and insisted he go home.

So the boy left. I mean, I didn't care if he had lunch with us, but I didn't want him there for every meal.

But every day for a week, he was at the house. And every day, he just happened to be there at lunchtime. And he'd worn the same filthy clothes for a week.

Finally, I couldn't stand to look at him anymore. "Look, buddy," I said, "the next time I see you, I want to see you scrubbed and with some clean clothes on. I'm tired of looking at your filth."

And the next time he came back to the house, he was clean and had on different clothes. The clothes weren't very clean, but, at least, they were an improvement over the ones he'd worn the week before.

He made a regular pest out of himself. He always

seemed to be at our house. At the table. In front of the television. Occupying the bathroom. Near the pool. And he often stayed until it was time for the girls to go to bed.

One Saturday afternoon, I happened to be in the kitchen, teasing my wife, when I looked out the window. Sean was sitting at the edge of the pool with his arms wrapped around his knees. I was struck by the fact that it was almost exactly the same position he'd been in the first time I'd seen him.

The girls seemed to like him, but I couldn't help but wonder if he really liked them or their pool. Then it occurred to me that I'd never seen him in it.

"Honey," I said to Yvonne, "doesn't the kid ever go swimming?"

"He doesn't know how, Larry," she replied.

I gave Yvonne a quick peck on the cheek, and told her I had to run downtown for a minute. I'd be back by the time she had lunch ready. I returned fifteen minutes later.

I don't know what possessed me to do it, because I still didn't like the kid. He was a nuisance. But I had gone to a local store and bought two pairs of swimming trunks—one red and one blue. I wasn't sure what size to buy the boy, so I got two pairs. I figured, I could always return the pair that didn't fit. But I never did.

When Sean and the girls came in for lunch, I had to remind him, for the umpteenth time, to wash his face and hands. When he returned, I saw one big mark that he'd missed near his eye.

"Hey, old man, you missed a spot," I said as I reached out and touched it. He flinched as my fingers touched his skin. Then I took a closer look and saw that it was a big bruise. "I'm sorry, kid," I said. "I didn't know it was a bruise. How'd you do that?" It was really a nasty-looking bruise.

He stood staring at me for a moment, as though deep in thought. Then, finally, he said, "I was climbing a tree and slipped. I hit my face on a branch."

"Well, you ought to be more careful," I said.

The girls loved the pool, but it was Yvonne's and my rule to make them wait for at least an hour after lunch before they could go back in the water.

When the hour was up, I handed the package I'd purchased to Sean.

He looked at me skeptically. "What's this?" he asked.

"Well, open it and see," I replied.

He opened the bag, looked inside, then pulled out the blue trunks. For a brief moment, his eyes sparkled, and then clouded again. "But I don't know how to swim, Mr. Summit."

"I know," I said, "so I'm going to teach you. Now, go take a shower, then see if one of those will fit."

He looked at me incredulously. "But why do I have to take a shower, if I'm going to get wet anyway?"

I scowled at him and leaned forward slightly. "Because I don't want all that dirt in my pool. Now, get going," I barked.

When Sean emerged, a little while later, he looked like a different kid. He was wearing the red trunks—the smaller of the two.

I was shocked when I looked at him. His frail chest and rib cage were a mass of bruises. "Same tree?" I asked, pointing to the bruises.

He looked down at this chest, and then answered

simply, "Yeah."

But I wasn't so sure about that. Some of those bruises were old and had started to turn yellow. Others were recent and were still pretty blue.

"Laura and Lauren, you girls and Sean go on out to the pool. I'll be along as soon as I change into my trunks."

The children hurried out to the pool, and I turned to Yvonne. "Honey, what do you know about Sean?"

"Not much. I know he's an only child. Oh, and he was born on Valentine's Day. That's about it. Why do you ask?"

"Because he's either the most accident-prone kid I ever saw, or somebody's been beating him. He's got too many bruises on his body for it to be from one slip in a tree."

We talked a few minutes more, and then I went out to the pool to begin giving Sean his first swimming lesson.

By the time school started, he had learned to swim quite well. I hadn't liked the kid at all, and had only tolerated him, because the girls and Yvonne seemed to like him. Yet, he seemed so eager to please me. I really believed it was his eagerness to please me that had allowed him to learn how to swim so quickly. But the day I saw all those bruises, something seemed to melt in my heart, and I felt pity for the kid.

Then he really made me feel guilty when I overheard him talking to the twins. "You guys sure are lucky," he had said. "You got the best dad and mom in the whole world."

When autumn came so did the chill winds and the

nippy air. And also a new annoyance from Sean. He began to pester the girls to ask for overnight stays for him.

On a few occasions, I'd permitted him to sleep over, but as the weather got colder, the requests became more and more frequent.

Finally, one night, I'd been a little irritable, and I'd flatly refused. "Look, girls," I said, "we aren't running a boardinghouse here. Sean has his own home, and he can sleep there for a change."

He'd been to my house every single day since we'd first moved into the house.

One night, in mid-November, it had been bitter cold. The wind was blowing fiercely. Sean was wearing a thin little jacket. When I refused to let him spend the night, I felt guilty about the cold and offered to drive him home.

Before I could even go get the car out of the garage, Sean had disappeared. "Where's Sean?" I asked as I buttoned up my coat.

Lauren just glared at me. "You told him to go home, so he went."

"Well, where does he live?" I asked, feeling even more guilty, to think that the boy was out on such a cold night. I figured, with the car, I might be able to catch up with him and take him the rest of the way home.

"We don't know," Laura said. "He lives down that way." She had pointed her finger as she spoke.

I drove around the neighborhood for an hour, looking for the kid, but I never found him.

The next morning, when I went out to get in my car to go to work, I was startled to see Sean curled up asleep on the backseat.

"What are you doing in my car?" I asked. I could feel my anger rising.

He looked at me with scared, sleepy eyes. "It was so cold and so dark, I was scared to go home. So I got in your car to sleep."

Then I was furious. "You mean to tell me you were in here all the time I was looking for you?"

He nodded his head.

I was so angry, I doubled up my fist and shook it at him. "Get out of here. Just get out of here and go home!" I yelled at him.

His eyes widened, and I could tell he was really scared. But he opened the door, eased past me, then started running in the direction that Laura had pointed to the night before.

For three days, I didn't see Sean, and it was kind of nice to be alone with my wife and daughters for a change. But, at the same time, I discovered that I sort of missed the kid. He'd been around every day since shortly after we'd moved there.

"Where's Sean been keeping himself?" I asked as we ate our supper.

"Around," Lauren said, and her words were tinged with a trace of bitterness.

"Around where?" I asked, pretending I didn't hear the tone of her voice.

"The girls tell me you really scared him the other night," Yvonne said. "He's afraid to come back."

"I was angry and frustrated. I looked for that kid for an hour, and all the time, he'd been hiding on the floor of the car." My voice elevated as I thought about it, but then I lowered it again and added, "But I'm over it now. You can tell him he can come visit once in a while, if he wants to." I hoped the girls caught the inflection in my voice when I said, "once in a while," because I didn't want him there constantly.

We lived in an area that didn't get much snow, nevertheless, a few flurries had left patches here and there on the ground. When Sean came back again, a week later, he was just as filthy as the first time I ever saw him. I knew he hadn't had a bath since the last time he'd been at my house. And he was wearing that same thin jacket he'd worn that night.

"Honey, don't you have a heavier coat?" Yvonne asked him as he removed his jacket and hung it on the back of a chair.

"No," he said. 'But it's okay, Mrs. Summit. I don't get very cold."

The next day, at work, I couldn't get it out of my mind that Sean didn't have a heavier coat. The weather was getting worse, and, at times, I got cold just walking to the garage to get in the car, and I had a heavy coat. So I knew, despite what he said, that Sean must have been cold, too.

That afternoon, when I came home for lunch, I gave Yvonne some extra money. "Hon, I don't know anything about kids' clothes. When the kids get home from school, I want you to buy Sean a coat. It bothers me that the kid walks around half-frozen."

I'd given Yvonne the car for her shopping, so when she picked me up after work she still had the kids in the car with her.

Sean's eyes shone as he sat there in his new coat, cap, and gloves. For a minute, it looked like he was going to cry. I guessed he was happy, because Yvonne had gotten him a nice coat.

I was pleased to see that, obviously, he had taken a bath before Yvonne had taken him shopping. After that, I didn't have to tell him to wash up. He did so without being told, yet, he still arrived at my house dirty. But he would always take a bath before he left. He knew that it pleased me. Sean would often come to me and say, "Am I clean, Mr. Summit?"

I'd check his neck, behind his ears, and look at his hands and fingernails. "Sure are," I'd say and smile. Then his eyes would light up with pride.

Since we didn't get much snow in the wintertime, the twins decided that they'd wanted bicycles for Christmas. So Yvonne and I had gotten them each one, along with numerous other gifts. I told Yvonne that I thought it might be nice if we got Sean a shirt and a pair of slacks. "And maybe a football," I'd added. I was a football enthusiast and thought he might be, too.

I figured the boy would probably be with us Christmas Day anyway. He was here every other day, and I wanted him to have some gifts.

On Christmas Day, just as I suspected, he was there, bright and early, wearing the thin little jacket he'd worn before Yvonne bought him the coat.

"Sweetie, where's your new coat?" my wife asked.

He hemmed and hawed around for a minute or so, then finally said, "I lost it, Mrs. Summit."

I was a little angry that the kid could be so careless, but it was Christmas Day, so I didn't say anything, and kept my anger in check.

Lauren and Laura were really excited when the saw their new bikes on each side of our tree. And Sean's eyes sparkled even brighter than the tree when he saw all the gifts.

His eyes misted when four of the packages—bearing his name—were given to him. I got him some socks, too.

"What did you get for Christmas?" Laura asked him.

"Oh, you know, the usual stuff. New socks. Some shirts and jeans." Then he added, "And a new bike. My dad got me a new bike."

"Good!" Lauren said. "Go get your bike, and we can all go riding together."

His eyes suddenly darkened, and he said, "My dad doesn't want me to take it away from the house. He's afraid someone might steal it."

As I listened to the exchange between the kids, I thought it was strange that the boy's father would buy him a bike, then not let him ride it away from the house. But I thought about it for only a moment, and then dismissed it from my mind.

Naturally, Sean was there for dinner, too. I mean, it was Christmas Day, and I sure couldn't turn the kid away, and still keep a clear conscience, and for some reason, he wanted to stay. I thought it odd that he'd rather be with us instead of being with his own family.

"What's that?" he asked as Yvonne placed a golden-brown turkey in the center of the table.

"Be serious!" Laura said. "That's a turkey."

"Oh, yeah! I saw one on Mark's television once. But I ain't never seen a real one."

"Haven't seen a real one," I corrected him.

I was incredulous. I couldn't believe that Sean had never seen nor eaten a turkey. I wondered what his family had for the traditional holiday meal, but I didn't ask him.

That night, when I went in to kiss my daughters good night, I found Lauren in tears.

"What's the matter, cupcake?" I asked as I sat down on the edge of her bed.

She raised up and hugged my neck, as I wrapped my arms around her. "Oh, Daddy," she sobbed, "I feel so sorry for Sean. Except for the things you and Mom got him, he didn't get anything for Christmas."

I felt like someone had hit me. "But, honey, I heard him tell you and Laura about all the things he got." I couldn't believe what she was telling me.

"Oh, he just said that. But when we went outside, he kept asking Laura and me if he could ride our bikes. Laura told him to go get his own bike. That's when he told us he didn't get one."

As I sat in front of the fireplace, with my arm draped around Yvonne's shoulder, I began to tell her what Lauren had said.

"That poor little thing," she said. "Larry, I feel so sorry for him. He's such a sweet little boy. But he's so terribly neglected. And he's just starved for affection."

She was silent for a minute, and then she said, "I wish he were ours."

I'll admit, I didn't like the kid at first, yet, he just kind of grew on me. But, even so, I wouldn't go so far as to wish he were mine. Yet, at the same time, I didn't think any little kid should go without a present at Christmastime.

I squeezed her shoulder affectionately. "Then it wouldn't upset you, if bought him a bike?"

She turned and threw her arms around my neck. "Oh, Larry, I love you so much. You're such a good man."

I didn't know about that. I still felt a little guilty, because I'd been so short-tempered with Sean, and had just tolerated him. Yet, in spite of it, he had told the girls I was "nice." If he thought I was nice—at my worst—then his home life couldn't have been very good.

It still troubled me that the boy could be so careless as to lose his coat, but, at the same time, it was too cold to be without one. "Honey, see if you can find Sean another coat. He really seemed to like the first one you got him."

As I thought about it, I realized something just didn't make sense. I had seen the look in the boy's eyes in the car that day. He was so happy that it didn't stand to reason that he'd lose the coat. But I only thought about it for a minute or two, and then promptly dismissed it from my mind.

Two days after Christmas, the twins helped divert Sean's attention so Yvonne and I could get the bike and coat into the house and placed near the tree.

When Sean saw the bike, his eyes widened, then darkened. "Who's the bike for, Mr. Summit?" he asked.

I smiled down at him. "Now, what little boy hangs around my house all day and half the night?"

His eyes sparkled. "This ain't a joke, is it, Mr. Summit?"

"Isn't," I corrected him. "And, no, it's not a joke. It's really yours."

Sean seemed surprised when he got the second coat. "This is just like the other coat that my dad"—he paused, and then added—"that I lost."

Sean walked over to me and stood looking up at me. He acted like he wanted to hug me, but was afraid to. "These are the nicest presents I ever got," he said.

I couldn't resist any longer. I reached out and hugged him, and he wrapped his arms around me and hugged me back. It was a warm feeling.

Even though it was a lot of work for Yvonne, she made a second Christmas dinner, especially for Sean. I hadn't paid much attention to how he ate in the past, but it suddenly occurred to me that he ate as though he thought he might not ever get another meal.

That night, when it was time for Sean to go home, he said, "Mr. Summit, can I leave my coat and my bike in your garage?"

"No, Sean. I think you ought to take them home."

"Please, Mr. Summit. Please, let me keep them in your garage."

That puzzled me. "But why, Sean? Why don't you want to take them home?"

His eyes misted, and he started to cry. "Because they are the nicest presents I ever got. And if I take them home, my dad will just sell them like he did my other coat."

I was sick inside. How could a man deny his son the warmth of a coat?

"Why did he sell your coat?" I asked.

"So he could buy some beer."

"All right," I said. "You can leave the bike here, but you need the coat." I decided it was about time I meet his parents and see just what kind of people they were. I should have done it when I first saw all the bruises on the boy's body.

Yvonne shooed the girls off to bed, and I told Sean to put on his coat. He put on the thin little jacket, leaving the new coat behind. "No, Sean. You wear the new one. It's too cold for that one."

He did as I told him, and then walked with me to the car.

"Where are we going?" he asked as we walked toward the garage.

"I'm taking you home."

"No!" he shouted, and started to run, but I caught him before he could get very far.

I grabbed him by his shoulders and turned him to face me. "I don't know what you're afraid of, but I sure intend to find out. But I can't, if you don't show me where you live."

So reluctantly, he directed me to his house.

I knocked on the door and waited. Sean stood timidly behind me.

The door opened and a dirty, unshaven man said, "What do you want?" His breath reeked of alcohol. "I brought your son home," I replied.

For the first time, the man looked beyond me and saw the boy. "Where've you been for the past week, you little brat?" he asked. He reached out and grabbed the front of the boy's coat. He made his other hand into a fist and raised it high in the air. At the same time, he let loose with a long list of vile names.

Quickly, I jerked Sean boy away, and the man's fist found only empty air.

Hatred filled my eyes and my voice. "You don't deserve this boy," I said, "and I'm going to see about taking legal steps to take him away from you. In case you don't know it, there's a law against child abuse."

"You don't have to see a lawyer. Take the little

brat. He's not even my kid, and I'm sick of taking on someone else's troubles." He slammed the door in my face.

For a moment, I just stood there in a daze. But I quickly regained my senses and turned to Sean. His eyes were large and frightened. I ruffled his hair, and said, "Come on. You can spend the night with us."

Yvonne was surprised when I walked in with the boy. I could see it in her eyes, even though she didn't say anything. I instructed Sean to sit at the table, and then Yvonne and I sat down with him.

"Okay," I said, "let's have a man-to-man talk. And I want the straight truth. No lies about falling out of trees and losing coats and new bikes that your father bought you."

Then Sean began to tell me about the horrors of his life. His mother was seldom home. He didn't know where she went nor what she did. His father was drunk more than he was sober. He had never had a meal in his own home. Usually, there was nothing at home to eat. So, Sean stole food from the local market, or dropped in to see his friends at mealtime. But his friends' parents had gotten tired of his frequent visits and wouldn't allow him to come around anymore. He tried to escape his father's beatings by staying away from home for weeks at a time. If he couldn't find someone that would let him sleep over, he would sleep in the park in the summertime, and in unlocked cars in the wintertime. He went to school every day, because he knew it was someplace to keep warm.

I was physically sick when I heard all those things. And I knew that there was no way I could ever let the boy go back to that kind of life.

THE BOY NOBODY WANTED

I sent Sean to bed in the guest room, and then Yvonne and I sat down and had a long talk. "Oh, Larry," she said, "that poor little boy. How can anyone be so cruel and uncaring?"

"I don't know," I said. Then I remembered what Yvonne had said about wishing he were our son. For the first time, I realized that I wished the same thing.

"Honey," I said, "you said you wished he were ours. Were you serious?"

"Yes, Larry, I was. He's a nice little boy. He doesn't deserve the life he's lived."

"Then it would be all right with you, if he lived with us?"

She looked at me and smiled. "You old softie. You act like you don't like him, but you really do, don't you?"

"Yeah," I admitted, "I guess, I really do." I squeezed her shoulder, and then said, "Let's go tell him."

Sean was still awake when we entered the guest room. Yvonne sat on one side of the bed, and I sat on the other side. "Sean," I said, "my wife and I've talked it over and have decided we want you to live with us. How do you feel about that?"

His eyes widened. "This ain't . . . isn't"—he corrected—"a joke, is it, Mr. Summit?"

"No, Sean. It isn't a joke. We really want you." He broke into a big smile.

"Oh, and Sean, do you think maybe you could call us Aunt Yvonne and Uncle Larry?"

"Sure," he said, and grinned.

Sean lived with us for a year, and all during that time, his parents never once made any effort to see him. Nor did they ever call to inquire about how he was doing.

Yvonne and I treated him as though he were our son, and he gave us the same respect that our twins did.

A year of proper food and rest turned him into a healthy-looking boy.

Shortly after Christmas of the following year, I began to think about the fact that his birthday was on Valentine Day. We had bought him new clothes, and just about everything else a boy could want or need.

His height had really shot up. I wrapped my arm around his shoulders. "So tell me, old man, what do you want for your birthday?"

Yvonne and I contacted a lawyer, who in turn contacted his parents. Since only his mother was his legal parent she was the one who had to agree to the adoption, and she signed the papers without batting an eye.

As we sat at the table on Valentine Day, Sean's eyes twinkled. He was eager with anticipation. I'm sure he must have been remembering his last birthday.

Yvonne finally entered the dining room carrying a decorated cake with candles on it. Lauren and Laura were anxious to give Sean his gifts. But before we allowed them to, I wanted to give him the gift that Yvonne and I had gotten him.

I handed him a gaily wrapped, shallow oblong box. He opened the gift, and his eyes widened, then misted. Then his lips broke into a broad smile. Inside the box were his adoption papers—changing his name to Sean Summit and listing his parents as

THE BOY NOBODY WANTED

Yvonne and Larry Summit.

As I thought back over the past eighteen months, I remembered all the changes that had taken place with our move and my new job. I remembered the things we all had to give up. But I knew we stood to gain more than we would lose. Yet, as I thought about it, I never once dreamed the change would bring us a son!   THE END

I'VE NEVER
BEEN ALONE
LIKE THIS BEFORE

The sun poked its fingers through my bedroom window, rudely prying open my eyes long before I was ready to get up. Pulling the covers over my head, I tried to sink back into the floaty comfort of our waterbed, but it was no use.

Assorted flushes, gargles, and splashes told me Tom's morning rites were fast reaching an end, and soon he'd be rummaging noisily through our bedroom closet. Then it would only be a matter of minutes before Jenny, our nine-year-old daughter, would burst in, demanding to know why breakfast wasn't ready.

I moaned, pulling the sheet even tighter around my head to block out the hot rays. July was beginning, and the thought of dragging myself through another lonely, tedious day, let alone the rest of the hot summer, was more than I could face. If only I could just sleep a little longer.

"Up and at 'em, Sunshine," Tom said, playfully swatting my seat. "Hey," he said as I made no effort to surface, "you're still not mad, are you?"

Guiltily, I mentally replayed last night's argument. For months now, I'd been moody and depressed—and, I suspected, a colossal pain in the neck.

This new Reno job had been everything Tom both needed and deserved—advancement, challenge, and stimulation—in short, an opportunity too golden to ignore. But it also meant leaving behind my hometown, my mother, and the lifelong friends Corpus Christi had given me, and that hadn't been easy. Logic told me it made sense to move, but logic was cold comfort against my stinging homesickness.

"I'm okay," I lied, throwing back the sheet.

Balancing himself on the bed's padded side rail, Tom leaned over and kissed me. "Good. Maybe it's too soon for you to love this as much as I do, but if you'll just give it a chance—"

"Yeah, yeah, life's an adventure and all that."

"Well, it is," Tom insisted, returning to his morning assault on the closet. "It's just as dull or as exciting as you want to make it."

"Look, if I wanted lectures on positive thinking at seven o'clock in the morning, I'd have married a motivational speaker."

"Go ahead, make fun," Tom said. "But like my family's always said. . . ."

Mentally, I stuffed cotton in my ears. I wasn't up for any more lessons from life as told by the "Swiss Family Bradford." Besides, it always boiled down to the same inescapable truth: Tom and I were different, and with good reason.

To say that Tom's family was the adventurous type would be an understatement of the first order. I mean, if they'd been around for the settling of the American

West, you can bet that the Bradford wagon would have blazed the trail.

But, as far as they were concerned, the pioneering spirit hadn't died with that era. New horizons beckoned, and the Bradfords answered the call, following Tom's father whose job kept them zigzagging around the globe for nearly thirty years. One by one, the Bradford children returned to the United States for college, but Rob and Shelly were still going strong—somewhere in Africa, according to their last letter.

Ironically, it was that same spirit of adventure and zest for life that attracted me to Tom in the first place. I was an only child, coming rather late in the lives of my parents. They were gentle people who'd seen as much excitement as they cared to, and who wanted nothing more than to settle down and lead a quiet, orderly life. I grew up pampered and protected, secure within the family nest. But, as content as I was with my life, Tom represented a vast and exciting world beyond my own. Tom Bradford captured my imagination.

After graduating from college, Tom found work nearby. For a time, I had the best of two worlds: the comfort and security of friends and family, yet a vicarious window on the world as well. Still snug within Corpus Christi, it was easy to dream Tom's dreams— dreams which included eventually working in exotic foreign lands, raising strong-minded, independent children who'd be as much at home in Istanbul as Texas, Tibet as Tennessee. It was a grand plan, but for me, a part of the very distant and very fuzzy future.

Deep down, I knew Tom wasn't the type to log a quiet thirty or forty years until retirement, but I'd grown complacent, comfortable in our Corpus Christi life.

Even after signs of Tom's discontent became too blatant to ignore, I still argued long and hard in favor of staying. My father's sudden death two years earlier had brought my mother and me closer together than ever before, and the thought of leaving was simply too painful.

"She'll be fine," Tom assured me. "I know she's not used to standing on her own two feet, but she's stronger than you think. Besides," he reasoned, "it isn't like she'll be completely alone. She's got friends all over the place, and there's always your Aunt Pam."

I snorted. The thought of my mother's complaining, neurotic sister providing any comfort was ludicrous. "You should've quit while you were ahead," I said, a begrudging smile tugging at my lips.

And so it was decided. With talk of frequent visits and promises of long letters, I mournfully packed each box and crate, and through misted eyes, said my good-byes, sure that I'd faced the hardest part of leaving.

Now, though, five months later, the painful ache for familiar people and places was still present.

Feeling the beginnings of a dull headache through the fog of my morning depression, I stumbled from bed, aware that Tom was still talking.

" . . . go back for a visit, if you think it would help."

"You know we can't afford the cost of a plane ticket right now," I snapped.

"True, but last time I checked I discovered the most marvelous thing: They actually have roads connecting Nevada to Texas. Imagine that!"

For the first time in months, my heart filled with sudden hope. "Oh, Tom, do you think you could get the time off?"

As he looked at me in questioning silence, the confusion on his face turned to irritation. "Of course not. It'll be months before I've built up any vacation time. I was talking about you going by yourself."

I was stunned! I'd as soon set out for Mars. "Corpus Christi's a world away from here!" I wailed.

Saying nothing, Tom ran a comb through his hair, then headed for the door as though in a hurry.

"You'd really send me on a trip like that alone?" I asked, my voice shrill, following him down the hall. "Don't you know how many weirdos prowl the freeways just looking for easy targets?"

"How many?"

I ignored his sarcasm. "Is that what you'd want to have happen to me? Well, is it?" I grabbed his arm just before he cleared the front door.

"You know, Maggie," Tom said in icy, even tones, "you're sounding more like your Aunt Pam every day." Then, shaking his arm from my grip, Tom walked lightly down the front steps and strode toward his bus stop without once looking back.

Slamming the front door, I wiped away the couple of tears that were trickling down my cheeks. The men in my family had protected their women, cherished them. I could almost hear my father's fitful turning in his grave.

The day passed with the same monotonous certainty I'd come to expect. The combination of Jenny, haranguing to join the neighborhood baseball team, plus the strain of functioning in Reno's energy-sapping locale, sent me dragging from room to room, feeling bluer with each passing hour. By the time we all sat down to supper that evening, my mood was darker than any I'd had since leaving Corpus Christi.

"No daughter of mine is going scrambling after baseballs in a park filled with muggers and perverts, and that's final!" I shouted.

The ringing telephone waylaid any rebuttal, father and daughter settling instead for an exchange of sympathetic looks.

"Margaret?" the voice whined through the connection's fuzzy hum. *Margaret*. Only one person stubbornly refused to use the nickname I preferred.

"Aunt Pam?"

"Now, I don't want to worry you. Your mother didn't want me to call at all, but I couldn't see the sense in that. I always say—"

"What is it, Aunt Pam? What's wrong?"

"Margaret, your mother has had a heart attack."

I sank into the nearest chair. Then, trying to collect my wits, I asked, "What does the doctor say? How serious is it?"

"Listen, Margaret, I can't hang on here all night— long distance, you know. City General Hospital, room 318, in case you want to send flowers. I'll call you again in a few days and let you know how everything's going. Try not to worry." And with that, the line went dead.

Clustering around me, Tom and Jenny begged to know the news that had shocked me so much. I told them what little I knew.

"She shouldn't go through this alone," I said suddenly. "I've got to go."

"You mean drive?" Tom asked.

"There's no other way." Then, my mind awhirl with a thousand details, I said, "Jenny—who'll look after Jenny?"

My neighbor, Lisa Phillips, had offered friendship as

well as help when we moved in, they reminded me. There'd be no problem there.

Tom slid his arm around my waist. "Are you sure you want to do this? I mean, I know I was encouraging you to go, but this is so sudden. Couldn't Pam handle things at least until—"

"Would you want her as your only source of comfort if you were sick?" I asked. "She's probably filling Mom's head right this minute with every story she's ever heard where the patient died!" Then, squaring my shoulders, I took a deep breath. "Don't worry," I said, kissing Tom's cheek. "I'll just do whatever has to be done to get me there."

I hardly slept at all that night, my mind as restless as my body. Up with first light, my eyes feeling as though they'd been sandpapered, I headed downstairs, eager to get started and dreading leaving all at the same time.

Handing out instructions and saying good-byes for the tenth time, I could delay no longer, but rounding the corner at the end of our block, I slowed for one last glance. Both father and daughter still stood in the driveway, holding hands and using their free arms to wave their last good-byes. Then, not trusting myself to sit there one more moment for fear of turning back, I shifted the car into gear, and with eyes so full I could hardly see, drove off into the morning.

Early morning traffic swooshed around me, and soon my entire concentration was focused on finding the freeway entrance that would eventually bring me back home. The signs were large, though, and their meaning clear. Almost before I knew it, I'd joined the northbound lanes of Interstate 25. As five lanes narrowed to three, then eventually to two, the big signs soon announced I was leaving my home state.

The panorama of endless sky, and hot, windy fingers raking my hair, became my tonic. The day slipped rapidly beneath my wheels. Finally, with evening appearing on the horizon, I left the eastbound traffic along Interstate 84, and prepared to stop for the night, tired but strangely satisfied, too. Checking the car's odometer, I realized I'd gone more than four hundred miles.

"Not bad for a six-year-old kid who had to ask for directions around the block," I said to myself, smiling.

Selecting a motel, I walked inside, feeling the mild fluttering of butterflies. Tom had always handled this end of things, so I felt a bit anxious.

"Yes, ma'am, may I help you?" the man asked from behind the desk.

"I—I want a room," I stammered.

"You alone?"

My eyes narrowed suspiciously. The place looked respectable, but you could never be too careful, to quote my Aunt Pam. "What difference does that make?"

"About twenty-five bucks."

I stared stupidly.

"Rates go up with each occupant," he explained.

I stifled a giggle. Maybe you *could* be too careful.

Parking in front of room number nine, I quickly unlocked my car's trunk and unloaded the heavy bags. But juggling car keys, motel key, purse, and suitcases was too much. Stuck over four hundred miles between one home and another, I couldn't risk losing my precious car keys in the shuffle between auto and room. Tossing the keys into the front seat for temporary safekeeping, I finished the task of unloading.

Everything at last unpacked and my stomach growling threateningly, I decided to live dangerously and walk across the street to a little restaurant I'd noticed earlier. Eating alone in public was another life-long hang-up of mine. I'd been known to skip meals altogether rather than face a crowded restaurant on my own.

But today had been spent like no other, and the roads were littered with cast-off fears. It simply made no sense to go hungry with a perfectly good restaurant only a few yards away. In a day filled with purges, what was another dragon, more or less?

Stepping into the broiling heat of the motel parking lot I paused, hearing the vague whisperings of Aunt Pam's horror stories. I'd heard tales of strange men lurking in the backseats of women's cars too many times to leave my doors unlocked all night in a strange town.

Quickly opening the passenger door and pressing the lock into place, I slammed it with a resounding thud, then moved to the driver's side. Instead of locking securely, however, that door bounced back a bit as I slammed it. It closed, but without the usual snug fit.

"Good enough for now," I said under my breath, and headed across the street for supper, making a mental note to lock things up properly when I returned.

The cool restaurant air patted my face like an old friend as I stepped out of the evening heat. Aunt Pam had always complained of the notoriously poor service women traveling alone receive, but listening to the rustling approach of the hostess in her crisp uniform, I wondered for the first time just how Aunt Pam had come by that bit of wisdom. She didn't even drive, much less travel.

"Just one?" the hostess asked pleasantly.

"One." I repeated, confronted with yet another of life's little details. I felt as though I'd spent the past twenty-nine years swathed in cotton, and was just now really beginning to see and hear.

I ate hurriedly at first, intent only on completing my meal and returning to the privacy of my room. But somewhere along the way, I made an amazing, discovery: No one even seemed to be aware of me, much less stared. Many of my fellow diners were alone and far too wrapped up in their own concerns to pay any attention to me.

Returning to my room, I stretched across the bed, momentarily depressed by my total loneliness. I missed Tom. But then a pleasant exhaustion, the kind that comes from a day filled with challenges met and problems solved, came over me. In no time at all, I was asleep.

I woke next morning to the sounds of slamming car doors and idling engines. I showered and dressed, then quickly gathering my belongings, I locked the door behind me and stepped out into the bright morning.

Setting the cumbersome bags on the pavement beside my little car, I fished in my purse for the car keys. My fingers came up empty.

Trying to remain calm, I rummaged through first one compartment and then another, telling myself that at any moment I'd hear their reassuring jingle. But pocket after pouch revealed nothing.

My fingers clawed the purse's dark interior with a

panicked urgency of their own until, in utter frustration, I crouched low to the pavement, dumping out the bag's entire contents. Pencils, lipstick, and stray pennies littered the ground. But no keys.

Running a trembling hand through my hair, I stood up and leaned against the side of the car, trying not to cry. I wasn't sure of much, but I did know that hysteria wouldn't solve my problems.

Closing my eyes, I thought of Tom. Independent, sure-of-himself Tom. What would he do in a case like this? Maybe if I could remember the last time I'd seen the keys. . . .

I took a few deep breaths and tried to steady my whirling mind. Mentally, I was again parking the car in front of room number nine. Had to have had them then, for sure. I'd unlocked the trunk, and then, afraid I'd lose them—

Whirling, I stooped to peer through the car window. There on the seat sat my keys, gleaming up at me from the car's sun-drenched interior. The *locked* interior!

Well, I thought wryly, *at least nobody's crouching in the back.* Instead, I stood isolated and vulnerable in the middle of a strange parking lot in the middle of a strange town, locked out of both motel room and car.

"Thank you, Aunt Pam," I muttered.

Closing my eyes once more, I tried to think logically, sensing that my failure to secure the half-locked door the night before could prove to be a blessing.

To lock the car in the first place, you had to press the lock into place and slam the door while hanging on to the handle. If you didn't grasp the outside door handle while slamming the door, the lock would pop up again, and you'd wind up with an unlocked door.

Therefore, I reasoned, since the door hadn't been shut tight to begin with, if I could force it closed without touching the handle. . . .

I gave the door a sudden, sharp push. It clicked firmly into place. I held my breath and reached for the door handle. The magic worked.

"Open sesame," I said, smiling, and climbed inside.

Winding slowly down the highway, I was only dimly aware of the beauty that surrounded me. With the morning's growing heat came a new worry—my car's temperature gauge was climbing steadily higher with each uphill grade.

Nervously monitoring the insistent hissing beneath the hood, I stopped each time the gauge reached a dangerous new high, now measuring progress in yards rather than miles.

Finally after much driving and dust, limping into Texas, I gave a small sigh of relief. I was still more than two hundred miles from Corpus Christi.

The sudden thud of something breaking loose squelched all illusions of home and safety. With steam pouring from under the hood, I had no choice but to stop.

I was still staring forlornly into the car's hissing depths when a state patrolman pulled up alongside.

"Having a little trouble?" he asked, emerging from his car.

No, I thought testily, *this is just a hobby of mine!*

"A bit, I'm afraid."

"Looks like you've blown the upper radiator hose," he said, indicating a gaping tear in the black contraption spewing steam like a geyser.

"Can you fix it?"

"Got any duct tape with you?"

Of course. Doesn't everybody? I thought.

"What's duct tape?"

"Well, never mind," he said. "That'd only be a temporary solution at best. It's too hot to do much with now, anyway. Besides, you'll probably need some water to replace what your radiator lost. Your best bet is to let me take you to the nearest tow truck. It might not be easy, though," he mused, "with the holiday, and all."

"Holiday?"

"Yeah, you know," he said, looking at me strangely. "It's the Fourth of July. Say, how long have you been on the road, anyway?"

We drove for over an hour, stopping at every hamlet claiming a gas station, but the story was always the same. Most were closed, and the ones that weren't had no tow truck at all, or one that was already out on call.

"Well, we might as well go on into Burley," the officer said as we pulled back onto the freeway. "There's bound to be somebody there with what you need."

There was. That is, there was—if I had money to burn. But if I wanted to have enough for the return trip to Reno, I'd have to find another solution.

"Well," the mechanic said slowly, "I could sell you the hose you need and show you how to fix it yourself. All you need is a screwdriver and some water."

I looked at him, speechless. I didn't change light bulbs if I could help it, much less work on cars.

"You've got to be kidding!" I cried. "Anyway, how would I get back out there? My car's probably fifty miles from here."

"You could buy a bus ticket, I suppose, and tell the driver to let you off when you come to your car. I'd take you out there myself, only I'm alone here today and I can't leave unless it's for a tow. So, do you want a demonstration?"

"It's no use," I said miserably. "You could demonstrate till you died of old age, and I still wouldn't be a mechanic."

Then, with a practicality that reminded me of Tom, the fellow said, "Looks to me like you've got three choices, lady: You can pay for the tow, catch the bus out and fix it yourself, or stand here all day and wring your hands."

Then, softening slightly, he said, "Tell you what, if you're not back by the time I close down the station tonight, I'll come looking for you. Now, what's it going to be?"

I sighed. I said I'd do whatever had to be done to get me to Corpus Christi. The time had come to make good on my promise.

"Show me," I said.

Timing in buying my bus ticket couldn't have been better, the first decent break of the whole lousy day. In a matter of minutes, I boarded the large bus, self-consciously clutching the tools I needed for the job that lay ahead.

I suppose it wasn't every day that a passenger boarded with nothing more than a paper sack and a gallon of water for luggage, but that didn't make the barrage of curious looks any less embarrassing. Picking the first empty seat nearest the driver, I busied myself with the view, growing more and more uncomfortable under my seatmate's pointed scrutiny.

It intruded on my thoughts dimly at first, then bubbled to the surface all at once. What in the world did I have to be embarrassed about? For the first time in my life, I was taking full responsibility for myself and my problems. Instead of slouching like a timid child, I should be sitting tall and proud!

Patting the jug of water in my lap, I looked squarely into the probing eyes of the woman sitting next to me. "In case I get thirsty," I said, winking.

The moment I spotted my car, I asked the driver to let me off. I watched the bus until it disappeared from sight, feeling more alone than at any other time in my life. Then, wiping my misting eyes with the back of my hand, I set the jug of water on the ground and lifted the car hood.

The mechanic's instructions still echoing in my ears, I slowly twisted each screw, loosening the clamps that held the tattered hose in place. Still it wouldn't budge.

Forcing the tip of my screwdriver into the end of the hose nearest the radiator, I pried and dug, finally breaking its stubborn grip. Twisting and tugging, I removed the battered hose and threw it in the back of the car. Then, placing the new hose in position, I slipped each clamp into place and firmly tightened the screws.

So far, so good, I thought, releasing a small sigh. But there was more.

Twisting off the radiator cap, I carefully poured the precious water into its black depths, then replaced the cap. Unlocking the car, I climbed inside and, with trembling fingers, started the engine. I was to let it idle for five to ten minutes, the mechanic had said, then check for any leakage of water or steam from the newly installed hose. If I'd done everything correctly, things should appear perfectly dry and I could then drive on into Burley to have him check my work.

Taking a deep breath, I climbed out of the car, almost afraid of what I might find. Gathering my courage, I looked inside. The engine purred routinely and the area around the hose was dry!

Letting out a whoop that could shatter glass, I leaped around the pavement like a deranged grasshopper. I'd done it!

The lights of Corpus Christi winked their greeting through the descending twilight as I rounded the freeway's last bend and found myself home at last. Relief flooded my senses. Soon, too trembly to drive, I pulled onto the shoulder and sat like some sort of lunatic, laughing and crying all at the same time.

"Everything okay here, ma'am?"

Jumping at the sound of the voice so near my window, I jerked to attention, seeing for the first time the patrol car parked behind me.

"I noticed your Nevada plates. Are you lost?" the policeman asked, still taking stock of my disheveled appearance.

My mind whirling through the events of the past two days, I searched for an adequate explanation. How could I possibly convey the exhilaration, the pride I felt at having finally come to terms with my own adulthood? This man had probably faced down dragons such as these a full twenty years ago without thinking twice. No, he probably wouldn't understand. Few men would, I suspected.

"No, I'm not lost," I said, smiling. "If anything, I'm more along the lines of found."

"Well," he said, eyeing me carefully, "if there's no real emergency, you'd better move along. Holidays bring out the weirdos, you know."

I smiled, wondering which category he'd filed me

under: those needing protection, or those to be protected from.

"That's right, I keep forgetting. It's Independence Day, isn't it?" I said, laughing at the utter appropriateness of it all.

Still chuckling, I pulled slowly onto the freeway, leaving him shaking his head in the middle of the Texas desert.

Parking in the hospital's busy lot, I hurried inside just as a recorded voice intoned the end of visiting hours. Remembering the room number Aunt Pam had given me, I moved quickly down the third floor hallway, scanning the numbers alongside each door. Rounding the corner into Mom's room, I ran smack into Aunt Pam.

"Margaret! What in the world? Where's Tom and Jenny?"

"They didn't come, Aunt Pam. I'm alone. How's Mom?"

"Alone? Oh, Margaret, what a foolish—"

"Maggie? Maggie, is that you?" my mother's weak voice called from inside.

Waving my aunt aside, I stepped into the dimly lit room.

"Yes, Mom, it's me. I'm here now, and everything's going to be fine," I said, gently squeezing her outstretched hand. "Tom couldn't come, but—"

"I know. I heard. Oh, Maggie, you shouldn't have come," she said, her eyes filling with tears, "but I'm so glad you did." Then, gathering her composure, she asked about Jenny.

"Spunky as ever," I assured her. "Really has a mind of her own."

Kissing Mom on the forehead, I told her I'd be back

the next day. I wanted to call home before Jenny went to bed.

"Nothing wrong, is there?" Mom asked, gazing at my thoughtful expression.

"No, just a matter of a little summer baseball."

Days slipped quickly into weeks, and as Mom grew steadily stronger I felt a longing to get back to Tom and Jenny—back home. With the last suitcase wedged into my little car, we stood on the sidewalk, hugging our good-byes.

"I'm proud of you, Maggie," Mom said, looking deep into my eyes. "I know it took a lot of courage for you."

"I just did what I had to," I said quickly. "What Tom made me believe was possible."

"I'm so glad things are different for you. Your father and I . . . well, it wasn't anybody's fault—more the times, really. I was too young to question things, and by the time I got it all figured out it was too late. Too late for me, anyway." Putting her arm around my shoulders, she gave me a tender hug. "Cherish Tom, honey. He loves you enough to let you discover your own strength, and that's rare."

Mom's words rode with me all the way back to Reno. For the first time, I felt I really understood what Tom's family was all about. I guess I'd finally become a Bradford. From now on, our love for each other would mean encouraging flight, not clipping wings.

I knew I had a lot of catching up to do if I wanted to join the world of fully functioning adults, but heading south into Reno's rush hour traffic, I knew I'd started. I couldn't wait to get home.   THE END

LOVE ON
THE WILD SIDE

The world can be a beautiful place—so beautiful it sometimes hides its deadly traps. I fell into a couple of traps myself. And I guess that's why I ended up where I did. Trap number one was a wonderful guy named Harry. I'd graduated from high school and was taking some college courses while I tried to decide what I wanted to do. I was into the outdoors—botany, zoology, and ecology. In zoology class, Harry was assigned to be my lab partner.

He was smart, hardworking and had a great sense of humor. By our third session, it hit me like a blow to my heart—I was in love with Harry. There was definitely something between us. I had never been in love before, and I was overwhelmed by the sheer joy of being with Harry and of being alive. Halfway through the semester, Harry finally invited me for a cup of coffee after lab. We settled at a corner table in the cafeteria. Our talk was light, but I gradually sensed that something was wrong.

Harry set down his cup with a clatter. "Oh, Lara,

I—I..." He paused, running his finger around the rim of his cup. "You've made me feel so alive these last weeks. I could get very serious about you."

"But—" I prompted nervously.

"But," he interrupted.

The words hung in the air between us. I felt everything inside me begin to close up. I could only stare at him. "I was eighteen and she was seventeen when we got married two years ago." He gave a mocking laugh. "I knew she had a dragon or two on her back, and I thought that by riding in on my white horse that I could kill them for her. Well, I've learned we all have to kill our own dragons." He was silent a moment. "I can't desert her. We have a baby on the way."

I don't remember what I answered. I'm sure I said something reassuring. In the nights that followed, I shed a lot of tears, but during the days, I continued as if nothing had happened. The next term, I made sure Harry and I didn't share any classes.

That was my first, and not very happy, experience with love.

A couple of years later, I met Dan. He was trap number two. I'd finished college and signed on as an apprentice at a high-tech company. I was barely scraping by in my own little apartment. My folks had retired and moved to Florida, but I was learning a lot about computers and related matters. Dan was lean and good looking, with a laid-back quality that very thoroughly hid his high-flying ambitions. He was a young man on his way to the top, but I didn't pick up on that for a long time.

We dated. I was flattered by his interest in me, and overwhelmed by his presence. He was very unique—it made people notice him and pay attention. When he said he loved me, I didn't know how to answer him. He was foreign to the world I'd grown up in, and he knew it. The night he decided to break it off was the night I decided to tell him I loved him.

We looked at each other silently for a few moments, and then he grinned. "Well, it's obvious we can't have it both ways. I withdraw my suggestion." We were sitting in his car, and he pulled me into his arms. "Do you really love me, Lara?" he asked.

"Yes," I murmured. "I don't know what to make of you, but I know I want to be with you—for the rest of my life." His arms tightened around me and we kissed.

Two nights later, we were in his apartment making love. It was all new to me, and he led the way gently and patiently.

He whispered my name over and over, and, when at last we were one, I felt the tears on my cheeks. I was profoundly moved by the experience.

Dan's world, I came to realize, was hard work, game playing, and political flimflam. I bided my time for four years and finally forced a showdown—marriage immediately or I would walk.

He wouldn't budge. The time wasn't right for him to marry. I guess he really hadn't loved me.

I was stunned. I couldn't believe that he could say he loved me, and then just walk away. He wasn't trying to call my bluff; he said he understood that I wanted to get on with my life—that he knew his attitudes and orientations were different—and goodbye and good luck.

If I had ever thought I knew what love was, Dan had shattered that certainty.

I quit my job and drifted for a few weeks. I ran through a series of emotions from hurt to anger to self-doubt and finally to withdrawal. The message was loud and clear: maybe I was desirable, but not that desirable. I wanted to connect, share, and be needed. Love—a man-made notion—apparently hinged more on opportunity and expediency than emotion. So who needed it? Not me.

My one thought was to get away. Finally, a bunch of factors came together, and I was offered a job I couldn't turn down. The state forestry program needed several fire lookouts. I had enough knowledge and education to qualify and the idea of living high on a mountain in the beautiful forest was exactly what I needed for my bruised soul.

I was hired, and briefed on procedures. I packed outdoor clothing, my MP3 player, and a couple of boxes of books. Ranger Yulesman drove me up in his four-wheel rig. It was a six-hour drive.

High up on a rocky ledge stood the forty-foot lookout tower. We parked beside its steel legs. Beyond, sheltered by scrub brush, was a shed that contained a toilet and shower, water pump, and generator.

I looked at the open work stairs, growing smaller and smaller as they spiraled upward.

"Good thing you're not afraid of heights," Ranger Yulesman said.

I smiled wanly.

Ranger Yulesman unlocked the solid security gate three-quarters of the way up the stairs, and handed me the key. "If you get nervous just lock this gate—no one can get past it."

We made several trips up with my stuff. When everything was stacked on the floor of my new home, I made sandwiches and coffee, and Ranger Yulesman showed me how to use the equipment.

"Everything's computerized," he said. "You take your sighting on the smoke, and this dandy little machine gives you the exact distance, heading, and location. Ninety-nine percent of your fires will be the result of lightning strikes. But over there," he said, pointing, "there's public access. So there's always a chance of a careless match or a campfire that's not properly doused starting a fire."

He then briefed me on the two-way radio. "Aside from emergencies, you can give us a call if you need supplies." Then he added, "You can even call us if you get lonely."

"Thanks," I said.

"But you'll have visitors," he reminded me. "Four-wheel drivers and hikers. It seems everybody's fascinated by lookout towers."

We said good-bye, and I watched him go down the stairs. I waved to him as he swung the rig around and disappeared down the dirt road.

I stood still as the silence settled over me, a silence so intense it was audible. I was absolutely alone, and the feeling gave me a bit of panic. But, in a moment, it was displaced by a sense of awe at the rugged, endless wilderness that surrounded me.

I checked out my new home—thirty square feet, steel walls that came up to my waist, then glass up to the heavy pointed roof, surrounded outside by a metal catwalk. Inside, I had a narrow wooden cot, a refrigerator, a two-burner stove, a sink, an armchair, and by the electronic equipment, a tall, wooden stool with a backrest and legs grounded in glass booties. Ranger Yulesman had told me I should sit without touching anything during a lightning storm in that specially-made unit.

Beyond the glass panels that could swing up to let the breezes in, was a dark green sea of endless pine trees riding up mountainsides, spilling into valleys, broken only by occasional outcroppings of granite. The sky above was an intense, clear blue. In every direction, I could see for miles. I took a deep breath and felt a new kind of peace begin to grow in my heart.

My routine took getting used to. I think the hardest part was in the early morning, scrambling down the cold metal stairs to shower and brush my teeth. I always shivered, my fingers felt like ice. Back in my glass nest, I'd warm up with steaming coffee and a hearty breakfast. I learned to frequently interrupt whatever I was doing to take a three-hundred-sixty-degree scan out the windows.

By the end of my first week, I realized I had neighbors—woodpeckers, crested jays, and a red-tailed hawk. If I still felt an edge of aloneness, they began to fill it. The birds were truly my friends.

By the end of the first month, I also discovered that there were raccoons, deer, and bobcats. Sometimes, in the hours before dawn, I'd hear the high, yapping bark of a coyote.

My first human visitors were a young couple in a bright, shiny rig, who wore bright, shiny wedding bands. They stood in my glass house, looking at the view.

"Just married?" I asked.

"Yes," the girl answered, taking her husband's hand. "Eight days, two hours, and thirty-three minutes.

". . . but who's counting?" her husband continued.

They asked me about the weather and the wildlife and about the fires.

"There haven't been any fires in this region for thirty-four years," I told them.

"No wonder it's so green and beautiful," the woman said. "I hope there's never a fire here."

"Well," I said, "on the other hand, without occasional fires to clear out the debris, the mountains become burdened with the thick undergrowth, rotting logs, and dead trees."

"Fuel waiting to burn," the young man put in.

"Exactly."

I congratulated them on their marriage and watched them clatter down the metal stairs. They honked and waved as they drove away.

Seeing the two of them together, holding hands, the pain washed through me. Dan! How could you have done what you did? That could have been us. I allowed myself to feel the hurt, to let the tears slip out from under my eyelids.

Then, a few minutes later, I roused myself and wiped my eyes. I ran down the spiral steps to the shed. I pulled out two mousetraps and set them. Maybe I could catch a field mouse and offer the tidbit to my hawk. I wanted to entice him, to get him so he wouldn't be afraid of me. It was something to do.

As my second month came to an end, I had the signatures of twelve people in my visitors book— the young couple, of course, two rangers, three middle-aged couples in a camper caravan, and two young backpackers.

By that time, I was running out of supplies. I radioed in to ranger headquarters, read them my list, and asked them to include a dozen new paperback books.

When I saw the ranger's rig pull up at the foot of the stairs, I ran down. I hadn't realized how glad I would be to see a familiar face—even if it was just Ranger Yulesman. As the man climbed out, I almost threw myself into his arms—before I realized it wasn't Ranger Yulesman.

"Oh! Excuse me!" I said, feeling my cheeks redden. "You're not Ranger Yulesman."

"I'm afraid not," he said. "I'm Todd Halstead." He held out his hand, and I shook it.

"I'm Lara McCafferty."

"Well, I've got these boxes for you in the back," he said. "I expect you could use a hand."

"Yes, thanks," I replied.

When the boxes were stacked in the lookout, I offered him coffee and sandwiches.

"I don't want to put you to any trouble," Todd said.

"It's no trouble," I told him.

After I boiled the water and stacked cheese slices on the fresh bread, I said, "What's your station? What do you do?"

"Wilderness patrol, four-wheeling, or backpacking," he answered, and then he gestured to the west. "I work out of the main camp over there, but mostly I stay in the backcountry, just keeping an eye on things."

"You backpack in for days at a time?"

"Weeks, usually," he answered, taking the sandwich I handed him.

"That must be as lonely as my job," I said.

"I don't get lonely," he replied. His voice was steady, his eyes keeping their watch on the distant mountains. "What's lonely is the city. At least for me. Clots of traffic, air that gags you, noise enough to scar your eardrums, everybody moving in his own little space trying to keep his sanity—that's lonely."

I looked at Todd in his ranger's uniform as he took a big bite of his sandwich. He was tall with a strong jaw. He spoke like a person who didn't say much, kept his own counsel, and wasn't bored by his own company. He was a self-sufficient man, with interests outside of himself and I was sure he had a great imagination.

I handed Todd his coffee. "What are you doing delivering supplies to a lookout?"

He turned his eyes on me with a slight smile. "I just came back from the city. My mother died; I went home to go to her funeral."

"I'm sorry."

"Don't be. She hated being confined to her room. And she was in pain." He paused, blinked, and then looked out at the mountains again.

"How about your dad?"

"He's put the house on the market, packed his clothes, and gone back up to Alaska. He's going to be a trapper again, after all these years. You think this is lonely? He'll be visited by a bush pilot with supplies once a month in summer, and then he'll go six months with no visits at all in winter."

"I guess it runs in the family," I said.

He turned his eyes on me. "I'm glad my parents raised me to love the wilderness. You know, it's what we're taught, what we're used to, that we come to love. I expect that's why some people love the big city and begin to feel panicky when they see more than six trees together. Me? I get panicky when I see more than six blocks of tar and brick."

I laughed, and he gave me a slow smile.

"Anyway," he said, "I was on my way back to the head camp and, when I stopped at the ranger headquarters, they asked if I'd deliver these boxes to you."

"Well, I appreciate it," I said.

He finished his sandwich and drained his coffee mug. "Thanks for the snack," he said. He headed for the door and turned. He gave me a grin. "Thanks, Lara. No one has made me talk my head off in years and years!"

I went and leaned over the railing and watched him go down the stairs.

"If you ever come this way when you're patrolling, stop by for a cup of coffee," I called.

He waved and climbed into the rig.

I put away the tins and boxes and supplies. As the sky took on its translucent twilight, I fried myself a steak and ate it hungrily. Then, I curled up in the armchair and thumbed through my new books. When I went to bed, the full moon was just rising over the eastern ridge. It shone in my face. *Like God's flashlight,* I thought. It wasn't until I was drifting off that Todd came into my thoughts again. Rugged, reticent, simple. What an extraordinary person.

Two days later, I spotted my first fire. I was doing

my three-hundred-sixty-degree scan when I spotted smoke. I followed the prescribed procedure and pinpointed the area. It wasn't coming from a campground, but from an area three miles into the wilderness. I radioed the nearest campground to alert them, and then I radioed the headquarters.

I continued my scan, and then focused on the smoke again. It had increased measurably.

At last, I heard an old propeller plane lumbering overhead. I looked up. It was a bomber heading for the fire, followed in a few minutes by another bomber. With my binoculars, I watched the first one make a low run over the treetops and drop its load of red powdery matter, labor up into the sky, and head out. Then the second bomber made its run.

Apparently, that's all it took. Within a half hour, the smoke was gone. I got a call on my radio from headquarters.

"According to the supervisors, the fire was caused by an illegal campfire not properly extinguished. You did a good job, Lara."

"Thanks," I said. I felt really good.

The following week, on a sunny morning, my hawk came soaring into sight. I hadn't had much luck with the hawk, but I went down the stairs to check the mousetraps again. Maybe this time he'd take a tidbit.

I opened the shed door to the generator and sure enough, one of the traps had a catch. I took out the mouse and was resetting the trap when I heard a motorcycle approach. I stood and turned.

I could sense the vibes were bad.

The driver wore mirrored sunglasses and a sweatband to keep his long hair out of his face. He had on jeans, heavy boots, and a black leather jacket with the sleeves ripped out, exposing his huge arms. He dismounted, kicked down the stand, and rested the bike. Then he saw me.

"Well, well. You the little lady that runs this place? Or have you got an old man upstairs?" he asked.

"I run the place," I said.

"Well, now, ain't that dandy!" A slow smile spread on his face, but there was no humor in it.

"Did you come to look at the view?" I asked, trying to be pleasant.

"I came to get some food. Haven't had any for a while, either." His smile turned to a leer.

A cold knot settled in my stomach. "I don't have any food to sell," I replied. "You can take the road ten miles to the next camp. There's a store there."

"Can't wait that long," he said, moving toward me. "I'm as hungry as a bear. Now you wouldn't deny a hungry man a sandwich, would you?'

I didn't answer as my mind raced. If I can beat him up the stairs, I can slam the security gate and radio for help.

I turned sharply, but his hand clamped down on my arm. "Not so fast now. Let's just keep it slow and friendly," he said to me.

He pushed me up the stairs, keeping a grip on my arm. I had to shake him free! I had to get that security gate closed between us!

I bided my time. His hand relaxed a little. Three steps from the gate I caught him by surprise, suddenly wrenching myself free, whirling up the steps, and ferociously slamming the gate.

There was no reassuring click. Instead, there was a heavy thump as the gate hit his shoulder. Slowly, he forced it open.

In a panic, I ran the rest of the way up, swung into the lookout, banged the door shut, and bolted it.

He arrived on the catwalk puffing. He didn't even try the handle. He leaned against the railing and with a booted foot, he kicked at the glass. At the third kick it shattered and he slowly reached in and unlocked the door.

My heart was pounding in my chest.

"Now, I don't like your attitude," he said. "I don't like it one bit."

I knew better than to challenge him. I kept my eyes down. "I'm sorry. I—I'll make you a sandwich."

"And get me a beer," he said.

"I don't have any beer."

"Yeah?" he growled. "Well, we'll see about that." He flung open the refrigerator. There was nothing but canned juice, soda, and milk. He kicked the door shut. "You're not making any points with me, little lady."

"Sorry," I said. "Try this." I handed him an enormous double sandwich stacked with cheese and sliced meat.

He took a bite. "That's more like it." He perched on the high stool and propped his booted feet on the small sink. He had a grin on his face that sent shivers down my back.

I poured him a glass of milk and handed it to him. Without changing his expression, he swung his arm and knocked the glass out of my hand. Milk went flying over the floor and the chair, the glass shattering against the wall.

I didn't blink. "Perhaps you'd prefer some cola."

"Perhaps," he mimicked.

I popped open a can of cola and put it by his feet. He shook his fingers at me. "Here," he said. "Bring it here to me like a nice little lady."

I picked up the can and held it out to him. He grabbed my wrist and pulled me close. "You're going to feed it to me. A sip at a time. When I ask. Like a right proper little lady."

He finished the sandwich, belched, and wiped his mouth with the back of his hand. He took the last swallow of cola and released my wrist. He stood up and stretched.

"I've seen corpses with more life in them than this place," he said.

I was sure he had, and it did nothing to ease the sick tension in my stomach.

He turned back to me. "So, what do you do when you want a little action?"

I didn't answer. I kept my eyes down.

"Look at me when I talk to you!" he snapped.

I raised my eyes, and he grinned. "I said, what do you do when you want a little action?"

"I . . . I read, or listen to country-and-western music," I stammered.

He laughed and moved toward me. "Well, I guess you don't know what action is. I'm going to have to show you."

I backed away from him but he kept coming until I was flattened against the window. I forced my voice to be steady. "Why don't you just take yourself out of here? You've had your sandwich. You're overstaying your welcome."

"I don't think so. I think that you're just dying for a little action."

He was right in front of me. His left arm circled my

waist, his right hand captured my jaw, and he crushed his mouth down on mine.

I wanted to scream as the fear and revulsion tore through me. Instead, I went limp. His kiss got no response. I hung limply, hoping he couldn't feel the pounding of my heart.

"You little . . ." More filthy words came stringing out of his mouth. He slapped me across the face, sending me staggering across the room. I fell in a heap by the bed and cried.

"Okay, punk," said a voice by the door. "You've had your little bit of fun beating up a woman. Now get out."

I looked up. It was Todd.

The man snarled. "Well, look here! It's a boy scout to the rescue!"

Todd moved from the door to stand between the man and me. "Get out!" he said, his authoritative voice hard and even.

"Just who do you think you're talking to?"

"You, you slimy tub of lard. Now move!"

The man's eyes popped out with anger. I stayed against the bed. The man bent quickly and straightened. A switchblade knife flashed to life.

"You say that again, and I'll cut your little uniform to ribbons!" he snarled.

I gasped.

In a motion so fast I didn't even see it happening, Todd had a gun in his hand. "You try to use that knife, and you'll be dead before it hits me."

The man hesitated.

"Come on. You're so tough!" Todd said. He took a step toward him, and the man backed away a step. "You know your problem? You're only half a man without that motorcycle. So, why don't you go on down to your alter ego and just ride away?"

The man let out another burst of awful words, but he backed up another step.

"Go on!" Todd suddenly shouted. "Get out of here before I lose my cool!" He crowded him to the doorway. "Now," he said, "you're going to fold up that blade and put it back in your boot. Then you're going downstairs. Backward. And if you so much as think about reaching for that blade again, you're going to be dead. Do I make myself clear?"

The man, his face boiling red, did as he was told. Todd followed him halfway down, keeping the gun on him, until he reached his bike and kicked it to life.

"I'll get you for this!" he yelled.

"Yeah! Sure you will!" Todd yelled back.

The sound of the motorcycle receded into silence and Todd reappeared in the doorway. By then, I was sitting on the bed, clutching my hand, and shaking violently, the tears sliding down my cheeks.

Todd went immediately to the radio and called headquarters. He gave his location as he slipped the gun into the holster on the back of his belt. "We've had a little trouble here. A biker with a switchblade, now heading south. Maybe the sheriff can pick him up for carrying an illegal weapon."

There was more talk. I hardly heard it. Afterward, Todd sat beside me and held me in his arms.

"Are you okay, Lara? Did he hurt you?"

"No, he . . . he didn't. I . . . I'm okay."

He stroked my hair and said awkwardly, "Best you should let it all out."

It was ten minutes before I began to calm down. Todd handed me his handkerchief and rose to make coffee. When he spoke, his voice was tight with anger.

"That's another reason I hate the city."

"I thought I was so safe here." I moaned softly. "I never dreamed those types came into the woods."

"They usually don't," he answered. "Lately, well . . . . It probably won't happen again."

Suddenly I remembered. "That gun! I didn't know rangers carried guns."

"We never used to," he said wearily. He poured the coffee into two mugs and handed me one. "It's only been recently. Rangers used to give directions and information, aid in emergencies, and manage land use. Seems now we're nothing but a branch of the police—breaking up rowdy parties, having drug busts, and protecting against vandalism."

I gave a little sigh. "Well, I'm glad you had a gun. I don't know what would have happened if you hadn't."

"Don't think about it," he said gently, "Just put it out of your head, if you can."

"Why did you stop by?" I asked.

He gestured with his cup and smiled. "Your invitation. Remember? You said if I was in the area to drop by for a cup of coffee."

A laugh burst from my lips. "I'm so glad you accepted." Then I was giggling hysterically, and Todd held me in his arms again.

The sun was lowering in the western sky when I finally got myself composed. The menace of that awful man was raveling at the edges. The wilderness was looking beautiful and serene again.

I rose and washed my face, and then I turned to Todd. "Would you—would you stay the night? I mean . . ."

"I know what you mean," he said gently "You don't even have to ask."

"Do you like creamed tuna on rice?" I asked.

Todd retrieved his backpack from the bottom of the stairs where he'd dropped it when he'd suspected trouble. I cooked dinner. We ate, talked, watched the sunset, and then talked some more.

He asked me about myself and I told him, touching on Harry and Dan, but I kept it light. "Just unlucky in love, I guess," I joked.

"It's not luck so much as timing, I suspect," Todd said. "So many things have to come together at the right time—attraction, opportunity, plans. With me, the plans didn't jibe. She liked the mountains, but she wanted the convenience of city living. A ranger cabin somewhere was what I wanted. It was an area of no compromise."

"And there has to be compromise, doesn't there?" I mused, thinking once more of Dan's raging ambition. And even as I thought of Dan, he seemed to fade beside the reality of Todd sitting across from me.

I rose and went to him. "Thank you, Todd." I bent and kissed his cheek.

Our eyes held a moment. His were unreadable. Then he said, "Let me help you clean up this mess."

I scrubbed the milk from the armchair and the floor as Todd swept up the broken glass and fitted cardboard over the gaping hole in the door.

"That ought to keep the cold air out until they can get a new pane of glass up here," he said.

I gave Todd a pillow and some blankets, and he made his bed on the floor. We said good night and turned out the lights, and I slipped into my pajamas.

I was awake a long time, looking at his silhouette in the bright moonlight and wishing he was in my bed, holding me close, keeping me safe, and warming me with his arms and his love.

Then I reminded myself that I didn't know what love was. I turned over on my side and finally went to sleep.

In the early morning, I awoke to the aroma of coffee. Todd stood by the bed, a steaming mug in his hand.

"Hi," I said, pushing the tangled hair from my eyes. "You are an early riser, aren't you?"

"Well," he answered, "it's almost five-thirty."

I took the coffee and scrunched up my knees so he could sit down. "Did you sleep okay?"

"Sure," he said. "I sleep okay anywhere." Then he smiled. "Teddy bears."

"What?" I glanced down at my pajamas and laughed. "Yeah, teddy bears." My pajamas were thick, warm flannel and happened to be decorated with teddy bears. I thought ruefully that I probably looked about as sexy as somebody's grandmother.

"Well," I said, "maybe I should cook us some breakfast."

"Let me help," Todd said.

I made the bed quickly, and then left him slicing bacon from a thick slab, while I ran down the stairs to shower and dress.

We lingered over the meal and Todd told me about some of the marvelous places he'd discovered in the mountains.

"I'd like to show you those places sometime." He rose and strapped on his backpack.

I was really sorry to see him go. "I hope you'll

drop by again soon."

He looked down into my eyes. "I will, Lara."

In two short days, a ranger and a worker showed up to replace the pane of glass in the door. On the following day, Todd came back.

"I brought some things from the camp store," he said, and he pulled out a couple of steaks, a bottle of red wine, a loaf of fresh bread, and an apple pie from his pack.

We chatted through the afternoon as the sky slowly grew overcast and the first drops of rain splattered against the glass. We took turns doing the three-hundred-sixty-degree scan, and I pointed out my hawk when he flew by.

As it grew dark, I turned on the lamp by the armchair and set about making dinner. Todd opened the bottle of wine and poured two glasses. We settled with plates on our laps and made a toast.

"To the wilderness," he said.

"To the rain," I said.

"To . . ." He didn't finish. Our eyes held as we clinked glasses and sipped.

We dug into our steaks, sopping up the juices with the bread. For dessert, we had forkfuls of apple pie. The rain came down steadily and made a rousing rattle on the metal roof, shutting away the world. Occasional lightning flashed in the distance.

"Cozy little place you have here," Todd said. "We could be in the crow's nest of a ship."

". . . or in the tower of a Bavarian castle . . ." I added.

". . . or on the inside of a kettle drum!" he cried as a burst of rain practically drowned out our voices.

I rose to clear the dishes and Todd said, "Let

me help."

We stood side by side at the sink, me washing, him drying. His shirt sleeves were rolled up above his elbows and I was suddenly acutely aware of his strong arms and his broad shoulders. Our conversation had stopped, and it wasn't just because of the noisy rain on the roof. When he took the scrubbed skillet from me, his hand touched mine and we both jumped. Todd put the skillet down and leaned on the sink a moment.

He took a deep breath and turned to me. He pulled me into his arms, and I went to him like it was the most natural thing in the world. He held me tightly, and then he looked at me as I raised my face to his. He took tentative little kisses, needing more, but not wanting to be greedy. He kissed my nose and my eyes, and then returned to my mouth.

Then Todd said, "I love you, Lara," and stopped any words I might have said with a kiss.

We moved the few paces to the bed and fell on it. All my caution and reserve vanished. Maybe I didn't know what love was, but I knew what lovemaking was. Todd, with his mixture of tenderness and passion, had me crazy with desire.

The next morning, I woke suddenly, and then I knew what had roused me. The rain had stopped. There was just the barest hint of dawn. Todd murmured and moved in his sleep. I just watched him as he slept. A few hours later, he strapped on his backpack and he was on his way. "I'll be back in a few days," he said. "Then we'll talk."

The sky was a brilliant blue; the pine trees showed off their trapped raindrops like sparkling diamonds. I watched Todd disappear into the forest. What did he want to talk about? I didn't want any surprises—things were just fine the way they were.

I cleaned up my quarters, discovered some steak trimmings, and went out onto the deck to find my hawk. "Come on, you dumb bird," I grumbled. "It's time to start being friends."

I draped the trimmings over the railing. And suddenly, he was swooping down out of the sky, squawking at me.

He landed on the railing some distance away and regarded me and then the steak trimmings. He took off in a rush of wings, made a wide circle, then shot down, snatched the scraps in his talons, and flew off into the treetops.

I laughed with glee and the laughter turned to tears on my cheeks and I whispered, "I love you, Todd."

It turned out that what Todd wanted to talk about was marriage. We sat on the metal deck, on the shade side, our legs dangling over the edge, our arms resting on the lower bars. The ridge dropped steeply away and the treetops were below our feet.

"Marriage is a big step," I said, balancing my tone between the seriousness of the subject and my desire to keep it light. "We still have a lot to learn about each other."

I grinned at him, but he didn't return the grin.

"Do you love me, Lara?"

I looked away "I loved you when I was crying and you were holding me. I loved you when we were making love. I loved you when I was in the sunshine with my hawk." There was a short silence. "I think."

I looked at Todd. "What is love, Todd? Do you

know? There seem to be as many definitions as there are people. I'm not sure I know what love is anymore," I said, and then turned away.

"I didn't know you hurt so much," he said.

"It's not that," I said. "It's just that I don't know anymore." We looked out over the trees at a ghostly moon rising in the blue sky.

Todd rubbed his chin on his hand and swung his feet out a few times. "So, you want time. We'll be together, get to know each other. And in a few months, or years, you'll let me know if you love me and want to marry me."

I sighed. "I guess it's something like that. For a while."

"So you'll look for forest fires and cook your meals and read your books and watch your hawk and see me every so often."

"Very often, I hope . . ."

". . . and we'll wait."

Todd looked at me. He said in a low voice, "Lara, life is something that happens to us when we're doing something else—like waiting."

I returned his look. I wanted to say, "I love you, let's get married." But I couldn't. I needed time, I needed some sort of sign that this was really love.

His stern look softened slowly. "But I'll wait," he said. "Because I love you."

We sat there, smiling at each other, holding hands.

Two more months passed. Spring warmed into summer, and with it came occasional dry lightning storms off to the south. The days were longer now, twilight lingered after nine in the evening. Todd dropped by two or three times a week and we made wonderful love and talked.

"One thing I have to know about you," he said. "Is this attraction to the wilderness something real to you? Or is it just an escape for you?"

"Both, to be honest," I replied. "Okay, I ran away; but I've always loved the mountains.

"Because I have to know if you're going to miss the supermarkets or the movies or parties or having girlfriends."

I laughed. "Oh, please."

"So you really haven't been lonely up here?" he asked.

"Really, I haven't."

He pulled me into his arms and held me tightly and sighed. "I've never been put on hold before."

Suddenly, I felt a squeezing in my heart. I had been put on hold—by Dan—for four years. Sure, we'd had good times; I'd been promoted at my job, I'd matured. But it had rankled me. I'd felt like the kid on the outside of the window looking in at all the candy she wanted and couldn't have.

I couldn't do that to Todd—it wasn't fair. I pushed out of his arms and stood up.

"I'm sorry, Todd. I'm very, very sorry."

"Hey, I didn't mean anything." He swung his feet over the edge of the bed and sat up. "I was only kidding."

"No, you weren't. I mean, I can't bring myself to make a commitment, but I'm keeping you on a string. That's just not right."

"I said I'd wait."

"Well, you shouldn't," I said, almost crossly. "I'm being fickle and selfish, and I don't like myself very much."

"Hey, Lara, come on."

"If I've got a problem I shouldn't saddle you with it."

"Look at it as our problem," he said, standing to take me in his arms.

"But I can't!" I answered, pushing him away. "It's my problem and here you are, a perfectly wonderful guy, and I can't . . ." Tears suddenly clogged my throat.

Todd stepped to my side and took me in his arms. "Just stop fighting, Lara. That's all you have to do."

We made love, but for the first time, there was constraint between us.

Todd didn't come around for two weeks after that. I missed him and I worried about him. Finally, I called the ranger at the head camp and was informed that Todd was out in the backcountry and wasn't expected for another week. I figured Todd was trying to give me space, and time to think things out, but I only seemed to get more confused.

I was sitting in my armchair one cloudy afternoon, eating crackers and trying to think things out, when there was a flash of light and a simultaneous explosion of thunder that just about sent me through them in a mighty leap. I was on my wooden stool with the glass booties, hugging myself and cringing. I was right in the middle of a dry lightning storm!

There was another flash and burst of thunder.

And the lookout tower is just one great big lightning rod, I thought frantically. I recalled Ranger Yulesman telling me the stool was perfectly safe as long as I didn't touch anything.

Finally, I took a deep breath and opened my eyes.

If I was going to be in the center of some wondrous force of nature I might as well enjoy it. The landscape was dull and gray, jolting into brilliance when the lightning flared, and the thunder following rumbled in my breastbone. Occasionally, jagged bolts of lightning zapped the ground.

I must have huddled on the stool for an hour before the storm moved on. I stayed still another twenty minutes just to be sure, and then I gingerly stepped down.

Everything seemed serene and normal. I turned a slow circle, scanning carefully. Nothing.

I ran down to the shed to freshen up. When I returned, I took another look around, then decided to relax with a sandwich and a book. To all appearances, the storm had done no damage. I felt vastly relieved.

I shouldn't have.

I'd forgotten how long a patch of dry duff or a stump or a tree smoldered before it burst into flames. Three hours after the storm passed, I saw smoke.

I plotted its exact location and radioed in to headquarters. "Keep your eyes peeled, Lara," they said, "this storm was a lulu."

An hour later, I saw two more wisps of smoke. I felt a flutter of nervousness; the storm was a dangerous one for sure. I took my readings carefully and radioed them in. Firefighting bombers began thundering overhead.

It was eight-thirty and beginning to grow dark when I spotted a fourth patch of smoke rising. When I radioed in its position, I got some startling instructions.

"Lara," the ranger said, "we don't know what we've got here. New spots could erupt during the night. Just as a precaution, I think you'd better start digging that survival trench, get the tarp out, and water it down. I don't mean to alarm you, but its better to be safe than sorry."

"Right," I said, keeping my voice calm.

I bolted down the spiral steps with an electric lantern and pulled a pickax and shovel from the shed. I went to an area that was about at the center of the large clearing, beside the road, and started digging. Almost immediately, I struck granite. I moved ten yards and tried again. Too hard. I moved closer to the trees where the ground was covered with pine needles. That was better. I started working by the light of the lantern, as the sky grayed into black. Every half hour, I went up and did a scan. It was impossible to see smoke now, of course, so I looked for fire. I saw five glowing spots. Another fire had broken out. I called it in, then went down and continued digging.

By midnight, the trench was dug and I was exhausted. I did a scan—there were four spots of fire now. I made a big pot of coffee and got something to eat. It was going to be a long night.

By three in the morning, two spots of fire were out, but the other two fires appeared out of control. I stared at the two thin jagged lines of orange as they moved closer together against the enveloping black.

I must have slept, finally, for a couple of hours. When I awoke, the sky was growing light, but there was something eerie and unnatural about it. I ran out onto the deck. The sky was canopied by brown smoke, the sunlight struggling through had painted everything an unreal pinkish orange. Underfoot, the catwalk was sprinkled with white ash. The two fires had joined, and with a knot in my stomach, I realized it was heading this way.

I radioed headquarters for an update on the situation and was told to sit tight.

Great, I thought, *just sit tight!*

Two hours later, a wind had sprung up—a strong, hot wind that sometimes plagued this region in summer. If there had been a prayer of containing the fire, I knew it was gone now. That wind could whip the fire along, swinging it from treetop to treetop, jumping firebreaks and rivers. Nervousness clawed at me.

I was on the deck watching the fire race down into the valley below my ridge, when I heard a faint noise. Startled, I listened closely. It sounded like someone calling my name.

I stuck my head inside the door; it wasn't the radio.

"Lara!"

I ran to the deck where I could look over and see the foot of the stairs. No one was there. Anxiously, I scanned the edge of the woods.

Finally, I saw who it was. It was Todd.

My feet hardly touched the treads as I flew down the stairs. I ran across the dry ground and flung myself down beside him.

"Todd! My God, Todd, what's happened to you?" I cried.

He was cut and bruised, his backpack was gone, and his clothes were torn. And then I saw the blood. His torn jeans were soaked, with his leg at an odd angle, the tip of bone jutting through.

Tears sprang to my eyes. "Oh, Todd!"

His voice was tight with pain. "Did a foolish thing—trying to get to you—crossing a creek—slipped on a boulder."

"Tell me what to do."

"Get me some water—a blanket—radio for a helicopter." I started to move and he stopped me. "Wait," he said.

"Yes?"

"We'll get you out of here."

I ran up the stairs. In a minute, I was back. I propped him up as he drank some water, then put a pillow under his head, and covered him with the blanket.

"Do you want an aspirin?"

He attempted a grin. "I don't think that will help."

I called headquarters, fighting to keep my voice steady.

"There's a helicopter ambulance in your area now," the ranger informed me. "We'll radio them to come in and pick up Todd."

"How soon?"

"Twenty minutes."

"Sooner." My voice was gritty. "He's in such pain."

I returned to Todd. He clung to my hand, digging in with the pain. "Soon," I said, wiping his forehead. "They'll be here soon."

The white ash was shrouding Todd's blanket. The wood smoke was unpleasantly pungent.

It seemed like hours, but it was only fifteen minutes, before I heard the helicopter. It came in low over the trees. It found the center of the clearing and hovered. The backwash of the huge propeller sent dirt and twigs stinging into our faces. The craft settled slowly to the ground, the thump and whine of the engines deafening.

A man scrambled out, undid the basket stretcher from the pontoon, and ran toward us. He put the stretcher beside Todd and gestured me to help. Todd grunted with pain.

We carried the stretcher back to the helicopter and the paramedic secured it to the pontoon. I noticed that the basket stretcher on the other side already had a person strapped.

The young man turned to me, his forehead glistened with sweat. "We're full," he shouted over the noise. "We'll have to come back for you."

I nodded numbly even as I heard Todd's hoarse shout. "No! She goes. Leave me here, and take her out."

I turned to Todd, an angry tone in my voice that surprised me. "Stop being heroic! You're helpless with that broken leg. If I have to, I can walk out."

"I won't leave you here, Lara."

The paramedic cut in. "This is very touching, but we've got injured people in this craft and—"

"Go!" I shouted, backing away from the helicopter.

"We'll be back to get you," the man yelled as he swung up and settled into the seat. "In one hour."

He slammed and locked the door, and I ran back to the edge of the woods as the engines whined into high gear. I thought I heard Todd shout my name. I blinked back tears.

The helicopter rose slowly straight up above tree-top level, turned, and lumbered off, the sound gradually fading away.

As the silence closed over me again, I was aware of a new sound. I raised my head sharply to listen. I heard sizzles, cracks, and small explosions as trees burst with the heat. The fire was so close I could hear it!

The man in the helicopter said they'd be back to get me in one hour. *Lots of luck, Lara,* I thought.

I climbed back up into the tower to get an idea of my situation. The fire was burning on three sides. If I wanted to run for it, I could head south down the county road. And then I told myself to stop being foolish. Experienced firefighters had been trapped by the sudden caprices of raging fires. The best thing for me to do would be to wait for the helicopter.

But I couldn't wait in the tower. Already, it was becoming uncomfortably warm. The fire seemed stalled at the foot of the ridge, but that condition could change at any moment.

I filled my canteen with water, stepped out the door, and locked it. As I ran down the stairs, I realized what a silly, futile gesture that was.

I hauled out the tarp from the shed, watered it down, and then dragged it over to my survival trench. I had the crazy notion that I wished I'd brought a pillow with me. I put the canteen in the trench, and then began pacing nervously. The sinister crackling and explosions grew louder, the air was getting hotter. I checked my watch. A half hour to go. They'd never make it back. I forced a steady grip on my nerves.

I heard a loud rushing noise like an express train passing. I whirled to see the trees across the clearing dissolve into raging fire. My heart leapt to my throat. *There's no time left,* I thought.

I heard another sucking, rushing sound. I whirled again. Flames were topping the ridge and licking at the tower.

And then, above the noise of the fire, I heard another noise. It was faint at first, then louder. It was the helicopter. I raised my arms and waved frantically as it came into view.

But it didn't come over the center of the clearing to land. It hovered just down the road, turned one way, then another. It seemed like some alien creature, timid and afraid.

Then I realized what it was.

The helicopter couldn't rescue me. The fire was too close, its heat was raising such turbulence that if the helicopter tried to land, it would crash. I stared at it helplessly as the reality washed over me.

Suddenly the helicopter rose sharply and, as it did, I heard a roar like the opening of a thousand furnaces.

My mind clicked off. Instinct for survival took over. I ran and threw myself into the trench and pulled the tarp over me. I don't know if I prayed. I couldn't hear the helicopter anymore. All I could hear was the booming thunder of the fire. I wondered what it would be like to suffocate to death. And then, I thought bitterly that I was going to die before I'd given myself a chance to live.

I was in the trench for an eternity. I guess at one point my mind went numb. But sometime later, I was aware of a strange silence. Slowly, I pushed the tarp aside and sat up.

What I saw was a scene from the moon. The

ground was white with ash, ghostly trunks smoldered sullenly, and the shed was gone. The lookout tower was an ominous black, its windows burst from the heat. The air was acrid and stinging to the nostrils.

I climbed out of the trench and stretched my cramped muscles. I took a long drink from my canteen. To the south, the fire burned on relentlessly. I went suddenly weak as I realized that if I'd walked out, I'd be dead now.

The strain of the last twenty-four hours washed over me, and I sank exhausted to the ground.

I wasn't there long. Soon I heard the faint thump and looked up into the thick brown sky. The sound grew closer, and the helicopter was overhead. I shielded my face as I watched it settle to the ground.

A man jumped out. It was the same paramedic who had rescued Todd. He walked toward me, a smile of obvious relief on his face.

"Nice day for a picnic," he said.

"Yeah," I answered, rising to my feet. "But it's a real shame when you run out of potato chips."

He grinned and I grinned.

"You okay?" he asked.

Tears pricked my eyes, but I kept grinning. "Sure."

"Well, then, let's go home."

I buckled myself into the seat and stared out the window as we rose high above the devastated forest. We made a wide swing around the fire line and headed toward the nearest city and the hospital.

I kept thinking of what Todd had said: Life is something that happens to us when we're doing something else.

At the hospital, I curbed my impatience as I was checked out, then I got directions to Todd's room.

He was sleeping as I stood beside him. Then slowly he opened his eyes. "Lara!" he said, reaching for my hand. "You're okay. They got you out!"

"I'm here, aren't I?" I smiled. "How are you?"

"The leg will be okay. I was so worried about you, and then they knocked me out." He grinned at me. "You had a pretty rough time at your first forest fire."

"I've decided to give it up."

"I don't blame you."

"To marry a tall, tough ranger. After this, backpacking through the wilderness will be a piece of cake!"

His eyes grew intense. "You—you really mean it, Lara?"

"The only thing in this world that means anything to me is you, Todd," I answered. "I love you. I've loved you all along. I couldn't love you more."

His face lit up with a smile.

Todd was still hobbling on his crutches when we got married. We were assigned to one of the damaged areas of the forest, working to replant the watershed against winter rains, setting out seedlings, and managing what wildlife was left. We worked out of the main camp, with our own cabin.

We've decided to have two children. We're going to show them the beauty of the mountains and the deserts. We're also going to let them know that life has its traps and pitfalls. But most importantly, we're going to teach them that every minute of life is to be lived to its fullest, because it passes quickly never to come again.

I thank Todd for verbalizing that idea for me. And I have to thank the fire for teaching me that lesson.

For my children, I wish a gentler teacher—and much love always. THE END

NIGHT NURSE

"You have a date." Les eyed me accusingly as I adjusted the blinds, then turned to see if the afternoon sun still bothered him.

"Yes." I pretended to sigh. "Ashton Kutcher called and said he was in town doing nothing tonight and I simply had to have dinner with him."

"Him, I can compete with! It's the local Romeos that worry me," Les said, reaching for my hand as I deftly moved away from his bed. "That's not fair," he moaned. "You know I can't get to you!"

I laughed. "Honestly, Les, you like to think of yourself as the lecherous patient, but you're not. You're—" I stopped.

What was he? A handsome, blond giant of a man who didn't belong in a hospital bed, held prisoner by weights for the slipped disc in his back. The first few days he'd been in the hospital, he had been in agonizing pain. I had seen it deep in his eyes whenever I had come to give him medication, help him to ease the weights, ask him if he needed anything.

Once, I suspected there had been tears in his eyes, because he had turned his face into the pillow.

"Get me something, for God's sake," he'd mumbled.

The doctor had given him morphine injections. These had helped. Then, he'd given him a pain-killing pill to which he'd had a violent reaction. I remembered Les's panic when I had answered the call. He hadn't been able to get his breath; he felt as though a giant hand had pressed down on his chest and was crushing him. I had rushed out for help, and the resident physician had come immediately. He had been given an antidote, and in a half hour he was breathing normally again.

"Hi, angel," he'd said the next time I came into the room. "I'm alive!" He'd let out a small yip.

"Don't let it go to your head," I teased.

I couldn't help but like Les, he took his pain so well and he never complained to anyone. He was even good for the other men in the ward. He seemed to get a kick out of them too. Even when a semiprivate room became available and his parents wanted him moved into it, he refused. He said he didn't want to leave the "gang."

But after two weeks he was able to move around, and he began to make noises about going home.

"Don't you like us?" I asked him.

"I love you, but I feel shy in my pajamas," he said. "Listen, do you like to dance?"

"Ummm—want to try it?" I said.

"Go on, Les, dance with the lady," one of the other patients said.

"I'll get you yet!" he threatened me." Wait until I get out of here! I'll come back and haunt you."

"Promises, promises," I said, laughing at him.

I found myself going into Ward C more and more often, though my duty took in the entire third floor. The wards weren't big—there were eight beds in each one. I liked talking with Les, seeing his eyes light up when I came near him. I even liked the pretend passes he made at me while the other men egged him on.

Then one day, he went home. His mother and father came to take him. He was still far from one hundred percent well, but he claimed he had to get home and practice his guitar. Actually, he was a talented musician and played in a small combo—the guitar was only one of the instruments he played. I imagined he missed making his own music and was glad to be leaving. But I must admit I felt a twinge the day I went into Ward C and his bed was occupied by somebody else.

"Hi, Miss Burns, miss your boyfriend?" old Mr. Perkins asked.

"How can I? You're here," I said. But deep down inside I liked the idea of being identified with Les, even though our relationship had been nothing more than nurse and patient.

I had always been careful not to allow myself involvements. And it wasn't just because of our nursing supervisor's admonitions. I didn't need to fall in love with patients. If it was dates I wanted, I had plenty of them when I had time off and felt like fun. And I had something else too—a disinterest in rushing into marriage and giving up all that I had studied and worked so hard to get. On the other hand, I wanted to get married by the time I was twenty-seven and then devote myself full-time to being a wife and mother. Later on—well, then I'd resume my nursing career.

Oh, I had it all figured out. But I hadn't figured on meeting a guy like Les, or feeling as I did after he was gone. I actually felt deserted. I was snappy, unlike myself around the hospital and at home, and I'd catch myself standing still as though waiting for something to happen.

It did. One morning, there was a flurry in Ward C and the patient elevator doors opened to admit a new patient. It was Les, back again! He hadn't heeded the doctor's advice. Thinking the surgical support he wore around his middle was enough, he'd bent over to pick up a book and his back had gone out again. This time, his agony was mixed with fear. He had lost mobility of his right leg because of a nerve being pinched and closing off circulation. I knew this could be bad. There was always the danger of blood clots or neurological problems.

That day the doctors worked over him with medicines and weights, and a regimen of therapy was put to work for him. He saw me, but he didn't see me. His eyes were glazed with pain. And fear. In the next few days, he was to need all the cajolery and good humor I could muster for him. Each day he expected that his leg would be all right, and by the end of the week he was in an unhappy, dark mood.

"I'd rather be dead than crippled," he said to me one day as I changed the position of the weights.

"Stop feeling sorry for yourself," I snapped, knowing he needed to be shaken up. "There are lots of other sick people in this hospital, you know."

"I'm sick and I'm me—that's all I know," he said darkly.

"I'll bring you a crying towel," I said, leaving him.

I wasn't being cruel. I was every bit as worried about him as he was, because he had come to mean more to me than I dared admit. But I had to help him by not feeling sorry for him.

Then one day, he was all smiles. He had felt a tingling in his leg, and he had felt pain when the doctor pricked the leg with a needle. He was getting better. And he was a changed man.

"Come here and kiss me!" he cried. "Now that I've decided to live, I need some loving."

"Go ahead, Nurse," Mr. Perkins egged me on. "That'd be better than watching television."

"All right," I said suddenly, and I don't know where I got the nerve. "Pucker up, boy, I'm coming in!"

I had meant it to be a joke, a light kiss, a laugh, and that was all. But Les's arm went around me, and his mouth beneath mine held me to him for what seemed an eternity. Vaguely I heard someone clapping and chortling behind me. When Les released me, my face was burning and I felt like anything but a dignified nurse in a big hospital. I felt trembly and weak and in love.

"And that will show you!" I said, turning to flee.

Les hadn't been laughing, either. His eyes had been hot and intense on mine.

In the supply room down the hall, I leaned against the wall and it felt cool and good to my hot cheeks. How dared I do such a thing? If the charge nurse had seen me, I'd have been in real hot water.

I went about my duties the rest of the afternoon in a kind of mental fog, glad that I was almost through for the day. I knew I had to sort out what was happening to me. Didn't I know better than to fall in love with a patient? I could almost hear Mrs. Welch, our supervisor, saying: "Male patients fall in love with their nurses and female patients fall in love with their doctors because we are their only world and we are also their hope. They lose track of what it is like to be outside the hospital. They become like children suddenly, and although some rebel, most sink into the child-parent relationship. We feed them and bathe them and take care of them, and so we become special people to them. But once they are gone, a day or so back in their own environment, they forget what we even looked like. Remember that!"

Les would leave and forget about me. I must not let myself think of him as anything but a patient, I reminded myself over and over again.

The day after that, Les said to me, "Why don't you come and visit me some evening?"

"Visit you?" I said. "I see you every day. That's enough."

"You hustle in and out of here in that white uniform and your hair pulled back in a silly ponytail. What do you really look like?"

"That's for me to know and you to find out," I teased.

"All right—come and see me tonight," he said.

"I can't." I pretended to sigh from the burden of my social life.

That was when he said, "You have a date."

"Yes, I have a date," I said, turning away.

"I hope you have a rotten time!" he called after me.

"I wouldn't say that to you," I said.

"I'm sorry." He was a contrite little boy. "I've got no business asking you such a question anyway."

Perversely, I didn't tell him where I was going that night—as a matter of fact, right after I got off duty at three-thirty. It was a Saturday in March, and spring was giving us a preview.

"Behave yourself and I'll bring you some candy," I told him.

On my way down to the nurses' restroom where I planned to change into my flowered sheath and high-heeled pumps, I wondered idly if Les had a girlfriend. His parents visited him evenings, I knew. Did a girl come then too? I didn't know, because I had day duty and was never around at that time. The thought bothered me all the time I was getting dressed and going out the wide doors of Parsons General Hospital. But I managed to shrug it off when I got on the bus that was to take me to my brother's apartment and my "date."

What I hadn't told Les was that my young nephew had been christened that day, and I was going to a family gathering at Paul's house. Since this was their first child, Paul and his wife, Myra, were making a big thing of the christening, and I knew there'd be a huge group of people there when I arrived.

I was right. I could hear the laughter when I approached the door of their apartment. I didn't even ring—the door was open. I walked in and went over to say "hello" to Mom.

"I'm so glad you came," Mom said. "The baby was so sweet, Janet. He didn't cry once. Do you want to see him? He's sleeping, although how he can in all this noise—"

I followed Mom down a small hallway to a bed-

253

room. The baby was awake by then, chuckling to himself and reaching for a mobile hanging over his head. Mom started to croon. I smiled as I looked down at him. All this for him, and he didn't even know what was going on.

Just then my sister-in-law came buzzing into the room.

"Hi, Janet," she said. She was a tiny girl, with red hair and blue-gray eyes. Paul adored her. "What are you doing in here? The men went thataway, girl. Come and snag one of them. These are the best kind—healthy ones!"

Myra was always teasing me about getting a husband who was on his feet rather than on his back, so I just grinned. "Who do you have in mind today?" I asked her.

"Come and see." She took my hand. "Mom, I'll get the baby his orange juice in a minute."

"That's all right, dear. I'll just stay with him a bit," Mom said.

Myra took me into the living room and up to a bushy-haired man with fierce eyes who was talking about isotopes.

"Stop showing off, Mel, and make pretty for the lady," Myra said. "Janet, he's not as mean as he looks."

Mel was fun and terribly clever. I found myself laughing at his jokes and letting him pry hospital stories out of me.

Around six-thirty, Mel took my arm and said, "I know a place with the prescribed red-checked tablecloths and spaghetti and candles in dirty wine bottles. Let's go."

I'll never know what made me refuse. "I'm terribly

sorry," I told him. "But I have a date."

I'd said that twice that day. I was beginning to sound too terribly popular for the everyday world.

"Break it," he urged.

I wish I had. I wish I hadn't been so foolish and that I'd gone with Mel. I'll always wonder what kind of man he really was.

As if I had thought it all out, I decided that I would surprise Les and go back to the hospital for a short visit with him. I knew I looked nice, and, womanlike, I wanted him to see me all dressed up for once. I whispered to Mom that I had a date and would be home early, then I slipped out.

As I neared the hospital, I felt myself getting excited. I anticipated Les's big grin, his surprise at seeing me. And I anticipated more—his treating me as a girl and not his nurse.

I didn't anticipate that there would be a girl sitting on the edge of his bed, contrary to regulations, smoking a cigarette and laughing. She had long blond hair, the straight kind that falls like a soft blanket on a girl's shoulders, and every eye in that ward was on her. I was grateful for that much, because no one saw me, no one recognized me as I turned and walked swiftly down to the stairway and out.

I felt crushed. Les hadn't really meant it when he asked me to visit him. And I'd been acting like a student nurse over a rich patient. I was so angry with myself that I walked three blocks before I realized that I would have to backtrack in order to get the right bus for home.

When I got there, Mom and Dad hadn't come home yet, and I was just as glad. I went into my bedroom and undressed quickly and then took a hot shower. I felt better then. I got a glass of milk and made myself a sandwich of cold roast beef and mustard. When I finished that, I cooked myself a fried egg and ate that. Then I had a piece of chocolate cake—and suddenly realized that I wasn't all that hungry at all.

I was hurt and I was angry. And somewhere deep inside me, I felt a little humiliated, even though Les hadn't seen me. Nor had the shining girl sitting on his bed. That would have been final and utter humiliation.

I was in bed when my parents came home, so I didn't have to discuss anything with them. And before they were up the next morning, I was gone.

All the way to the hospital, I told myself I would be very cool to Les. I'd treat him just as though he were any other patient. Well, that was the idea, wasn't it? He was just another patient. He wasn't someone special. He didn't belong to me. Whatever had given me the idea that our relationship was any more than a patient-nurse relationship?

I postponed going into his ward until I absolutely had to. Then I was as cool and efficient as I knew how to be. When finally I came to Les, he grabbed my hand.

"How was the date last night?" he growled.

"Wonderful." I forced myself to smile sweetly, dreamily. "Just too wonderful for words." It was on the tip of my tongue to say how was your date, but I didn't. That would have given me away.

I slipped away from him and went to Mr. Perkins. He was going home, he told me. He sounded happy, and I told him how wonderful it was that he felt so well. I didn't quite look into his eyes when I told him that. I knew he was a terminal cancer case and that the treatments he had been receiving had only prolonged his life by a few weeks, maybe months.

"I leave you in good hands," Mr. Perkins said, winking at me. "Go get that young fella, Nurse. He's a fine boy."

I shrugged. "I like men myself, men about your age."

He beamed. He didn't believe me any more than I meant what I said, but I had learned to talk that way when it would boost a patient's morale.

That day, I avoided Les as much as possible. When I heard his doctor talking to the charge nurse about discharging him the following morning, I felt a kind of thud where my heart was. But I told myself I didn't really care. It was the end of something that hadn't even got off the ground, if I was honest.

I didn't go to the hospital the next day—it was my day off. I slept until eleven, then had coffee and scrambled eggs with Mom.

"What are you going to do today?" Mom asked.

"I'm going to have my hair done, for one thing," I told her. "Then I'll do a little shopping. Want to come along?"

"I can't. Your father's chair is being delivered today," she said. "It's an anniversary present for him. Think he'll be surprised? He's been hinting like a little boy."

I smiled at Mom. How lucky she was! She and Dad really got along well. Sometimes they were like two kids going off together to do their grocery shopping or to see a friend or to take a ride. They really enjoyed being together. It must be heaven, I caught myself thinking enviously, to find that kind of love. Then I remembered Les and determined not to be a sentimental ninny.

For a week, I went about doing what I had to do, being as good a nurse as I knew how, finding time to buy my parents an anniversary present, going to the movies on Friday night with a fellow named Kevin. Kevin and I had gone to high school together, and our dates were hardly romantic episodes. I had a notion Kevin was afraid to get involved with a girl and that he enjoyed being with me because he knew he was safe.

Two weeks later, as I was coming out of the hospital around four o'clock, there was Les parked at the curb in a convertible.

"Taxi, lady?" he said, grinning.

I stopped. He looked so well, so healthy and tanned and virile. And so unattainable.

"Hello, how are you?" I was as formal as I knew how to be.

"I'll be a lot better if you get in this car," he said. "The cop's been by here twice, and a third time will cost me fifteen bucks."

"Oh, sorry to keep you," I said. "Nice seeing you," and I started to walk away.

He was suddenly out of the car and grabbing my arm. "What's the matter? What have I done? I got the freeze the last day like I was in that mausoleum, and when I left you weren't even around. Okay, what'd I do? Hock some thermometers?"

"It took you a while to ask," I said pointedly.

"Oh, that. I went down South to get some sunshine," he said. "I meant to write you a card, but I'm not much on letter writing."

"I see." I didn't see, but I was glad he hadn't forgotten me—that he'd been away, not just too disinterested to look me up. I even felt a little warm glow. "Come on, please?" he begged. "We've got some talking to do, and that cop will be giving me a ticket any minute. Oh-oh! Here he comes! Jump in!"

I got in the car, and Les waved to the cop and roared away from the curb. He was laughing, and suddenly I was laughing too. I tried to forget the blond girl and remember only that I was the one sitting beside Les, and that must mean something.

Les drove madly through traffic, out past the country club and beyond to a section of lovely homes with wide green lawns. It was so different from the tiny house I lived in with my folks, the small patch of grass out front that Dad tended so seriously each summer. Suddenly, Les pulled off into a wide driveway that led to a large English-type home with small leaded windows and the look of wealth written on it.

"Where are we going?" I asked.

"The old homestead," he said. "Remember, I'm a patient—can't go gunning around all the time."

"You don't act like a patient," I said to him. "But, Les, look at me, I'm in uniform."

"There's no one home," he said. "My folks stayed down South for a while. Come on, you're safe. There's a woman who comes in to clean and cook for me."

We went in through the kitchen—I'll always remember that. Les parked the car near the garage, and we walked into a huge square kitchen, where a woman in a gray uniform was cleaning salad greens.

"Hello, sweet Sue," Les said to the woman. "Meet my girl, Janet, the nurse. She brought me back from the jaws of death." He laughed and grabbed a carrot. "Come on," he said to me. "I want to play some of my CD's for you."

If I had been Alice stepping through the looking glass, I couldn't have stepped into a more alien world for me. The carpet was thick and plush, the living room a muted blend of beiges and greens and blues, and beyond it was a huge sun porch with brightly colored furniture. Les went over to a CD player and flicked on the switch.

"Remember I asked you to dance?" he said. "Now we dance."

"You idiot!" I protested. "I wish you'd have let me go home and change at least."

"It's not your clothes I love, it's you, you, you!" he murmured, pulling me into his arms, burying his face in my hair. "Mmmm, that beautiful, marvelous smell of formaldehyde," he said, and I jumped back, annoyed and a little hurt.

"Aw, don't be mad again," he pleaded, taking both my hands and leaning toward me. "Do you always get mad so easily?"

"Do you always get your way?" I demanded.

"Come here, let's sit down and talk." He pulled me along with him. "Are you really angry because I brought you here? Really? Can't you see that I don't care what you wear? I only want you, not a dress or a uniform. I keep remembering how you took care of me in that hospital. You're sweet, Jan, sweet."

His voice was low, filled with an emotion I dared to think was love. Then he kissed me, a soft, warm kiss that lingered on my lips. Suddenly, he got up and put a new CD on, holding his arms out to me. "Dance? You promised!"

I laughed. He held me close and we danced, and the music and the house and Les all became more than a dream —they were the only reality. Was this the way it felt to love someone? Was it a sense of timelessness, a wanting only to give of myself so that he would know forever how I felt about him?

In a little while, the woman in the kitchen came in softly. "Will that be all?" she asked Les. "Dinner is ready, and if you like I can stay and clean up."

"No, you go along, sweet Sue," Les said to her. "I'll handle that, and what I don't do, you can finish up in the morning. Thanks."

I didn't know what Les expected me to do. I stood there, suddenly feeling very foolish in my uniform. "Les, maybe you can take me home now," I said. But I suppose my voice told him I didn't really want to go.

He laughed and pulled me to him. "Just when we're getting to know each other the right way? You're staying and staying," he said. Then he looked at me and grinned. "Listen, why don't you go upstairs and put on something of my mother's? She's pretty much your size. Go on—get out of that thing so I can forget I'm entertaining a nurse."

I protested, but weakly. I didn't want to go home. Les took me upstairs to a huge bedroom, and he slid back a closet door to reveal all kinds of dresses and suits hanging there.

"I can't!" I held back.

"Sure you can. Mom won't mind," he said. "Put anything on and come down."

When he had gone, I touched the clothes gingerly, feeling like an intruder. Finally, I selected a button-down shirt and a cotton skirt, both washable. The skirt was a little large, but I cinched in the belt and it fit. Before I went back down with Les, I called Mom to tell her not to expect me for dinner.

Later, after Les and I had eaten and piled our dirty dishes in the sink, I had the oddest feeling that we were married. It would be like this, warm and close and thrilling.

It was dark when we went back to the sunroom. Les put some music on, and he took me in his arms and didn't pretend anymore.

"All the time I was South, I kept thinking about you like this," he whispered. "I promised myself that when I came back I'd find you. Jan, I'm crazy about you, I want you—"

"Oh, Les," I cried, my mouth on his. "This isn't just a grateful patient talking, is it?"

"Shhh," he said. "You're my girl now."

Yes, I was his girl, then and in the weeks that followed, weeks that turned my life upside down. It was a kind of madness. I worked and I tended to my patients, but always with the eager expectancy of seeing Les again. I didn't think it was wrong for us to have an affair. I was a nurse. I knew about emotions and I knew about love, didn't I? And Les and I loved each other.

Les's parents came back, and we no longer met at his house. But there were nights when he made love to me in his car, and I didn't think it was wrong. I became a night person for Les, meeting him at a small club where he played four nights a week, sitting at a table near him and waiting.

Mom began to worry about me, that I wasn't getting enough sleep, that I looked thinner. She wanted to know more about Les.

"I love him, Mom," I told her.

"Does he love you?" she asked.

I nodded. He did, didn't he? And one day, we'd get married and I'd have his children. We'd live happily ever after.

Days passed in a haze. I was alive only when I was with Les. And Les would rumple my hair or kiss me suddenly and say, "How's my girl?" But nothing more.

Any girl who gives herself to a man without any commitments must learn to live with this. She can't say to the man, "Marry me. I love you." She has to wait and hope and stifle the little fears that creep into her heart.

One day, there was a picture in the newspaper showing Les with the blond girl I had seen sitting on his bed. The girl's name was Lydia something or other. She had been named chairman of a county drive for some fund-raising project, and Les was playing at a kickoff dance.

The next time I saw Les, I mentioned the picture.

"I'm a celebrity, how about that?" he said, grinning. But he didn't say anything about the girl, and I was too proud to mention her.

In July, I came down with a bad cold and stayed home for a week. Les didn't call, so I called his home. I was told he was out of town. I thought that was odd, because he hadn't said anything to me about going away.

The following week Les called. "Miss me?" he said into the phone.

"Where were you?"

"I was in Memphis," he said. "Got a good deal cooking. I'll tell you about it."

"When will I see you?" I asked, hating myself for having said it.

"How about I call you?" he told me. "I'm kind of busy right now with some loose ends. I'll get to you by the end of the week."

Get to me by the end of the week—like I was some kind of unpleasant duty. It bothered me, and it had me so upset that my mind was only half on my work at the hospital. Twice, my temper snapped at a patient, and the charge nurse reprimanded me. I didn't care. Something was happening between Les and me. I felt it, a kind of premonition.

Then on Friday night, he called and asked me to meet him. I was so overjoyed I almost cried, and I didn't stop to consider that our love affair had been just that, Les calling the tune each time. I went to the club where he was playing that night and sat at a table waiting for him.

It must have been about midnight. I had gone to the restroom to freshen my lipstick and fix my hair. When I came back, Les wasn't on the bandstand. He was sitting at a table with the girl named Lydia, laughing and holding her hand.

I sat and waited. His back was to me, and it was almost as though he didn't know I was there. I felt as if everyone else was staring at me, laughing at me. Then, I began to shed my embarrassment and feel only anger that Les should treat me like this.

Suddenly, I couldn't take it any more. Les hadn't even gone back to play, waving away the piano player who came to talk to him. He was still engrossed with Lydia. I got up and left, going home in a cab and lying in bed for hours just staring at the ceiling.

I was angry with Les, but also afraid. What had I done wrong? Had he tired of me? He had known I was there. When he'd finally remembered me, had he worried about me?

All day at work I fretted, and I began to pray that he'd be waiting for me when I came out of the hospital. *Just let him be there,* I thought frantically. I don't care what he did last night. He has to be there. I love him. I was beyond feeling shame. I just wanted Les. He wasn't there, nor had he called when I got home. But late that night, the phone rang, and it was Les.

"Hi, what happened to you last night?" he asked as though it had been something I had done.

"I didn't think you noticed," I said coldly. "You were too busy."

He laughed. "Aw, come on, Jan, don't be like that," he said. "When am I going to see you?"

"When are you going to have time?"

"Well, I'm kind of tied up tonight," he said. "But let me call you about tomorrow, okay? Don't be mad now." It was an unsatisfactory call. I wanted him to say so much more to me. I tried to tell myself I wouldn't see him when he called. I'd pretend I was busy, that I had another date. I wouldn't chase after a man who showed so little respect for my feelings. But I was a woman in love, and I still hadn't admitted to myself that Les was a man who was just having an affair.

When he called the following night, I agreed to go out with him. He picked me up, and we drove to a small club where we sat at the bar. Les kept drumming his fingers on the table and acting like a man in a hurry.

"Les," I said, "I'm sorry about the other night. I guess I was just jealous of that blonde." I was doing the apologizing.

"What for, honey?" He grinned, taking my hand and stroking my fingers. "You're my girl, aren't you?"

"Am I, Les?" I felt like crying. "I love you. I want more than just—you know—making love in a car."

His eyes got kind of blank, and he turned away from me, hunching over the bar. "Listen, Jan," he said. "You're terrific. I mean, no one knows that better than I do. But don't push me, okay? I mean, I'm grateful and all that for what you've been to me. Hell, I'd have given up in the hospital if it wasn't for you. But take it easy now, will you? It's a big world, honey. Let's not rock the boat."

I heard him, and yet his words washed over me like words uttered on a television screen. I was his girl, but it didn't mean the same thing to him that it meant to me. And I was too proud to say, "Marry me. I want you to marry me."

But I couldn't close my mind any longer to my stupidity. To Les, I was the nurse who had helped him, and for a while, he had clung to me that way, then enjoyed me as a woman. But that was as far as it went for him. I had been the stupid one to let myself fall into this trap.

"Take me home," I said.

"Come on, Jan, don't be like that," he begged. "What're you angry about?" He didn't know. And I wasn't going to let him see me cry. I was a nurse, wasn't I? I had learned to be tough my first time in surgery; I had learned not to flinch when preparing a patient who had just died. I was just a nurse. What made me expect I could be anything else to Les?

All the way home, he was quiet. Then, at my door, he tried to kiss me. "Look, I want to see you again," he said.

I didn't answer. I just said good-bye and went into the house. Three weeks later, I read in the paper that Les and Lydia had got married. I cringed. Did he tell her about the silly little nurse who'd been good to him? Who had fallen in love with him while he was a patient in the hospital? Had they laughed together about me?

I didn't let anyone know how I felt inside, like a cold weight was pressing down on my heart. If all I could be to my patients was just a nurse, that's what I'd be—and the best nurse they ever knew. But that was all. If they wanted their souls healed, they could call in their minister. If they wanted their hand held, they could call on their family. I'd be there only to see to their physical needs. That was my job, wasn't it?

Mom noticed the change in me, and once she asked me about Les.

"What happened with him?" she said. "I thought you were in love with him."

"Oh, Mom," I said. "You know how every male patient falls in love with his nurse on those television shows! Well, it was fun for both of us for a while, but nothing permanent."

"I just don't want you getting hurt," she said quietly.

Being hurt is part of growing up, I wanted to tell her, part of wising up to the ways of the world. To some nurses, it happened when they were students. They fell for a med student or intern, and nothing ever came of it. I'd had to learn my lesson with a patient.

A few weeks later, the supervisor of nurses called me into her office one day. "Mrs. Allison is going to have a baby," she told me. "She's taking a leave of absence, and I want to do some switching around. How would you feel about night duty, Miss Burns?"

"I haven't thought about it," I said. "But I guess I could do it."

"As you know, there's more money for you, and I imagine you could be charge nurse in a short time," she said to me. "Why don't you give me an answer tomorrow? You know the hours, eleven-thirty to seven-thirty. More responsibility too."

I made up my mind. What else was there to do with my evenings except stay home and think of Les? This way, I could fill both my days and nights. And there were other opportunities too. If I was going to make nursing my life's work, then I ought to start thinking in terms of advancing my status and not being a floor nurse all my life. I might even be supervisor of nurses in a hospital someday. That was a challenge worth working for.

I took a few days off to rest, and on a Wednesday night I reported for my first night duty.

Anyone who has ever been hospitalized knows that a hospital at night is like a giant in restless sleep. The corridor lights are dimmed and sounds are muted. A night nurse walks with a flashlight in her hand to check on her patients or answer a call, her rubber-soled shoes quiet on the tiled floor, her aloneness a part of the night.

The first few nights I was on duty, I had the eerie feeling that day sounds remained suspended in the hallways. By the time I got on duty and checked the charts and silently went in to see if my patients were comfortable, most of them were sleeping. But there were always those who were lying in the dark, staring up at the darkness either in pain or in fear. I checked to see if they were hot or uncomfortable, if they required further medication. In any emergency, I had only to call the resident physician. Otherwise, I would sit at the charge desk and make out my night report.

The floor nurse with me was an older woman, widowed, who kept slipping down to the cafeteria for coffee almost every hour. Nell was not a talkative person for which I was grateful, and when things were quiet on the floor she'd do some needlepoint.

"Do you like doing that?" I asked her once.

"I don't like to just sit," she told me. "Is that why you chose night duty?"

"Yes, as a matter of fact," she admitted. "I was lonely."

"That doesn't make sense," I said.

"Oh, yes, it does," she told me. "When I finish here, I stop off and have breakfast and talk to Charlie across the way. Then I take a bus home and do my grocery shopping in my neighborhood, clean my apartment, and read the papers. I sleep until I feel like getting up, have dinner, and come here. That leaves me very little time to be alone. Besides, I kind of think that I belong here. I'm lonely and they're lonely." She nodded toward the corridor.

I could understand that. I was filling my hours too.

"But what about you? A pretty young girl shouldn't be a night nurse for long," she said. "What about your love life?"

I got up quickly. "I'll check on Mr. Perrini. He was restless," I said, walking swiftly away.

My love life! I had had it, love and passion and a man to hold me in his arms but not forever. Les—I didn't even like to say his name because it hurt. I stood at a corridor window and stared out at the night. Somewhere out there, Les was laughing and kissing the blond girl, and he no more thought of me than of a dozen other girls he'd known. I wanted to hate him, but instead I felt numb with grief.

Night brings with it a kind of special terror to hospital patients. I was to find that out. One night, I went into a semiprivate room to give a patient his five o'clock injection. The shades were still drawn in the room, although out in the corridor I had seen the first finger of dawn creeping into the sky.

I thought I'd have to awaken my patient, but I found him lying with his eyes wide open. I leaned over to speak to him softly.

"I'm going to give you another needle," I said. "Will you turn over a bit?"

He looked at me. I had put my flashlight on the night table with its beam shining on the wall, but I could see him clearly. He reached for my arm.

"It's so strange," he said to me softly. He was a terminal cancer patient, sixty-seven years old. "They don't want to look at me. Do I look like I'm dying?"

I tried to smile. "Nonsense," I said. "You're imagining things. Come on, turn over now. This will help you to sleep."

"You don't want to look at me, either," he said.

"My wife acts embarrassed and my son does too. It's like dying is something to be ashamed of." I sensed his fear, but I was only a nurse. It wasn't part of my job, I reminded myself, to hold his hand.

"I don't mind," he said to me as I finished giving him the shot. "I've got to die, just like everybody dies sometime. I just wish they'd look at me. Can you talk to me now?"

"I really can't," I said, adjusting the covers for him. "And we'd wake the man in the other bed. You don't want to disturb him by talking, do you?"

He shook his head. I became very efficient. "Just relax, you'll go off in a few minutes," I said. I turned to leave, and there was Nell, waiting for me.

"New admission," she whispered to me. "They're putting him in 220. Can you do a work-up? I have to give a look at that intravenous I started."

I nodded, following her out into the corridor. She touched my arm. "You were pretty hard on that old fellow," she said to me softly. "He's just lonely and afraid."

"I'm a nurse, not a baby-sitter," I snapped and went down to see about the new patient.

He was a young man, now being helped into bed by an attendant. He looked white, and beads of sweat stood out on his forehead. His eyes were glazed, and he doubled up suddenly in pain. The resident physician, Dr. Allan, came hurrying into the room followed by one of the young interns.

Just then, the man became violently ill. I grabbed the pan from the nightstand and held it under his mouth. He was gasping, and there were traces of blood in what he had thrown up.

"Take it easy—lie back now," the doctor said.

He began a quick examination. I could see that the man's abdomen was tense and boardlike, and his breathing was labored. Dr. Allan took heart and blood pressure checks, and I followed him out of the room to get his orders.

"Looks like ulcer perforation," Dr. Allan said. "Unless it's sealed immediately, he'll have to have surgery. Symptoms will intensify. We'll give him medication for pain and keep a close watch on him. Meanwhile . . ." He told me what I was to give the man, and I hurried off.

When I got back, Dr. Allan was with him again, questioning him about when the first attack had occurred.

"In my hotel. I'd had a big dinner, a few drinks, I was feeling okay. Then I started to get pain, and— Doctor, it's killing me!"

"Okay, calm down and don't do any more talking," the doctor said. "You have your wallet with you? We can get the name off that, Nurse."

I went to the man's clothes and hunted for the wallet. I handed it to the doctor.

"George Thorp. Okay, Mr. Thorp. Do you know anyone in town?"

The man shook his head. "I'm a book salesman," he whispered. "I'm here on business for two weeks. Mr. Wiley down at the Arcade Bookshop, he knows me."

"Family? Are you married?"

The man had closed his eyes, and Dr. Allan walked away. Outside the room, he told me he was going to get in touch with a specialist and have him see the man as soon as possible.

"Hard part here is we have no history on the

man," he said. "Dr. Meyers may be able to get something more out of him later. Keep an eye on him, Nurse."

I nodded.

When I went back into the room, the man was doubled up in pain. I got a towel and wiped his face, and when he reached for the pan again, I tried to hold it for him. He motioned me away.

"Boy, oh, boy!" he gasped a few minutes later. "What hospital is this?" I told him.

He lay back on the pillow and closed his eyes. "What happens now? Do I turn in my chips?"

"If you mean are you going to die," I said crisply, "obviously you're here so you won't die!"

"Thanks," he said. "Don't sound so unhappy about it."

I turned away. He was just another lonely, scared patient. The hospital had suddenly become his only world, and he was reaching out to us to hold his hand and smooth his brow.

"Do you want me to raise your bed?" I asked, ignoring his remark. He had his eyes closed, his dark hair was matted, and there were deep, blue circles under his eyes. I took him to be about twenty-seven.

"Yeah, a little," he said. I cranked up the bed until he signaled me to stop. "Here's the buzzer." I put it beside his pillow. "Press this button if you need anything."

"Man! If I need anything!" he said. "Where you going?"

"There are other patients on this floor," I said to him. "I'll be back shortly."

I turned out the lights, and the room was in darkness. As I went out, he reached up and put the light back on.

"You can't rest with all that light," I told him.

"I'm scared of the dark," he said. "My mother gave me a night light. Okay?" I shrugged and went out. The light was on over Ward C, and I hurried to answer it. Dawn was now spreading out over the sky. In a little while the hospital would begin to stir and the terror that night brought with it would be pushed back with the dawn. Even I had to admit that I walked with a firmer step when it was time to turn off the light in the corridor and daylight splashed across the tiles. The night vigil was over once more.

As I came off duty that morning, I ran into Nancy, a friend of mine with whom I had worked day duty. She greeted me warmly.

"I haven't seen you in ages," she said. "Why don't you come around when I get off here, and we can see a movie or have dinner?"

"You mean you're free?" I said and I laughed. Nancy was always in love with someone.

"In between loves," she said.

I flinched inwardly at her words. What was I in between? Nothing?

"I can't," I told her. "Not tonight. I'm having dinner with my brothel Paul and his wife. I haven't seen then in ages. Let's make it another time."

It was true about my not having seen Paul and Myra. Myra was even a little miffed with me because I'd walked out on Mel.

"How could you do it?" she had wailed. "He's such a catch!"

That night, however, Myra didn't mention Mel.

NIGHT NURSE

She was all wrapped up in herself because she was pregnant again. Going into the kitchen with her after dinner to give her a hand, I fell slightly envious. She was so darned placid, I thought.

"I'm glad about the baby," I said.

"I'm glad too," she said. "I want to have all my babies quickly and let then grow up together. Jan, I don't mean to harp, but what happened? For a while there, Mom was talking like there'd be wedding bells for you."

I started stacking dishes so she wouldn't see my face. "Oh, you know Mom. She's incurably romantic. There was this nice man I met at the hospital and we dated for fun and then it was over. He went away." I couldn't bring myself to say he got married.

"Jan, what you need is to meet men outside the hospital," she said. "Maybe you get the wrong perspective in a hospital, seeing all those sick people all the time, even sick men. Where's the chance for romance there unless it's with the doctors?"

"Who are already married, and interns who can't afford to be," I said "Stop sounding like Mom. I'm not the family old maid yet."

"That's not it. I just think a girl should give herself every opportunity to meet the right husband. Now if you took a job somewhere where you'd meet men, that'd be more like it."

"Like where?" I shook my head. "I'm a nurse and nurses usually work with sick patients."

"Oh, you know, get a job working for a big doctor, meet wealthy patients, that kind of thing."

"But I like working in a hospital," I said.

I was to recall those words that very night. I went on duty I found out the new patient had had to have surgery and was in ICU, the intensive care unit. A new cardiac patient, Mr. Cameron, had been admitted to Ward C and was facing possible surgery in two days' time. Meanwhile, he was having a great deal of pain and discomfort caused by phlebitis, which was attributed to the cardiac catheterization that had been done that morning.

As I answered his call for the third time that night, he asked me to give him an honest answer to a question. "If I can," I said.

"Will I have to have an operation? This arm business, does that make it worse? The doctors won't tell me the truth. They think I can't take it. I'm not a baby. I have a family to worry about," he complained.

"Mr. Cameron, the doctors always tell the truth to their patients," I told him. "As for the pain, is it really that bad? Isn't it better that you are here and you know that you are being taken care of?"

"I guess that's your way of looking at it," he said. "You see people die every day. It doesn't mean that much to you, does it?"

There's a way for a nurse to answer such questions. She mustn't hedge on her answer either. Patients aren't asking questions like that just to be talking. They're afraid, and they do want to know. But I had put on a shield that would protect me from any involvements.

"I'll ask the hospital doctor if you can have some medication that'll help that pain," I said to him, picking up my flashlight and going out to the desk.

It was time for me to eat, so I told Nell I'd catch Dr. Porter or one of the interns down in the cafeteria and maybe have him come in and soothe Mr.

Cameron for a while.

Dr. Porter was a resident finishing out his second year. I found him eating spaghetti and poring over a magazine.

"May I bother you a moment?" I said to him.

"Oh, hello," he said, smiling. He was a young, thin man, with heavy-rimmed glasses that gave him a much older look. "Sit down. What's on your mind?"

"It's Mr. Cameron, a new admission in Ward C. He's complaining of pain." I told him briefly about the patient.

"I know, and pain's twice as hard to take at night," he said, leaning on the table with both elbows. "There isn't much we can do about that. Did he have medication already?"

I told him what he had been given by his doctor.

"That's it then," he said. "Look, why don't you just go and talk to him a few minutes, kind of calm him down. He's probably scared to death."

I got up quickly. "If I sat and held every patient's hand when he was scared or lonely, I wonder how long I'd last in this or any hospital?" I said.

He grinned and got up to walk beside me. "Didn't they tell you in nursing school that holding hands is good, better, best in medicine?"

I didn't answer. I got into the elevator and went back to my floor.

Nell was not at the desk, and I saw a light flashing in one of the semiprivate rooms. When I went to answer it, I found the patient asleep on the button. He'd evidently called or had expected he might need a nurse and put the button under his pillow, then fallen asleep. I flashed my light against the wall where I could see his face but not awaken him. He stirred but did not open his eyes. Gently, I took his pulse and it was steady. I tiptoed out of the room.

For some reason the night dragged. There were nights like that when daylight seemed forever in coming, when the sounds of a sliding elevator door were like a roar and my footsteps seemed to echo in the corridor as I answered a call or made my rounds. I was glad when dawn came and I could start my last round of temperatures and charts before I went off duty.

Going home that morning, I felt the chill of winter coming in the air, and it came to me as almost a shock that four months had passed since I had seen Les, two months since I had been a night nurse. In that time my personal life had been nil except for a couple of dates with Paul and Myra and Paul's business partner, Marty. But I'd known Marty for a long time and it was too late for us to become romantically involved even though he often made noises that were supposed to make him out a player.

I need a vacation, I thought. *I'll take ten days off and go somewhere warm and bask in the sunshine and forget hospitals and patients and involvements.* The thought made me feel better, and that should have given me a clue as to why it was important for me to be more than a nurse to my patients, but it didn't. I even talked about a trip to Mom, and she agreed it'd be a fine idea.

When I got to the hospital that night, I found George Thorp established in my ward. I found him awake on my first rounds, and I asked him if he was feeling all right or if he needed anything.

"Sure. Talk to me," he said, grinning. "You're supposed to be sleeping," I told him.

"You're not," he reminded me. "I don't feel sleepy."

"Do you want a sleeping pill?" I checked his chart. "You were given medication earlier, at nine."

"I know. Here it is." He reached into the night-table drawer and took out the yellow capsule.

"You were supposed to take it," I said. The nurse always hands patients medication in a small paper cup and stands there while they take it. "How'd you manage that?"

"See?" He popped it in his mouth, put it under his tongue, then took it out again. "I'll decide when to sleep. Besides, I wanted to talk to you."

"Me? Why?" I asked.

"Well, the other night, I have a vague recollection I might have been bothersome," he said.

"You weren't, so you can take your pill now and go to sleep," I told him.

"Can't you at least talk to me for a few minutes?" he said. "Don't you feel sorry for me so far away from family and friends?"

I wanted to turn my back on him and walk out. So he was lonely. So he was reaching out to me because I was here, a part of this new world of his, and the other world out there had receded and become like a movie reel. I knew all about that, didn't I? While he was here, I'd be the most important female in the world to him. As soon as he got outside, I'd be just another girl. *No, thanks,* I told myself.

"Mr. Thorp," I said softly, "I'm busy. I have other patients to see, sicker patients than you."

"Are you really that cold?" he said.

I didn't answer. I handed him the glass of water

and waited while he drank it. Then I picked up my flashlight and went to the next bed. Quietly I made my rounds, but I had a feeling he was looking at me. It bothered me somewhat, and then I told myself not to be a fool. He was just another lonely man in a hospital ward at night. In the daylight he'd get to feeling pretty chipper and self-reliant again.

I was wrong about Mr. Thorp. A few nights later, as I was putting some equipment in the sterilizer in the supply room, the door opened and he stood there in his bathrobe and slippers, his face white.

"What are you doing here?" I said.

"Listen, it's that man across from me, Mr. Hamilton. He's going to die, isn't he?"

Mr. Hamilton was going to die, yes, I wanted to say to him. What was I supposed to do about it—broadcast it for everyone to hear?

"I think you'd better get back to bed," I said. "I don't want to feel responsible for your foolishness."

He looked at me and his eyes narrowed. "Would you ever feel responsible for anyone?" he said softly. And he was gone. When I went into the ward a few minutes later, his back was to the room and he looked as though he was asleep. Mr. Hamilton, meanwhile, was not asleep. I went over to his bed quietly and looked down at him. "Pain?" I asked.

"Some, in my chest," he said in a strained voice.

I knew that this man had had radiotherapy for his lung cancer, but now nothing could stop the cells from squeezing out his life. All we could do was try to ease his pain, which, I knew, went all the way up into his neck and made breathing difficult.

I went to the desk and called for Dr. Porter to come and give Mr. Hamilton something. Perhaps that would make George Thorp feel good, too, I thought.

From the very beginning, George Thorp seemed to be my tormentor. I felt as though he was watching me weighing my words, judging me, and I didn't like it at all. He recovered rapidly, but since he would have to travel a long distance to get to hi: home, he preferred to stay in the hospital until he was feeling good. But a: he recovered, he became more restless at night when I'd come on duty, I'd find him either awake or prowling the corridor in his bathrobe and pajamas. Sometimes he'd walk to the solarium and stand there.

Once I went up to him and said, "This isn't a nightclub. You really have to get to bed."

"Oh, I know what it is, all right," he said. "I have only to look over at Mr. Hamilton to be reminded what it is."

"Perhaps you're well enough to travel now," I told him. "Why don't you ask your doctor?"

"Every time I get to it, there's Mr. Hamilton listening. My God! I feel so—I don't know what!" he said to me. "You can't rule your life by Mr. Hamilton's," I said.

"I like him. He's a good guy. Why does it have to be this way? I wake up at night and I hear him trying to stifle a moan and it tears my guts out."

"Why don't you ring me then?" I said. "I can always give him something."

"Can you give him more life?" he said and walked away from me. Later, I talked to Dr. Porter about Mr. Hamilton. "Perhaps he ought to be moved to a private or semiprivate room," I suggested.

"Are the ward patients complaining?" he asked.

"No, but after all, it's hard on them. You know and I know what will happen."

"He can't afford a private room," Dr. Porter said. "And anyway, start pulling the curtain around his bed at night if he can't rest easy."

"Would that be such a good idea?" I asked.

"What would you suggest? It'll have to be that or nothing."

Two nights later—I had been off the night in between—I got to my floor to hear muffled sounds of laughter coming from Ward C.

"What's going on down there?" I asked Nell.

She shrugged. "Don't ask me. I have to give an intravenous to Room 306. And listen, check that dressing on Mr. Hamilton when you get in there, will you? They took some fluid out of his lung today."

"What in the world?" I said suddenly as the elevator doors opened and John, one of the hospital attendants, walked out with three large cartons of pizza. The aroma filled the corridor. "Is that really pizza?" I asked.

"Oh, boy, now he's gonna catch it!" John ducked around me. "Honest, he gave me some money! I gotta deliver it!"

"You just better wait a minute," I said to him, taking after him as he ran into Ward C.

There was a wild whoop, and then, as I entered, a groan. Mr. Hamilton was propped up and smiling, but he, too, looked guilty. "Who's having a party in here?"

"Where were you?" George Thorp yelled at John. "You were supposed to get here an hour ago!"

"Listen! You're lucky I got here at all," John said. "You think it's easy to get a cab driver to play pizza delivery boy?"

I stood there, staring. "And now will you answer me? Who's having a party?"

"We found out it was Mr. Hamilton's birthday and we were hungry, so we sent for pizza," George Thorp said to me.

"You plan to eat pizza?" I demanded.

"I plan to smell it. Okay, Nurse?" he said, and his eyes were hard on mine, pleading. I knew what he was doing, what they were all doing. Mr. Hamilton was going to die, so they were all going to pretend it wasn't going to happen if they had to stay awake the night to keep out the dark. I didn't know what to do. Nothing like this had ever happened before to me, not on the day duty anyway.

"I have a call to make, after which I will check to see if lights are out," I said, turning and leaving the room. I heard them fall upon the pizza like a bunch of boys eating their first meal on a camping trip.

When I met Nell, I told her what was going on.

She grinned. "Didn't you join them?"

"They didn't ask me," I said.

As I walked away, I wondered if they'd have asked Nell. I knew she gave the impression of being the motherly type, and she'd talk for an hour with a patient if he couldn't sleep. But, then, Nell was Nell. She'd had her love, and he'd been true to her. Nell could afford to give of herself. I couldn't.

On top of that, I felt a great irritation with George Thorp. How dared he let some of those patients eat pizza so late at night? If I went in there and stopped it, I'd be some kind of ogre because they were sick and they were lonely men. But I had every right to put a stop to it.

I went about my duties, seething. In a short while the noise in Ward C had abated. I was about to go in and see that every light was out when George Thorp came up to me in the hallway.

"Okay, let me have it now," he said. I turned to him in anger and disgust. "You think you're so smart, some kind of god, being nice to poor Mr. Hamilton because he's going to die. Why don't you go, wherever it is you go, and live your life and leave other people alone?" I said. "How do you know you haven't hurt someone in there with your idea of a birthday party? This is a hospital, not a nightclub. I told you that before!"

"I know it's a hospital," he said, and his eyes were hard on mine. "You've reminded me of it every time you come around. I feel sorry for you, Miss Burns. You haven't learned how to join the human race yet. A nurse? You're not a nurse! You're nothing, because you don't feel a thing in your heart. I don't know how you came to be mixed up with nursing. I thought nurses wanted to help people. Do yourself a favor and a bigger favor to your patients. You get out and stay out! I'd rather die with someone holding my hand than live with someone doing their duty by me. And don't worry about my going. This is our last good-bye."

He turned and walked off. I stood there, shaking with anger and humiliation. How dared he chew me out! What did he know about being a nurse? He was a good one to talk! Make people laugh, make them feel good—that's all he thought was needed in a hospital. I was so furious with him that I asked Nell to take Ward C for me. I pretended I wasn't feeling well, and I went down to have some coffee in the cafeteria.

When I came back, Dr. Porter was on the floor, and in a few minutes Dr. Simmons came striding off the elevator, shrugging out of his coat.

Nell rushed up to me. "It's Mr. Hamilton," she said.

"Probably that pizza party," I snapped. "I ought to tell the doctor about that!"

"Oh, Jan, what's the difference?" Nell said. "He was dying anyway." When someone dies at night, there's a special kind of poignancy to it. The doctor had notified the family, and in a half hour, a woman with a young man beside her, followed by two girls, came in. I knew it'd be a real picnic in Ward C. No one would get any rest. Dr. Porter came out to ask me if there were any empty beds on the floor. I shook my head no.

"Well, we'll draw the curtain," he said, going back into the ward. I followed. I tried to calm the other patients, purposely avoiding George Thorp. I saw him lying with one arm thrown over his eyes. Sleeping? I didn't know.

"I think I'd like a pill. I don't feel so good," Mr. Smith whispered to me. "Is he in terrible pain?" another man asked me. "Does it hurt to die, Miss Burns?"

"Poor guy! He was okay a little bit ago," still another one said.

"Maybe the doc's giving him something will help him," Mr. Smith said, catching at my arm to hold me by his bed. "You think that could be it? He was feeling better today than ever. It was his birthday!"

I could see they wanted to talk to me. Behind that curtain was the mystery that was life. Like little children, they were clinging to me because I was alive.

I was their protector. I would take care of them. But how long would that feeling last?

Oh, for that minute, for that night. I knew that no other world existed for them, not even for George Thorp. Even their wives and their children and their sweethearts were remote, a part of that hustling outside world. I was a part of their hospital world, their night world of illness. But when it was over, they wouldn't need me any more. I'd fade into that memory they'd call the time they were in a hospital. I dare anyone to remember the name of a nurse he had in a hospital six months after he is discharged. Six months! For no reason at all, I thought of Les. He probably had forgotten what I looked like!

Suddenly, there was a soft sob from behind the curtain, the sound of a chair being pushed back, and the rustling of bedclothes. I put a restraining hand on Mr. Smith, who sat up in bed with a cry.

"Let me rub your back," I said to him softly. "It'll help you sleep."

"No, it's okay. I don't feel sleepy," he said, his eyes straining toward the circle of light coming over the top of the curtain, trying to probe through and see death and what form it took.

"He's dead, isn't he?" the patient next to Mr. Smith asked. He leaned over and touched my hand, holding on. I stood there, unmoving. They had to touch me to feel alive themselves. No matter what the doctor had told them about their own health, in the dark of night, with death walking softly by them, they were afraid.

Dr. Porter came over to me. "See if you can get this crew quieted," he said to me. "I'll go get a stretcher and get him out of here."

I couldn't leave them now. I went quietly from bed to bed asking them if they wanted further sedation. I knew Dr. Porter would give me an okay on that under the circumstances. When I approached George Thorp, he turned over abruptly, giving his back to me. I didn't speak. I walked away.

The family walked out of the curtained enclosure. The young boy had his arm around his mother as they left the ward. Dr. Simmons came over to me.

"We're going to do an autopsy. Will you tell the attendant, please?" he said to me.

I nodded. And then because I had to, I went behind the curtain where Mr. Hamilton was lying still in death. The doctor had closed his eyes and I had to prepare him for the attendant. I won't go into that. It's probably the hardest thing a student nurse has to learn. I was glad when the attendants came, when they put Mr. Hamilton on the stretcher and wheeled him out. And yet the sound of those rubber wheels, moving almost stealthily among the beds, made even me feel the tenseness in the air. I knew that every eye in that room was on the covered form of the dead man on the stretcher. And I knew, too, that not one Ward C patient would sleep that night.

All of a sudden, I felt such a loathing for what I was doing that I wanted to run to the elevator and right out of the hospital. It was a prison in its own way, a physical prison and an emotional one, and why should I put up with it?

I wanted to be out of hospital work. Nights were meant for romance, soft lights, music, and a man who looked at me as a man should look at a girl, not someone he wants as a mother substitute to help him get well. That's what I had been to Les—someone to help him get well, to bind up his wounds, to make him whole again, and then he'd gone on to a real girl, not one smelling of formaldehyde as he'd kidded that night.

I hate it! I thought, going to the nurses' charge desk and clinging to the edge of it with sudden loathing. I hate all of it! The smell and the sound of it, the awful sliding back of the elevator doors at night, ominous and frightening; the soft ping of the doctor's calls on the intercom; the pale blue light in the corridor; my rubber-soled shoes on the tiled floor; the eerie feeling I've had since becoming a night nurse that I live in another world when I'm in the hospital and people who pass the big heavy doors downstairs are different from all other people in the world.

I'm going to leave it, I resolved. I'm going to join the world. I'm going to be a girl and fall in love and have a man fall in love with me as a woman, not a nurse.

I didn't even hear Nell come up to me. When she touched me, I let out a scream.

"Sorry," she said, looking at me. "Hey, this isn't your first postmortem, is it?" she said.

I shook my head. "I'm just tired," I said. "Those characters in there weren't exactly taking it lightly, you know. It was like a blow-by-blow film."

"Go on down and get something to eat, have some coffee," she said to me. "I'll peek in on them."

I was glad to leave the floor for fifteen minutes. I needed the hot coffee. For the first time, I really looked around at the empty cafeteria. This was part of it, too, the sterile cafeteria and the interns and doctors in their white coats, exhausted, harried, overworked. Romance! That was a laugh. This was the last place for romance. And I had had it up to my ears. Maybe that man George Thorp had recognized something in me that I hadn't. Maybe I was never really cut out to be a nurse.

I went back to the floor. The night stretched interminably because almost everyone on the floor was restless and demanding that night. I had noticed before that when death paid a visit to a floor, the other patients almost always sensed it. There was a new quiet unrest snaking up and down the corridor and into the wards. I felt it myself. Once, as I was making silent rounds shortly before dawn, I thought I heard someone call me and I turned quickly to stare down the long, empty corridor that ended in a wide, undraped window staring into the sky. From far away, a blinking light was the only living thing out there in that world.

I couldn't wait to get off duty, I wanted to get out of the hospital as quickly as possible. I had two days off, and I might never come back, I told myself, the way I felt right then. But first I had to stop off and collect my paycheck. The clerk felt gabby that morning, and it was after eight when I left the office. Then I met Nancy.

"I thought you were on days," I said to her.

"I am," she told me. "I just had to see someone, and if I don't sneak back, old eagle-eye will have my head."

I smiled at her. I liked Nancy. "New romance?" I said.

"The newest," she giggled. "Know him? That cute new intern on OB? OB! Can you imagine? Makes me feel funny when he kisses me. Like he knows me inside out, but who cares?"

She waved and ran off to go up via the stairway and not the elevator, which opened right at the charge desk. Nancy's romances never lasted long and she always came out unscathed. But Nancy was never really serious about her dates. She'd once told me she was a one-woman cheering section for lonely interns.

I started for the double doors that led to the street when someone called my name. I turned and looked right past a young man in a tweed jacket and dark-brown slacks. Then I looked at him again. It was George Thorp. I had never seen him in street clothes! He came up to me grinning a little self-consciously. "I guess you didn't recognize me in street clothes," he said and that, too, was the ironic part of my life, it struck me suddenly. The men I knew were always in hospital gowns or pajamas or bathrobes.

"Well, I didn't," I admitted. "You're leaving?"

He looked down at some cards in his hand. "That's what I said last night in my little speech. That's also something I want to apologize about. I'm sorry. I had no right to shoot off my mouth to you like that. I really am sorry."

"That's all right," I said. "A nurse learns to understand that too."

He looked at me. I had never noticed how black his eyes were or how warm his mouth looked.

"I think it was nice the way you stuck around last night. Most of the guys were scared. I guess I wasn't feeling too good either. I've never been close to anyone who has died," he said.

"I was doing my job," I said pointedly. "Well, good-bye and good luck, Mr. Thorp."

"Well, I'm not leaving right away," he said. "That is, I'm leaving the hospital. But since I'm okay, I thought I'd just pick up where I left off. I'm going to be here at least a couple of weeks. I thought you might let me buy you a dinner some night, show we're still friends."

I looked at him and I wanted to hurt him the way Les had hurt me. "You don't have to be nice to me anymore, Mr. Thorp. I'm not your nurse. You're well. You can take care of yourself. You don't need me any more. Good-bye again."

I skirted around him and walked straight out of the front door feeling his eyes boring into me. Well, there was some satisfaction in getting even, I told myself all the way home, even if it wasn't with Les. He made me laugh, George Thorp did. Did he think I could be burned twice? Or three times? Or ever again? Did he think I cared about him or any of them? Any more than they considered me a human being once they didn't need me any more?

Later that day I told Mom I really felt bogged down. "I think what I'd like is a change of pace, a new job maybe," I said to her.

"You mean leave nursing?" she asked.

"Well, maybe even that for a while," I said.

She laughed. "Now that's just plain silly. You trained for it. It's your profession. Why don't you just take some time off? Trouble with you is you haven't done anything exciting lately. Go out and have some fun. Get away from the hospital for a while."

I called up a friend I hadn't been in touch with for ages. "What's new?" I said to her.

"Where have you been?" she cried. "What's new is that I'm going to have a baby."

"Oh," I said. Then quickly I congratulated her. Next I called Myra. "I'm at loose ends," I said to her. "I'm taking a few days off."

"Ugh," she said into the phone. "I'm dying with nausea all the time. I keep telling the doctor I didn't have it with the first baby, why do I have it now? Jan, do you suppose it means I'm going to have a girl?"

That was a small penalty for being a nurse, I told myself. People told you their ailments seriously and expected that you could help them. "No, it does not mean you're having a girl. It means you aren't taking the medicine your obstetrician gave you. There are pills you can take to calm that, Myra."

"I know, but I hate them," she said. That night I felt terribly alone. How could I have dropped out of my friends' lives so quickly? That was part of being a nurse, too. Unless I worked days and had my nights free, I could have absolutely no social life.

I went to bed at eleven o'clock and slept the clock around. When I awoke, I felt much better. And it was just as well, because it was the last good sleep I was to get for a long while.

I was mulling over the idea of asking for a ten-day leave of absence when my supervisor called me.

"Miss Burns," she said into the phone. "I know it's your day off, but we're in a jam down here and I'd like to ask you to come in tonight."

"Oh," I hesitated.

"There's a very real danger of an encephalitis epidemic," she went on. "So far today we have admitted sixteen suspected cases. There may be more. We need all the help we can get!"

For a while, even people who didn't have the disease were panicky, since the symptoms were chills and fever, followed by a brief abatement lasting up to twenty-four hours. Then, seriously hit patients complained of fuzziness, and some went into a coma from which they were not to recover.

Cots were placed everywhere in the hospital. We nurses were pressed into double duty, and it was a nightmare for three days. Meanwhile, the city went into a crash program of mosquito control. Those patients who showed only mild signs of the disease were treated symptomatically and sent home.

One day after I'd been on duty for something like thirteen hours, I started to leave the ward when I noticed a child about eight or ten on a cot, crying. His parents were beside him, obviously distraught.

"Hi," I said, walking over to the boy's cot. "How you feeling?"

He looked at me with deep dark eyes and I realized suddenly that he didn't understand me. He and his parents were Mexican. I nodded my head up and down and looked at the parents. "Okay," I said, pointing to the boy. "Okay."

The boy smiled through his tears. "Okay," he whispered.

I smiled again and moved off. I'd been touched by the little guy, but after all, no one could watch a child cry and not be touched. I went on to get my things and go home and collapse.

As I was leaving the hospital, I met the parents of the boy, standing near the big front doors. The woman was crying softly and the man was trying to comfort her. I just didn't have the heart to walk by them.

"Your boy will be okay," I said, spacing my words

the way we do when we are trying to make ourselves understood in a foreign language. I kept smiling, hoping to convey some comfort to the couple. But the woman only cried quietly.

"Do you live here?" I asked. They stared at me. I remembered my few words of Spanish. "Casa?" I asked.

"*Si, si, gracias*," the man said, grasping my hand and shaking it up and down, then turning to his wife and letting loose a volley of Spanish. I nodded again and started to leave when I realized they were following me. I hadn't said anything to them about following me. Whatever had given them the idea?

As I stood at the curb, not knowing what to do, I suddenly saw George Thorp coming out of the hospital. "Mr. Thorp," I called to him.

He came running lightly down the steps toward me. "Hello," he said. "I was hoping I'd see you again. That's why I stopped by. This is a tough thing, isn't it?"

"Yes," I said, then quickly I explained about the two people standing patiently beside me.

"Maybe I can help," he said. "I know some Spanish. I've traveled the Southwest."

He spoke to them in Spanish then, haltingly, and the parents responded volubly, smiling and pleased. George Thorp turned to me.

"I'm afraid they thought you wanted them to go home with you," he said. "They're afraid and alone in the city. They've only been here two weeks."

"Oh, dear," I said. "Now what'll I do?"

"Come with me," he said. "We'll take them to lunch and I'll talk with them and make them feel better. That's all they want, a little reassurance, and they get it just being with you because you're a nurse."

I felt weighted under this responsibility, and yet as I looked into the mother's trusting eyes, a warm glow went through me. To know that I could enjoy such trust and such gratitude made me feel suddenly very small in the eyes of God and man.

I turned to George Thorp.

"I'd like that very much," I said, forgetting that I'd like sleep and rest more and wanting to make up to George Thorp for the way I had felt about him when he was my patient. In a way I ought to be grateful to him for coming along, for helping me understand these people and myself. Ever since Les had walked out on me—yes, walked out on me—I had taken out my disappointment and heartache on my patients.

Deliberately, I had tried not to listen to their needs other than the physical ones, as if I wanted to stop being the human being I was meant to be. Les was a weak man. He had used me, but I had allowed myself to be used. What made me think all men were like Les? Take George Thorp. He had asked me to have dinner with him, to be friends, and I'd ignored his plea, knowing he was alone and might have welcomed a friendly face outside the hospital. I can't remember much of the lunch. I do remember watching George's face, though. He asked me to call him "George" and I did. He was solicitous with the mother of the boy and spoke often to the father.

"Their boy will be all right, won't he?" he asked me.

"I'm sure he will," I told him. Finally it was time to leave. George told me the parents were going back to the hospital to see their son. I started to say good-bye when the woman quickly took my out-stretched hand and kissed it. I felt my face get red as I pulled my hand back. I didn't deserve such an accolade.

"She is only thanking you her way," George said. "Accept it."

That was when I leaned over quickly and kissed the woman lightly—a hello and good-bye and good luck. George took my arm then. "Let me drive you home," he said.

I hadn't realized how tired I was until I sat in George's car. I put my head back on the seat and closed my eyes.

"Tired?" George said.

"I've been on duty since eleven o'clock last night," I said.

"Holy crow!" He whistled. "It's four o'clock now. Why didn't you say something?"

I turned to look at him. "What could I say? You saw their faces."

George reached over and touched my hand. "I'm glad you said that," he told me. "Ever since I got out of that place I've wanted to see you and tried to find an excuse where you'd have to talk to me. I really am sorry for anything I might have said to hurt you. In there, a person gets to feeling like he's somebody else. I don't know, it's the one time in my life I kept thinking only of me and the people around me and being sick and dying. You know what I mean?"

"I know," I said.

"And I thought you didn't give a damn about any of us, not even Mr. Hamilton," he said. "But being away a few days, getting my feet back on the ground, so to speak, I know that you have to do it that way. Heck, you can't get involved with every patient. You'd be torn six ways to Sunday if you did."

"But I do have to be involved," I said. "I do have to care. You needed it when you were a patient. So do the others. It's part of being a nurse. The trick is to know just how far to go."

It was more than a trick. It was a must, I thought. Men like Les were everywhere, not just patients in a hospital. A girl in an office could meet a Les and give up what was good and right for her to follow a will-o'-the-wisp. The important thing was to be able to accept disappointments and heartbreaks and to go on to be a better person. Punishing oneself and those around wasn't the answer. I had withdrawn from the outside world by taking on night duty. I had further withdrawn from my patients by not allowing myself to recognize their loneliness and their fears. How dared I put myself on a little island like that? I was responsible for people in the same way they were responsible for me. None of us live alone in this world. We all have to do for each other.

George had arrived at my house. I turned to thank him.

"I'm going to see you again," he said. "But when you can stay awake." I smiled. "All right," I told him.

I went into the house and to bed, where I stayed until the following afternoon. Mom called the hospital to tell them I'd be in for my regular night duty. Meanwhile the danger of an epidemic had been blunted, and those who were only mildly ill were sent home.

That evening George came to pick me up. He met my parents and then he and I went out to dinner. I took my uniform along so I could change at the hospital. This time I knew that George was not seeing me as a nurse, a continuation of his hospital stay, but because he wanted to see me, Janet Burns.

That first night he took me to the door of the hospital and kissed me lightly as he said good night. "I'll be here in the morning," he promised.

And he was.

"I have to see you every minute you'll let me," he said. "I'll be going on the road at the end of the week."

How strange, I thought. A week ago I wouldn't have given it a thought, and now I don't want to lose him. . . . "When will you be back?"

"As soon as I can make it—two weeks at the most," he said. "Jan, we're going to mean a lot to each other one day," he promised.

"Yes, I know," I said, feeling a special kind of happiness come over me. Because I knew right then that I didn't have to wait for the one day George talked about. One day had already come for both of us.   THE END

MY BABY WASN'T WORTH SAVING

We never know when tragedy is going to strike us. It can come when we least expect it. I had always felt as though I was blessed in life. My parents were ordinary, middle-class people. They were good to me and I had a happy childhood. I married the boy next door, and settled down to lead a normal life. I was content.

My husband and I were close with both our families, and we had a nice group of friends. Sam was a wonderful husband and lover and a good provider. I'd worked for the first few years of our marriage, and then Sam was doing well enough for me to stop working and begin our family. In the year that it took for me to get pregnant, we bought a house—just in time to begin fixing up a nursery for the baby.

After some mild morning sickness, I had a comfortable pregnancy. In fact, I'd never felt better in my life, and I looked as good as I felt. Sam was so happy and excited about the baby that he was like a little boy himself.

I went into labor a little earlier than expected, but my periods had always been so irregular that we couldn't be too sure of the due date. We were at Louise and John Monroe's, looking at the pictures of their last vacation, when my pains started. I wasn't sure it was really happening until the pictures were finished and dessert was being served. Then I felt a hard one, and I gasped.

Louise looked at me in surprise, and then said, "Sam, I think you'd better take Michelle home and pack that bag!"

Sam immediately started running around in circles. John took him by the hand. "Hey, relax," he assured my husband. "We all go through it. It won't be that hard." He steered Sam to the door.

As we left the house, Sam grabbed me by the arm. "Are you okay, Michelle? Should we go right to the hospital?"

We were walking home, since Louise and John lived on the next block, and now I took Sam by the arm. I felt very much in control of the situation.

"Don't worry," I told him. "Everything is going to be fine. When we get home, we'll time the pains and I'll pack. Then you can call Dr. Benedict and she'll tell us when to go to the hospital."

Everything went as planned. I even drove to the hospital because Sam was so nervous. In a small town like ours, nothing is very far away from anything else, so in ten minutes I was pulling into the parking lot.

Dr. Benedict was waiting for us. She examined me, and then sent me to the labor room. Sam sat with me there until they gave me some shots and wheeled me into the delivery room. Sam got dressed and then came to my side to help me with the birth.

After that, things got a little mixed up. I was vaguely aware of a commotion after the baby was born and a feeling of fear swept over me. Sam was asked to leave, and I started to panic.

But then I was given another shot. And the next thing I knew, I was waking up in my own room at the hospital. Sam was sitting by my side, an expression of sorrow on his face where I should have seen joy.

A sudden terror took hold of me, and I tried to sit up straight. But I was so weak that I fell back. Then Sam was leaning over me, holding my hands in his.

"Michelle," he whispered.

"What's wrong, Sam?" I pleaded. "What's the matter? Is our baby dead?" I voiced my worst fear.

"No, honey." Sam squeezed my hands hard. "But there were problems. The baby needs to be flown to Boston for operations."

I felt hot tears running down my face. "But why, Sam? What's the matter?"

"She has a birth defect, an opening in her spine," he explained. "Her spinal cord has come through the opening. It's outside her body instead of down in the spinal column where it belongs."

"What?" I asked, too stunned to really understand.

"It's called spina bifida. Dr. Benedict says it isn't anyone's fault, honey. She says it happens because, for some reason, the bones of the spine just don't join up the way they're supposed to during the first three months of pregnancy. A lot of babies are born with it, but most of the time you never even notice it and there's no problem with the spinal cord. But sometimes—like with our little girl—the spinal cord is exposed."

Our little girl, I thought. "Marina," I murmured. And saying the name we'd chosen for our baby girl suddenly made her more real to me. "Oh, Sam!" I clutched his hand. "I want to see her. I want to hold my baby."

Just then, Dr. Benedict came in.

"Where is my baby?" I demanded. "I want to see her."

Dr. Benedict pulled up a chair and sat down near the bed. "You'll be able to see her soon, Michelle," she assured me. "But first I want to give you some information. You and Sam are going to have to make some very important decisions."

"All I want to know," I said, sobbing now, "is will my baby live?"

Dr. Benedict looked very serious. "For the most part, that's up to you," she said. "The baby has spina bifida."

"Sam told me that," I interrupted. "But what does it all mean?"

"It means that the baby has an open sore on her back, and her spinal cord is exposed. If she does not have an operation right away to cover the cord, the sore may become infected, and she may get meningitis," she explained. "Because of the location of the protrusion, even with the surgery—if she lives—she will probably be paralyzed below the waist. She also seems to have hydrocephalus," Dr. Benedict added.

"What's that?" I asked shakily.

"It's water on the brain. She's producing too much of the fluid that normally surrounds the brain.

It will build up in her skull and cause her head to swell. It also creates pressure on the brain which will eventually cause brain damage."

The room began to swim before my eyes. I felt sick and faint. My baby had such terrible things wrong with her, but she was alive. And Dr. Benedict said it was pretty much up to us whether or not she stayed alive.

"What can we do?" I pleaded. "Tell me, Dr. Benedict. How can I save my baby?"

Dr. Benedict took a deep breath. "First of all, you can have the operation on her back done immediately, so she won't get an infection. Then we can put a small tube called a shunt inside her head to drain that extra fluid down into her heart where her body will be able to get rid of it. After that, what happens depends on whether or not there are other complications."

"And the will of God," I put in. "Well, I don't think God will take our baby just yet. I want the operations done right away, Dr. Benedict. I want Marina to go to the hospital in Boston."

"Michelle," the doctor warned, "you need to know that these operations might not work. Your baby still may die. And if she does live, she will never be normal."

"I don't care!" I said. "I want her to have the operations. I want her to have every chance she can. You'll see, Dr. Benedict. Marina will live!"

Dr. Benedict smiled. "I'll go tell Dr. Morris—he's the head of our hospital. After he speaks with you, I'll come back and we can make arrangements," she told me.

I felt a ray of hope warm my heart. Maybe things

weren't so hopeless after all. I turned to Sam. Silent tears were sliding down his face. I reached toward him to comfort him. But just then, the door opened and Dr. Morris came in. I could see right away that something was the matter. He was frowning.

Dr. Morris sat down and immediately got to the point. "Sam, Michelle," he said to us both. "I will not beat around the bush. Your baby has a severe birth defect and I do not recommend the operations."

"What do you recommend, then?" Sam asked, and I felt my heart sink.

"I recommend that you leave the baby alone and let nature take its course."

"But that means our baby will probably die, doesn't it?" I cried.

Dr. Morris cleared his throat. "That's right."

"Oh, no!" I said desperately.

"Michelle," Dr. Morris reasoned, "you must understand how severely crippled your baby is. Even with the operations, we can't be sure of saving it. And if it does live, what would its quality of life be like? It wouldn't be able to walk. It couldn't be toilet trained. It could be mentally retarded and constantly sick and have infections. It would need medicines and more operations," he continued. "The costs of medical care would be outrageous, and it would be in constant pain. Think about what I'm saying to you. You and Sam are young and healthy. You can have other babies—healthy babies."

I felt a cold fury deep inside me. "Dr. Morris," I said angrily, "first of all, my baby is not an 'it.' She is a little girl. Second of all, she is going to have a chance—every chance we can give her. Marina will have those operations."

Dr. Morris looked over at Sam. "Can't you talk some sense into her? Let me give you a few days to think it over," he said.

I felt panic take hold of me. What if Sam agreed with the doctor?

But my husband replied, "Michelle is right, Doctor. And the longer we wait, the less chance our daughter is going to have. You make the arrangements to send her to Boston immediately!"

A few hours later, I was being prepared to be flown by helicopter along with Marina to the big hospital in Boston where the operations would be performed. Sam drove down in the car to meet us there, and he got an extra week off from work to stay with us.

The operations were successful. We were very fortunate because Marina didn't develop any infections. The sore on her back was healing, although her spinal cord would never grow where it belonged. And she would be paralyzed below the waist. The swelling of her skull had been stopped before it was very noticeable.

Marina had to stay in the hospital for several weeks, and I stayed with her. While I was there, I met with Mrs. Dean, the public health nurse who covered the county I lived in. She was going to teach me how to take care of Marina's special needs, and she would be available to help us as our baby grew.

"Why did this happen, Mrs. Dean?" I asked her.

"We really don't know what causes spina bifida," she replied. "Sometimes the condition seems to run in families. Other times, like with you and Sam, it appears suddenly. We just aren't sure why, Michelle."

"Will Marina be mentally retarded?" I asked hesitantly.

"Again, Michelle, we can't be sure. But she probably won't be. The shunt is working well, and it will keep pressure from building up in the skull and causing brain damage," she explained.

"But aren't children with birth defects always mentally retarded?" That was what I'd always thought.

"Oh, no. There are many types of birth defects, and only a few involve mental retardation," she pointed out. "Spina bifida is not one of those. Sometimes children with spina bifida are mentally retarded, but usually they're not."

"Well, if it's not that rare a condition, why haven't I seen any adults with it?" I questioned her.

"Until recently, babies born with spina bifida usually died from infections or from hydrocephalus. Now, with new improvements in surgery and with better antibiotics, most babies with spina bifida can live. They can lead relatively normal lives and grow into productive members of society," Mrs. Dean said.

"But what about Marina's—her paralysis?" I forced myself to say the word.

"Because of the location of her spinal problem, she won't have much use of or feeling in her body below the waist. Still, she'll be able to use a wheelchair to get around, and there are adaptations that can be made for her inability to be toilet trained. But you'll have to be very careful to watch out for urinary tract infections," she warned. "They can be major problems for children like Marina. I'll show you and Sam ways to meet her needs. You'll also have to learn how to care for her skin and her legs to make sure they stay as healthy as possible in spite of the paralysis. But once her health complications are under control, you can treat your daughter as much as possible like a normal little girl," Mrs. Dean assured me.

I will always thank God for helping us—for not permitting anyone to talk us into letting our baby die, and for sending us Mrs. Dean. I won't say it was easy. It wasn't. Marina was often in pain. But as she grew, she got better. When she was a year old, her shunt became blocked, and then got infected, and she spent the next month in the hospital.

While Marina was small enough for a stroller, people who didn't know us couldn't tell that anything was the matter with her. But once she was old enough for a wheelchair, we had to get used to the stares of pity from strangers in public places and learn how to respond to people who asked what was wrong with our little girl.

Finally we learned how to say, "Oh, there's nothing 'wrong' with her. She's a perfectly normal child who has spina bifida."

Marina was a bright, cheerful, pretty child, and we adored her. Mrs. Dean had told us about a program for babies with birth defects and their parents, and Sam and I took Marina there once a week. It was a sixty-mile drive, but it was worth it. We all learned ways of working with our children to help them as much as possible. After the training sessions, we'd have coffee and talk. Through our sharing, we found courage and hope.

When Marina was four, she had an operation to open her stomach for a urine bag so that she wouldn't have to be in diapers anymore. She was able to be bowel trained through a combination of careful diet, laxatives, and being taken to the toilet regularly. And we were assured that as smart as Marina was, she would soon learn to take care of her needs by herself.

When our daughter was five, she started in the local head-start program. The teacher had some training in working with special-needs children, and children with disabilities were encouraged to attend the program. The teacher didn't mind that Marina was not completely toilet trained. Instead, she worked to help her, so that by the end of the year, Marina was ready to go to regular kindergarten.

The teachers in her elementary school were a little nervous at first about having a child like Marina in their classes. But they were willing to work with us, and it didn't take long before our little girl was accepted by everyone. She made friends, and as the years passed, some of her best friends even had their parents fix their homes to accommodate Marina's wheelchair.

Our daughter was a straight-A student through grade school, and when it came time for sixth-grade commencement, she was chosen to give a speech as one of the outstanding students. I will keep forever in my heart the memory of my daughter, looking so beautiful and strong, sitting straight up in her wheelchair in front of all the parents, teachers, and other students. Speaking clearly and with feeling, she began, "I'm pleased to have been selected to express our gratitude."

And our gratitude as well, I thought to myself as tears of joy and pride streamed down my cheeks. THE END

I CHEATED ON JESUS

"Sabrina, have you ever been in love?"

Sister Marianna's question perked me out of my daydreaming. I'd been gazing out of the Toyota's window at the flat, sandy roads of the Texas countryside, which even the bright October sun couldn't glamorize.

"In love?" I asked, a bit hesitantly. "What kind of love do you mean?"

"Like loving a man. Of course, we love God—but different from *that* kind of love."

"Well," I said, "I just battled two impassioned attractions. Quite honestly, that's one area of life that I came here to escape from—attractive men, I mean."

My long-time friend seemed anxious to fill me in. "Sabrina, the really tough part of these past two years was inside myself. I became intensely attracted to another intern in my counseling program, a priest, who was not stable in his own vocation. I was quickly falling in love, though I didn't want to."

"What did you do about it?"

"Actually, I had the grace of a good supervisor. She helped me to face myself. I hadn't realized how lonely I was, how much pain I was still carrying from my father dying back when I was a teenager. It was all of that stuff."

"But you came through, right?"

"Yes. I hope I came out as a better sister than if I had not gone through it. I just wondered if anything like that has ever happened to you, Sabrina. After all, I've barely heard from you these past two years."

Suddenly, it seemed less crazy of me to leave my unpacked bags and take this whole morning to drive away from the place I'd come half a world to get to. My brother and his children had helped me move in just yesterday, after my eight years teaching English on a little island off the coast of China.

"Marianna, I'm sorry I wrote so little since my last visit home."

"I didn't keep up my end, either," she offered.

"About your question—during the same years you were struggling with your relationship, I was struggling with two attractions. I don't think they were really love, since Jesus is my love, at least I *hope* He is."

"For me, it really was love," Marianna clarified. "I saw that I could love this priest. I could see walking the rest of my life with him—of course, only if he went through the dispensations, and I did, too. Dear, sweet Lena, my supervisor, helped me before it was too late to see that I really did not want that path into marriage. It brought me to Jesus on my knees; I felt so sorry to imagine leaving Him, doing

310

some things I am ashamed of—not sexual things, but things that were definitely wrong. But now that I found my way back, I feel more compassionate toward the people I counsel and direct. 'There but for the grace of God go I' comes so often to my mind."

"I often think of the same line, Marianna, in battling my passions. Isn't it true, though? We feel what other women feel, and, in the surprise or the confusion, we sometimes forget that we cannot do what other women can do. It is so easy to forget the type of woman that you have chosen to be—especially with life swirling around us. . . ."

"Exactly," she agreed. "And you'll see how busy our center gets. Lots of people come here to talk about their troubles."

"Right up the alley of your training and certification, isn't it? I'm not sure what I can do to serve here, with my teaching background."

"Oh, there's so much that you'll be great at—welcoming people, leading them in prayer—sessions, giving talks about God—all of your natural gifts. And you'll be learning as you take in the meetings and retreats. How do you like it so far, Sabrina?"

"Oh," I·said, searching through my first impressions. "It's a marvelous place. I like the director. I guess I was disappointed to find that guy, Heath, who moved in. I hoped to build a quiet community life with you and Sister Joelle at first."

"I understand. Of course, I miss having Joelle here, too. I was so glad that you were coming. I don't know if the community would let me stay here alone."

As we talked, the strange flicker in my heart

became more clear. I might be having another one of those attractions. *God forbid*, I sort of prayed. *That's what I came to escape.*

"So, why are you upset that Heath moved in?" Marianna's voice punctured my thoughts.

"Marianna," I replied earnestly, "I really hoped for some breathing room, not only to build up my physical strength—my official reason for coming—but also to focus on Jesus so he can heal me inside."

"Some rough situations?

"Many," I summarized. "In one way, I could have stayed on that tiny island forever. I was so fulfilled in my ministry. But some of the conflicts with other teachers, and even with some of other sisters, all in a land where most people spoke the dialect or Mandarin, really overwhelmed me. It feels great just to be able to talk and joke without fishing for words inside."

"I can imagine. Look, we're in Austin already. I'll need to concentrate on the turns to the hospital. I want to hear more, though," she said.

Our visit with Sister Joelle, a dear friend to both of us, was a bit depressing, as we found her so feeble after such an active life. The doctors had hopes, as did the community of our sisters there, that she would bounce back, but it would not be quickly. On the return trip, Marianna and I turned our attention to her, and to community matters we learned of on our visit.

I forgot the flicker of attraction inside me, until it resurfaced at lunch on Monday. That man, Heath, sat directly across from me. Usually, he would be working in San Antonio, but it was the Columbus Day holiday.

"Your brother is a neat guy," Heath said energetically—the way he seemed to say *everything*. "He sounded like an engineer, giving directions to the restaurant. It was easy and exactly correct!"

"Yeah," I agreed. "James was our family pathfinder on vacations. Once at an information booth, my dad didn't even know where we were heading until he called James up."

Heath continued, "You have a lot of talent, too. I can see that. I can't even imagine learning Chinese!"

"Don't get too excited, Heath. I speak like a first-grader," I countered.

"No. The people at the restaurant understood you perfectly."

"It's no prize feat to get into and out of a building," I said.

"So, tell me about China. I was in Hong Kong once, when our ship stopped for a night. It ended up turning into four nights."

"Oh?" I perked up. "What did you do in Hong Kong?"

"You wouldn't want to know," he said cagily. "I didn't stay in the convent, you know."

From our introductions that first evening, I knew that he had been in the Navy for four years, but I had not imagined that he was a philanderer. I had put him in the seeker category, like myself and some of the others.

"It's my conversion story, Sabrina. I'll have to tell you someday."

"I'd like to hear it," I said.

The golden sun sent reddish rays onto the stone building as I entered it. In this main chapel, I'd found my perfect prayer spot under a big, bay window. I basked in the rising sun there longer in the mornings, and often returned before dinner if I had free time. Now, I closed my eyes and centered on my Lord.

A short time later, I felt someone come up beside me. After a tap of resentment, my wounded spirit warmed. Someone wanted to sit by me. Opening my eyes, I felt my shoulders flinch.

"Didn't want to scare you," Heath said. "Just wondered if you wanted to hear my story now."

No, I thought, but I didn't say so. Even though I liked conversion stories, I also liked my prayer time uninterrupted.

"We need to go in a few minutes," I said.

"I was wondering about after dinner."

Oh no, I thought. *I still have boxes to unpack. But he seems like a little kid who might get hurt if I say no.* "Okay," I agreed.

So later on in the evening, we returned to my prayer spot. Though Heath was so tall and muscular, he seemed pleased when I asked, "Would you pray with me first?"

Of course, he conceded. "Jesus, thank You for what You have done in Heath's life. Thank You for always helping us in our greatest difficulties, and pursuing us when we have strayed. Be with us, Lord, as Your sun goes down, to keep our eyes on You."

Heath went into intimate detail of his rebellious childhood, his signing on with the Navy, his women, his not-so-honorable discharge, his chance to go to college, his marriage, his children, his divorce, and then finally his return to mass, confession, and his search without bounds for God. He spoke so honestly and articulately that I was engrossed in very word.

"So now you know how far down a man can go before he starts back up," he finished.

"You are very humble to share all of that with me," I said sincerely.

"I knew from the night we first met, Brina, that I could trust you. I see that you love Jesus. I know that you won't do as some women have recently done to me—told me they love Jesus, but then got into bed with me without a qualm."

I tried not to look embarrassed at his frankness. "You're right—I came here, as you did, to seek the Lord first. I can't pretend that I am His if I put someone else on His throne in my heart."

"What did bring you here?" he asked.

"In short, I was sick, and our sisters gave me a six-month recuperation time. I also hope to get into a spiritual ministry, rather than continue teaching English. Now I have time to explore this."

"I'd really like to hear your story," Heath said. "But I don't want to keep you up too late. Promise me that you'll tell me another time?"

"Sure," I said. "And thanks again for sharing your journey, Heath. You must delight Jesus' heart. You know the parable of the lost sheep, don't you?"

"Yeah. Jesus really did look for me in the brambles, and if He hadn't picked me out, I certainly could have died there. I feel this intense gratitude bubble up inside me day and night. Did I tell you I like to get up at three-thirty in the morning and pray the night office? That's the most special prayer time for me."

"Good for you," I said. "You may be a monk someday."

"I stay open to anything," he responded.

We walked to our opposite quarters; I to the little house that Marianna and I shared, and he to the priest's house where he had a room. But he did not leave my heart, I soon realized. I felt very guilty about it, but the trust that Heath placed in me had overwhelmed my entire being.

All night, I battled this, between bouts of sleep and agonized prayer to the Lord, always telling Him: "I want you—I came here for You, not for some guy. Do anything You want, but keep me as Yours. I did not leave those great people in China where life was difficult to fall in love and lose it all."

I awoke with a desire to seek out Marianna—experienced not only in counseling, but in dealing with love and its counterfeits. After prayer and orientation matters, I knocked at her door.

Though she wasn't expecting me, she hugged me and led me to her meeting room.

"Sabrina, what's troubling you?"

"You can read me well, Marianna. Remember what we were talking about on the visit to Joelle last Saturday?"

"Ah, yes: men. Or is it something else?"

"No, men it is. Specifically, how to deal with attractions. I thought I knew. I applied what I thought would work, and it does not."

"Can you tell me more specifically? Not to make you say what you don't want to, but I do not get a clear picture where the problem lies."

"It's Heath. I never hoped to find such a man here, but here he is. There's something in the way he looks at me. It just gets to me. I feel I should be shutting him out, for fear he will—in a phrase I heard last weekend—'rent a room' in my heart. Am I over-reacting, Sister?"

"Does Heath ever do anything that is out of your boundaries?"

"Never. He even says that he can trust me. From what he told me of his past, I feel he probably acts this charming to many women. Maybe he doesn't have any reaction. But a magnet pulls me toward him—just to talk—but for hours! And after, like last night, I have these emotions pounding inside."

"What do you do with them?"

"I pray and pray: 'Jesus, I belong to You. I don't want to feel that kind of love for anyone else.' Stuff like that."

"What does Jesus say to you then?" she asked.

I hesitated. "I don't hear any answer. Maybe I don't really listen for one."

"Sabrina, try praying and then listening. Do whatever Jesus tells you. Since you came here seeking His Will, and He allowed Heath to be here, too, then Jesus must have something for you to deal with inside yourself—something you *are* ready for. As I told you about my life, through the painful process of attraction and love, I learned what was missing in me, what needed healing, and what I needed to find in a deeper closeness to Jesus. This can happen. Pray a lot, and try to see what's behind the temptations. Since you are a writer, it will help you to journal this."

"In one way, I fear to do as you say. But in another way, it sounds right. Always in my past, I have run from such men. But I will never escape them by running, I guess."

"I'm here, if you want to talk more. Trust Jesus. Let's pray."

Marianna then led me in such a beautiful prayer that my darkness turned as bright as the noon sun when we finished.

By late afternoon, I found myself in our breezy chapel with my journal in hand. I wrote my heart out, protesting my love to the Lord. As I paused for the answer, I heard one:

"Brina, my Brina. Yes; I love you dearly. I have brought you here for My purposes, and Heath is included in that, too. But I ask of you this: Watch how you look at him. Let your eyes carry the message you are telling Me, that you are My bride, and you are not available. Don't send him a mixed message."

Wow! How right that was! In my hunger for Heath's compliments, I literally looked with longing eyes into his. I resolved to work on this.

The first day went well. I spoke sweetly, but my blinds were tilted.

The second afternoon, I heard a knock. Heath stood at my door—as usual, he did not come in.

"Brina, I'm heading to the rosary walk. Want to pray with me?"

Something in me started to say, "No thanks," but then I reconsidered. Prayer strengthens us in being the way we need to be with each other, I reasoned. Our eyes and hearts will be looking together at Jesus. "Sounds good," I then answered.

So we prayed, starting with brief meditations, and came back to the prayer station where we'd originally started. It had gone well. I felt nothing.

The next afternoon, we went again. I felt a bit self-conscious speaking of Mary saying yes to the angel and Jesus being conceived in her, but I concentrated on my prayers, not forgetting to add a little prayer for Sister Joelle.

Heath got more personal than I. "Thank You, good Jesus, for bringing sweet Sister Sabrina from her far-away mission, to visit me here. You know what joy she brings to my heart. Help me care for her with Your Love, dear Jesus."

I was really touched. We continued praying, but the emotions came back. I was relieved when we had finished.

The next day, he knocked, and I told him that I could not go with him. I had prepared lots of little explanations, but my words stumbled around.

"Hey, Brina—*Sister* Sabrina, I mean. Did I offend you?"

"Heath, no—not you. It's just that I have something I need to do."

"Look at me—are you holding something back? You aren't acting normal lately."

I had imagined that I could just talk to him as I would to Sister Marianna. But I couldn't. I just wanted him to disappear, but he didn't. He always faced things directly—that much I had learned from watching him.

"Can we talk?" he asked sheepishly.

"Sometime, yes. But not now."

So I backed off into my little abode, but he took a chair there in my mind. *Oh God, what will I do with this?*

The next evening, I saw him after his work in San Antonio. Usually, I felt overwhelmed by his presence, but he looked tired enough for me to think I might have a chance to speak coherently.

"Heath, if you have any time this weekend, could I talk with you?"

"Of course," he answered. "After dinner?"

After dinner, we sat on lawn chairs in the green Saint Augustine grass. "Heath," I began, "what I need to say is not your fault, but it's something within me. You see, I have all of these feelings for you. Sometimes I feel that I just want your attention so badly . . . I am tempted to you physically, and I've been very upset by it. I'm so sorry."

He leaned forward until his face was close to my knees. He focused all that charming attention directly on me. "It's not just in you. I feel it, too. It's natural—you're a beautiful woman, and I have the normal passions of a man. Does that frighten you?"

"I don't want to lose my love: Jesus Christ. He's not just someone I'm dating—I've made a life-commitment to Him, Heath. He has never failed me. I could never leave Him, and I don't want to."

"And I don't want you to. Am I taking you away?"

"No, it's probably normal in your life, as a man whose marriage is annulled—uh, I guess it is?"

"It's close to that. But I don't want to marry again, Brina. I face a whole new world. God has become real to me, and it's the most exciting thing I've ever experienced."

"So it's not that you or I want the feelings. But when they are there, they become barriers in my prayer."

"For me, they help. Like I've told you, Brina, you are the first woman I can really trust. I love you, but I don't desire you. I just want to talk to you. I want to learn how to love like you do—love everyone, not just one person."

"Heath, thanks. But I love some more than others. If I judge it by time, I spend an overdose on you."

"Is it that bad?"

"I don't know."

That night, we were cleaning off some tables as a meeting was held in an adjoining room. I was not really listening to the drift of voices. Suddenly, Heath said, "Sabrina, did you hear that? Come outside with me."

I followed him to the little garden. "They were just talking about us—not by name, but in the same situation. Brina, we *are* playing games. We *are* getting too involved by talking to each other the way we did this afternoon. We need distance."

I felt both sad and relieved. "You're right, Heath. Let's back off."

For several weeks, we treated each other politely. I did not find the Lord as deeply as I thought I would. It seemed that I had been abandoned, both by people and by God. I questioned the Lord, but I did not hear that I was right or wrong. But I rejoiced that I had freed Heath for his prayer and life.

One day, we ended up praying in the chapel when no one else was there. He came and sat beside me.

"How are things with you, Sabrina?" he asked.

"Fine," I said unconvincingly.

"With me, everything is terrible. I miss our talks. I think I lost the best person who ever came into my life."

"Oh, Heath, I wish I could know what would please Jesus. You were a beautiful person in my life, too. Your kind ways healed me—I didn't even realize it until the other day. All the pain I came here with is just, gone!"

He reached over and put his large hand on mine. It was the first time he had ever touched my hand, except at the weekly prayer meetings when we all joined hands to say the Our Father. I felt so loved, so valued.

From that day, we resumed our friendship. Sometimes, I felt my heart jump as he stood next to me, or put his arm around my shoulder going through a door. He invited me to pray the stations of the cross with him, and took my hand very gently.

Sister Marianna said it was growth and healing, because we sought Jesus. Heath and I said it was God who let us share with each other. I felt less uneasy with the emotional side, but when the sparks came into my heart, I would go to confession and pray a little.

At our center, many fine priests, nuns, and lay people of various religious groups and the Anonymous programs led wonderful retreats. I felt bonded with each group and inspired by their messages. My health was improving, and I felt positive about getting into ministry here when my re-entrance time was up.

Over Christmas, Marianna and I went with our sisters in Austin. I tried to help Marianna get some things in order for our annual reports, and I got in touch with many friends. But in the privacy of my prayer, I always had this other man sitting beside me. I could not get Heath out of my mind. I so looked forward to seeing him again when our staff reconvened.

He and I immediately pushed the boundaries further out. First, it was a longer time holding hands. Then, it was longer hugs. Only my solemn promise to my Lord that I would not kiss any man kept my head bowed as he held me. Several times, he'd quip, "I guess I only get to taste your hair."

And because I kept checking everything out with Marianna as a guide and she kept encouraging me to know within myself when I was going too far, I rationalized that I was not betraying my commitments or Jesus. I had begun work at the center, and in the whirlwind, I did not take as much totally quiet time to realize the other man always in my inner chamber. It felt exciting to feel so valued by someone I admired and cared for so much.

Almost a month went by. One morning, I heard a decisive knocking.

"Heath! Hi."

"Brina, meet me in ten minutes in the conference room chapel."

I shuddered apprehensively, knowing that something was amiss. Heath greeted me with a stiff hug, then pushed me gently into a chair. "Look, Brina, we have to break this thing up. I need space. I keep thinking about you, wanting more of you—and there's no chance for that. I need a clean break."

"Heath!" I was shocked. "We said we can be friends—and we are. We'll work the kinks out. I know we will!"

"I can't hold it halfway like this. Can you?"

"I thought I *was* holding it. But I do worry that I am too attached to you." I sat silently for a long time. Then I admitted, "You are right. What will you do?"

"I will probably move out. But until then, I will stay more distant."

I agreed. We parted. I went to the chapel and felt intensely relieved—at first. For a whole day and night, I kept saying, "This is right. I'm glad."

But the following morning, it hit me. I was usually calm and collected, but I began to weep—then to sob. "Jesus, I will miss him so much. Help me."

The problem was that I could not get Heath out of my mind.

I approached Father Keith and told him of my personal crisis. He was very tender in his approach, really sympathetic. But he finished, "Sister, as director of this center, I will not be able to continue helping you with this, as it becomes a conflict of interest for me. I have a friend, a very spiritual priest in a desert house of prayer, whom I think could direct you well. Maybe it's time that you make the two-week retreat you have spoken of since you came."

"Thank you, Father Keith," I said. "Yes, I think you are right. Would you get me the name and number of that priest, please?"

That was how it worked. Lent started early that year, and the day after Ash Wednesday, I drove off to a spot outside of Corpus Christi. I did not know how much to say about Heath to the priest. But since he was so much a part of my thoughts and life, even with the distance, I certainly would need to say something—which I did not relish doing.

The house was really stark, far into the sandy, flat lands. A Sister Martine got me into a little cabin, and gave me the tour of the buildings and grounds. I would see Father Craig an hour before dinner.

Fr. Craig strode toward me with the composure of a praying man. He looked firmly into my face. "Welcome, Sister Sabrina. I am Father Craig, and I will be directing you. Please, have a seat."

Already, I was nervous. Could he read me? He seemed like a mystic. I told him who I was and why I had come. But I did not mention Heath at all.

"Sister, we will meet each morning at ten. So for tonight, why don't you pray over Isaiah, chapter forty-three. I'm asking you not to read anything but the Bible during these days. We get so many things into our minds; this will clear out your mind and heart to really hear the word of God."

My stomach was sinking, remembering the books I'd brought, hoping to enjoy reading them between the set hours for praying with the Scriptures. But I meekly shook my head in compliance.

"If you need anything, I'm sure Sister Martine gave you her number."

I shook my head affirmatively again. I took my Bible and notebook, and headed for their chapel. That passage cut to my heart. My loving God was telling me, "I have loved you with an everlasting love. I have called you by name. You are mine." I felt terribly guilty as I remembered how I had let Heath hold my hand and hug my willing body.

I had gone through many hours of anguish before my appointment. I no longer held back, but told Father Craig the whole story. At the end, I tried to put some perspective on it by saying, "I wanted Jesus through all this, and this man and I have now agreed that we need more distance. I want that, too, but I find myself thinking too much about him. I want to get beyond the whole situation."

Father listened without responding for what seemed an eternity. Then he said one sentence:

I CHEATED ON JESUS

"We may have a case here of a divided heart."

How those words pierced me! A divided heart! I did not want any lover but Jesus. I had never intended to give my heart to Heath. But had I really done so?

I kept reviewing all the weeks of the four months since I'd met Heath. Of what was I guilty? I had tried so hard, sought so much counsel, prayed so much. If I did have a divided heart, then I had committed sin. All that I did not want to do, I had done, even if I had not acted it out to finality.

This time of prayer that I had once so longed to have now became a burden. I felt that Jesus was distant. I called for Him and He did not answer.

In my session on the fifth day, Father Craig commented, "You are too much into your head. What are you feeling, Sabrina?"

"I seem to have no feelings," I replied. "I read the passages and cannot feel into them."

Craig then gave me one passage that I well knew, the Gospel of Luke, Chapter Seven, verses 36 to 50: The woman who was a sinner running into a banquet, throwing herself at Jesus' feet, and washing his feet with her tears and a spilled bottle of ointment.

I knew in my muddled head that this was me, but in the first two prayer hours, I could not get into any feelings. I saw me run in, but I felt only confusion. Jesus was there, but He did not move my heart. That gripped me with fear. *Why can't I feel Your love, Jesus?* I cried.

Father Craig told me to stay another day with that passage, but also to fast and get up during the night for one of the meditations. Fasting did not seem too hard, as I was not hungry. I set my alarm as a back-up for midnight, in case I did not wake up.

The southern summer air was chilly, so I wrapped a sheet around myself, lit my candle on the floor, and knelt on a throw rug.

"Jesus," I prayed sincerely, "Please have mercy on me. I have offended You, and I am not worthy of You. But You came to save sinners, and I need You to save me. Help me. Meet me here tonight. My heart is starving for You. Please, Jesus."

I imagined Jesus entering the house and being coldly greeted by the host. I felt sorry for Him. I was that sinful woman, watching from the street. I wished I were an invited guest, but instead, if I wanted to console Him, I would have to endure the scorn of all the wealthy men sitting around at the tables.

I kept watching Jesus. If He would look my way, I would take that as an invitation to enter. My heart pounded. I felt sad, but still, He did not look my way.

Suddenly, a thought stabbed my heart: *Maybe I am to be lost. Jesus won't look at me with His sweet mercy because I have known his love and thrown it away. I have sinned too greatly.*

"No, no, please Jesus, I did not want to sin. I never wanted to love anyone else in your place. Please look at me and give me another chance. Please look at me!"

I waited. I trembled, partly from the chill, but more from my cold heart beginning to thaw.

I saw His head turn, but not to me.

"Jesus, please," I cried.

"Brina, come over here." The words sounded clear, even though I could not see His lips move or

I CHEATED ON JESUS

His eyes look at me.

I imagined myself running into the room, unmindful of anyone else around him. I fell at His feet, and wet tears bathed those feet on which I felt and saw the red nail prints, even though I knew that He had not yet in this story suffered crucifixion. But the nail prints made me cry harder. I had put them there. Why did I hurt Him who never hurt me? Why did I play with fire?

"Jesus," I sobbed. "I am so sorry. I am sorry I ever opened the door of my heart to Heath. I am sorry that I did not close it when I saw he was moving in. I am most sorry that I disappointed You, since You have loved me so perfectly, so deeply. Please forgive me, and give me another chance, my Beloved."

I looked up and He looked at me. His eyes had tears in them, too. We looked at each other a long time, and I felt as if they became a flood of salty water flowing over my head and body, cleansing me as they washed the open sores, but dissolving all the dirt in the big crack of my divided heart.

In that prayer, I heard no words. But I knew Jesus forgave me. I felt the joy I had been unable to feel for months. My first desire was to run and wake up Father Craig. I could barely sleep, reliving now the scenes of my past as I wrestled to let them be taken away.

It was at dawn when I woke and ran down to the Sacred Heart Chapel. I threw myself down at the altar. "Jesus, I am so, so sorry. I am sorry for my divided heart. Please take those images away, and let there be only You." More tears.

It seemed as if Jesus came striding across the sanctuary. Standing before me, He looked long into my eyes.

"Brina, my dear Brina. Why are you crying?"

"Because I disappointed You, Jesus. I felt I lost You—You who are everything to me."

"No, Brina, you are crying my tears. It is I who would cry harder than you if I lost you!"

That merciful heart imaged in the church's statue seemed to be pressing me to Himself. He let me cry in sync with Him, and my tears ran down onto the railing and my skirt. "I do want to break with Heath. I only want You."

When I finally looked at my watch, I had to run to be back for my ten o'clock appointment. Father Craig affirmed that Jesus had graced me, and that I needed to write this, as well as the follow-up resolutions I would make and do.

First, I made a very thorough confession to Fr. Craig. Once again, the mercy of Jesus touched me as He gently guided me to accept forgiveness but to know my limits. I felt more waves wash me as Father put his hand on my head and pronounced those words: "And I forgive you, in the Name of the Father and of the Son, and of the Holy Spirit."

The final days moved me to the reality I so wanted to face, but so dreaded. I drank in grace at each Eucharist, praying that I could be strong. My stomach churned with fears lest my mended heart be too timid to act on the resolves.

Here I was, driving up the center's wooded lane again, so different from four and a half months ago when I'd first arrived, and even different from two weeks ago when I left on retreat. I was a bit relieved not to see anyone, but then wondered why the center looked so abandoned. I headed for the conference chapel, sitting there in the mid-afternoon light.

When I heard a door open, my heart flopped wildly. I felt someone there.

"Oh, Father Keith!" I exclaimed.

He bent over and hugged me. "Hi, Sabrina. I saw you drive in, and just thought I'd see you before the retreatants descend right after dinner."

"Thanks. The retreat was wonderful—you were right about your friend. He helped me immensely. I want to tell you about it when you have time."

"I'm glad for you, Sabrina. I want to hear all about it. For now, I just have one message: Heath said to tell you he's spending the weekend in the city with his sister. He will get back Sunday evening."

I felt immensely relieved. "Thanks," I said as calmly as I could, though my voice shook.

It felt good to go through that retreat without fear of bumping into Heath and having to finish my relationship with him. I drank in the talks by a very gifted preacher. I smiled at everyone; life felt so much better, with my Lord walking with me. I babbled on in my heart to Him over everything.

I even told Him over and over, "You are my King, my Beloved. Help me stay focused on You." On Sunday, it seemed as if Jesus carried me with tender, strong arms. It was Him preparing me, I reflected later.

Then with the glorious setting sun came that familiar sight: Heath striding down the walk. I watched him from the conference chapel, and wondered if he would find me, or if I would have to find him.

The door opened. Heath came beside me and sat down.

I had to grip my chair not to open my arms to him. That would be my undoing. I tried to not look at his face.

"Your retreat went well?" he asked. "What did the Lord tell you?"

"Heath, it was a hard retreat for a long time. I saw how much I love you—too much. You were so right that we cannot continue relating as we were doing. I so often thought of the wisdom you have about all this. So I finally was brought to my knees. Jesus showed me that it hurt Him for me to give half my heart to you. I cried and cried for His forgiveness, and He had pity on me and took me back."

My voice cracked, and I felt tears well up. I reached for my handkerchief.

"I understand, Brina. I really thought this would happen. But then, if you were willing, I thought I'd be willing to move it in another direction. I had to get away when this came last week."

He pulled out an envelope. "My annulment was granted. You realize that this makes me free to enter into another relationship, if I find one."

"Are you thinking that you will, Heath?"

"I won't if it isn't with you, Brina. I've told you already, you are the first woman I have really loved, besides my wife at the beginning. I only understand what love is because of you."

"Oh, Heath, I need to say something like that, too. Because of my love for you, I understand better how wonderful it is for a man and woman to give themselves for life—how it would not be dull, but new each day. If I had not been called to this relationship with Jesus alone, you would be the best man I could choose."

"But you did marry Him."

"Yes. And although I am so ashamed of some of the things I've done with you, I got into this deep water trying to find my way. I certainly would never be able to get into it again without serious guilt."

He sighed. "That makes me feel some comfort—that I will always be the only one who was this kind of friend to you."

I had discovered another key point that I needed to tell him. "Heath, I also need to assure you that the woman you love is only this way because of Jesus. If I ever left him, I would be a miserable lady, and you would soon get tired of me."

He seemed to be breathing all this in. We turned together to the tabernacle, sitting silently for a long time. For me, I was exploding with thanks to Jesus for getting me through the challenge. It was so difficult, but Jesus had guided me securely through the choppy waters. I felt His love again pour over my heart.

Heath stood and turned to me.

"Sister Sabrina, I will never forget you. I will be moving out soon now, but please pray for me. And don't forget—it would be dangerous and detrimental to your spiritual health ever to share with another man what you have shared with me."

"Heath, Jesus lent you to me for this time, and now He calls us to separate. He will guide you. I do pray for you. Please also pray for me. Send me a card sometime, and I will you."

The last ray of golden sun pierced my heart. It was the sundown of a special love, and now there was only Jesus with me in the brilliant darkness.   THE END

STARVED FOR HIS KIND OF LOVING

I married Bob the day Andy Pemberton went into the Army. It was a coincidence, I know that now, but it also became a haunting omen to me later—an omen that I had rushed into my marriage and hadn't given myself enough time to grow up and get over my teenage ideas of marriage. You see, Andy and I had been high-school sweethearts. The trouble with that, sometimes, is that you begin to take each other for granted. It was always Andy and I on Saturdays for football games, Sunday afternoons at the movies, and together any other time there was something special going on.

"I'm nuts about you," Andy would say.

"I'm crazy about you too," I'd tell him.

What did it add up to? Too much time alone in Andy's father's car. Too many dates that ended with both of us feeling tense and excited and scared. It got to the point where I hated being alone with Andy. I remember an afternoon we stopped by his house to pick up his sweater to go out to play miniature golf. His folks were away, and Andy pulled me down on the living room couch.

"Come on, Andy, don't start that," I said.

"Start what?" he asked. "I'm not going to do anything. You scared of me, Kay?"

"No, I'm not scared of you, but I think this is kind of silly," I said.

Actually, I wasn't scared. It was more that I was cautious. Well, we graduated finally, and I was thinking about my future with Andy when Florrie came into the picture. She moved into a house two doors down from Andy, and she was everything I was not—gorgeous and cuddly and not a bit cautious. As soon as she saw Andy, she put her mark on him as though I didn't exist. And he fell for it. First thing I knew, I was just good old Kay, that girl he used to be crazy about. Andy and I had a huge fight one night when he insisted on double-dating with Florrie and her boyfriend. I accused him of wanting to be with Florrie, and he told me at least she wasn't a wall of ice. That was the end of that—of Andy and me, I mean. Oh, maybe we didn't share the great love I imagined we did. Maybe if we had married, it wouldn't have worked out. But it's like anything else you lose—it suddenly becomes very precious. When I met Bob a few weeks later, I was sure I'd never fall in love again. I thought I'd never believe in another guy's love. Except that Bob didn't just love me—he adored me. I can't explain it exactly. He kind of worshiped me right from the start. I remember one day we were supposed to have a date, and I came down with a miserable cold. My head was stuffed, my nose was running, I ached in every bone. I crawled into bed with a pile of covers over me and just shook.

When Bob came over, Mom told him I was sick in bed. And he came up to see me!

When he came into the bedroom, I screamed. "Get out!" I yelled. "You want to catch my germs and die?"

"You look cute all bundled up that way," he said.

When I ordered him not to come near me, he crouched down at the foot of my bed. I can still see him, his dark eyes soft on me.

"Okay, I'll just adore you from here," he teased.

"How can you talk like that?" I wailed. "My nose is red, my eyes are swollen shut, and I sound like a crow."

"Let me get you something," he said. "Fruit juice? Aspirin? I want to help you get well, honey."

"Then go away," I begged, hiding my face in the pillow.

I heard Bob stand up, and then he was kissing me lightly. "You know, I never realized before how much I love you," he whispered. "Hurry up and get well. I want to ask you things."

I got well. And Bob did ask me things, as he put it. He asked me to marry him. I hesitated to say yes, but he kept asking me for weeks afterward.

Mom was delighted with Bob. She'd always thought of Andy as just a high school kid.

"Bob is steady and dependable, and I like him," she told me. "Now you be sure of your mind, honey. You know how you like to dream. Bob deserves the best. Make sure you can give it to him."

My own mother talking that way! But I guess she knew me better than I knew myself.

I agreed, of course, about Bob's steadiness and dependability. He had a good job as an insurance adjuster with a big firm, and he told me his dream was to work up into a more important job as time went by. He could do it, too, I felt. He was eight years older than I, but that wasn't a big deal. I was almost nineteen, and his twenty-six years only added to his qualifications as a husband. It was no wonder Mom liked him.

So Bob and I were married on a perfectly gorgeous September afternoon. And we went to Canada for our honeymoon.

Did my vague sense of dissatisfaction start then? I don't really know. What I do know for certain is that I had anticipated my wedding night for so long, I had built it up in my mind into such an impossible dream of romantic bliss that I was bound to be disappointed.

We'd driven all day to get to our hotel in Montreal, and by the time we'd finished dinner, I was tired. So was Bob. But I told myself I'd forget that when Bob held me in his arms, and I spent a lot of time taking a warm, relaxing bath and putting on my beautiful white lingerie.

When Bob saw me, he pretended to drop to his knees.

"Wow!" he said, getting that warm look of adoration in his eyes. "I don't know if I dare kiss you, sweetie, you look like such an angel."

"Silly," I murmured. "I'm not."

He gathered me gently in his arms. He held me as though I were fragile and would break. "I can't believe a guy could be so lucky," he said huskily. "I'm going to make you happy, Kay. That's a promise."

I didn't want promises, not really. I wanted to be swept up and kissed and carried away on that cloud I'd imagined every bride discovered on her wedding night. But Bob treated me as though I were too pure to be interested in passion. I don't know how else to say it except that while he was making love to me, I felt as though I were the aggressor and my new husband were the shy, inexperienced one.

"Do you love me, Kay?" he whispered later.

"What a question!" I snuggled close in his arms. "I love you, I love you, and I love you!"

"I adore you," he said.

He held me gently. I felt warm and protected and loved, but not conquered. As the days of our honeymoon drifted by, our relationship continued in that pattern. Bob deferred to my slightest wish. On our third day in Montreal, I decided 1 didn't want to stay there any more. It had rained for two of those days, and I told Bob I was sick of it and wanted to go to Quebec.

"I don't know, honey," he said. "I've already got tickets to the theater for tomorrow night, and we have a reservation here until Friday."

"Oh, you can cancel the reservation and sell the tickets," I said. "With the weather so bad, there's nothing to do here during the day except sit in our room or go down to the cocktail lounge."

"We can make love," he teased. "That's what rainy weather's for on a honeymoon."

"We can do that in Quebec, too," I said. "Please?"

"Okay," he said. "If that's what you want, we'll do it."

He canceled our reservations and we left. When we got to Quebec, the weather wasn't too much better, but I enjoyed the shopping there. We found the most marvelous shop with British tweeds, and went on a shopping spree, buying material for skirts and a suit. Mom had always made a lot of my clothes, and I knew she wouldn't mind sewing some more for me.

When Bob mentioned how much money I was spending, I wheedled him into letting me do it. "Think what I'll be saving in the long run," I said.

I remember how he looked that day, so big and tall and sort of out of place in the tiny shop. Then his eyes softened as he reached for his wallet.

"What the heck—a girl only gets one honeymoon," he said. "Go ahead, honey. Pick out the material you want."

The pattern was set for our marriage. I knew that I could get him to do anything I wanted. But like a spoiled child, after a while, I didn't know what I really wanted.

We returned from our honeymoon to a small house we had rented near my mother. I had wanted the house, and Bob had rented it for me. It wasn't even a house, really. It had been the carriage house on an estate that had been subdivided for development homes. It was tiny and run down, but I liked the location.

But after living there for a few weeks, I began to detest the kitchen. It had a relic of a stove that either got too hot or didn't heat up fast enough, and I found it much easier to walk the two blocks to Mom's house and kind of stay over for dinner.

I'd call Bob's office, and if he was in, I'd tell him to pick me up at Mother's. If he wasn't there, I'd leave a message for him. He never complained. But one night, he didn't show up at Mother's. I was furious, wondering why he hadn't called.

As it turned out, he'd had to drive way out of the city on a call to a client and hadn't taken time to get to a phone. By the time he got back into the city, it was so late he went straight home, figuring I was there by then.

I got home a little after nine, worried about him. When I found him asleep on the living room couch, I blew up.

"You could have called me!" I cried. "All you had to do was be a little considerate and think of me. When I didn't hear from you, I began to think you'd been in an accident."

He didn't fly back at me. He sat up, rubbing his eyes. "Gee, I'm sorry, hon," he said. "I guess I should have called, but I figured you'd be home soon."

I burst into tears—childish tears. Bob came over and tried to put his arms around me.

"You make me sick!" I screamed, struggling away from him. "Don't you dare touch me!"

For one second, I saw something come alive in his eyes. Then he turned abruptly and went out of the room. In another minute, I heard the car roar out of the driveway. *He didn't even have nerve enough to stand there and fight with me. I hate him!* I thought. *I wish I had never married him!* It never occurred to me that the whole argument was silly and baseless.

I was in bed, pretending to be asleep, when he got home. I turned my back on him, and he didn't even touch me. I was sorry by then that I'd acted childishly. I wanted him to talk to me, to try to make it up to me. But he went right to sleep. I didn't bother to get up to get him his breakfast the next morning.

It was in just that kind of mood that I went out at around eleven to hang some wash in the backyard. I faced a long row of backyards, all belonging to the development houses.

"Hi," someone called over to me. "Some day, isn't it?"

"Yes," I said. "Sun's nice and bright."

The girl's name was Marion Sanders, and she had three little kids who were forever waking up with the birds and playing out in the backyard.

She came over to the fence. "Glad everything's all right at your house," she said. "I was getting the dog in last night when I saw your husband high-tail it out of the house as though he'd been shot."

I was embarrassed. I didn't know her well enough to want to talk about it. How much had she heard? I pretended to laugh it off.

"He forgot his toothpaste and was rushing to get to the drugstore," I said, knowing she wouldn't believe me.

"How about a cup of coffee?" she asked.

I didn't want to be alone. I was bored and a little lonely and still angry at Bob. I went over to sit in her sunny kitchen. She poured coffee, after pushing cereal bowls aside and kicking at toys on the floor.

"Wait till you have kids," she said. "Boy, they're better than a demolition squad!"

But, actually, it was just talk. She didn't seem to mind the mess at all. Flopping into a chair, she grinned at me.

"Whew!" she gasped. "My husband had better stop making like a bridegroom every night! It's okay for brides like you, but I've got to get up with the birds and feed babies."

She laughed. I laughed, too, but a kind of uneasiness touched me.

"Have you been married long?" I asked her.

"Five years," she said. "You?"

"Just a few months," I said.

"Oh—oh, still honeymooning!" she grinned. "You know, I don't think I could go through another honeymoon!"

Just then there was a whoop outside, and one of the kids gave a high-pitched scream. Marion ran to the door, and then sagged against it.

"Oh, it's you!" she called out. "You scared me half to death! Billy, keep that wagon in the driveway. Don't take it out on the road."

She turned back to me. "My husband," she said.

STARVED FOR HIS KIND OF LOVING

I got up to go, but her husband walked in—a big, brawny man in work clothes.

"Ha! Caught you loafing!" he roared, pretending to he mad.

"What are you going to do about it?" Marion roared back. She started to turn, but he grabbed her, turned her around roughly, and kissed her with a loud smack on the lips. Crazy as it may sound, I felt that kiss. I felt the virility and manliness of Marion's husband in a way I had never known it with my husband. There was something about the way he held her that hinted of an intimacy I knew nothing about.

"Let me go, you lug!" she ordered.

He noticed me then. "Hi," he said, straddling a chair. I'd nodded to him a few times out in the yard, but we'd never had any other contact. "How about some coffee, honey?" he said to Marion. "Got a sandwich handy?"

"You said you'd grab lunch out," she wailed. "Oh, Pete, all I have is cheese. Settle for a toasted cheese?"

"I'll run along," I said quickly.

"No, stay." Pete picked up his coffee cup and drank. "I'll be out of here soon. Then you gals can get back to your gossiping."

"Really, I have to go," I said, edging toward the door. "I'm going shopping. See you."

I went back to my house, and began dressing to walk up to the small shopping area for some bread and milk. And all the while I was getting ready, I was thinking of those two next door. They had something special. A lusty, earthy something that was lacking in my marriage.

Bob adored me, he worshiped me, he loved me; but he wasn't exciting. I wanted to be Bob's wife, but I also wanted to be his mistress. I wanted thunder and lightning and the earth to move when he made love to me.

All that day, I felt edgy. That night, when Bob came home, he acted as though we hadn't argued at all the night before. That infuriated me. Why couldn't he get sore and yell the way I was sure Marion's husband did if he was mad? I could imagine Pete grabbing her in his arms and making her do what he wanted. Not Bob! He'd be too gentle and sweet for that kind of thing.

I didn't talk too much during dinner. Once Bob said to me, "Feeling okay?"

"Of course I'm feeling okay," I said.

"I've got some paperwork to do after dinner," he told me. "Hope you don't mind."

"Go right ahead. Why should I mind?" I said.

I did the dishes and then went out in back to dump the garbage. I couldn't help hearing Marion and her husband quarreling.

"I'm telling you for the last time that we can't afford a dryer!" Pete was yelling.

"And I'm telling you I'm sick and tired of hauling wash into the backyard! Besides, it'll soon be winter and where will I dry the clothes then?"

"Try the basement," he said.

"I'm going to get one soon," Marion said.

"You do and I'll—"

"You'll what?"

"I'll clobber you!"

"Try it! Just you try it!"

There was a scuffle. I stood still, scared, not knowing what to do. Then they appeared in the doorway of the kitchen a moment. Marion was struggling in her husband's arms. He had her arms pinned behind her back. Suddenly, her body went slack, and he leaned over and kissed her. Then both of them slid to the floor. In a minute, I heard Marion giggling.

I felt goose bumps running up my arms. *That's what I want out of marriage,* I thought. *I want a strong, masterful man who will overpower me.*

But my Bob just wasn't the type. We'd argued, and what had happened? He'd gone out in the car to get away from the quarrel, and when he came back, he acted as though nothing had happened.

I felt cheated. I went back into the house. Bob was bending over some papers on the coffee table.

"Hi," he said. "Any more coffee left?"

"I'll get you some," I said.

I went into the kitchen and got him a cup. I came back and picked up the evening newspaper. But I felt restless. "Let's go to a movie," I said.

"Honey, I've got to get these papers in tomorrow morning. This claim's been hanging over me, and I've got to get my notes into shape to present first thing in the morning."

"You care more about that stupid report than taking me to the movies," I said, egging him on to an argument.

"It's not a matter of what I care about," he told me. "It's what I have to do."

"And you always do the sensible, safe thing, don't you?" I snapped.

"Look, Kay, don't start up an argument, okay?" he begged. "We'll go to the movies tomorrow night."

"Don't put yourself out!" I said.

I was so furious with him for not fighting back, for not doing what I wanted to do, that I jumped up, picked up my coat and purse, and raced out of the house.

I drove around aimlessly for a while, and finally, I went to a movie by myself. It wasn't much of a movie, but I sat through it. I wanted to worry Bob. I wanted—oh, let's face it, I wanted Bob to be angry with me when I got home and then overpower me and make love to me.

It was late when I left the movie, and it had turned chilly. I started up the car, and I hadn't gone two blocks when it began to rain. Five blocks more and the darn car started to sputter and spit. A dozen blocks from home it just sort of gasped and died. I tried and tried to start it, and then I noticed the gas gauge was empty. I was so mad at Bob then, I could have slugged him. Why hadn't he told me? Why did he let me go, knowing the car was almost out of gas?

I got out of the car, slammed the door shut, and started hiking home. That was the wettest, coldest rain I've ever felt in my life. It went right through to my bones. On top of it all, I was scared to death walking those dark streets. Every time a car came by, I slinked in toward the hedges. What if someone saw me, a lone woman walking by herself at this time of the night? What if someone stopped and tried to drag me into a car? I began to shiver more from fear than from the rain and cold.

It took me forever to get home. And by the time I got there, I was blue with cold and rage.

I turned on the lights in the living room. Bob was in bed. He heard me, though.

"Kay, is that you?" he called out.

"Don't let me wake you up!" I called back. "I wouldn't want to disturb your rest. After all, what's it to you if your wife is out on the streets alone at night?"

He came into the living room in pajamas, looking sleepy and tousled. That infuriated me all the more. All the while I'd been dying a thousand deaths out there in the dark, he'd been sleeping.

"I thought you went to your mother's," he said.

"You left that car out there with no gas in it!" I screamed at him. "And I had to leave it up on Fourteenth Avenue and walk all the way home! Thanks for caring whether I was kidnapped or raped or killed out there!"

"Oh, come off it," he said. "I guess I did forget to get gas, but you went roaring out of here in such a huff I didn't have time to mention it."

That did it! If it had been Marion's husband, he'd have grabbed me, crushed me to him, scared me a little, but made me feel terribly wanted and important. Not my husband. He was always so reasonable.

I ran past him into the bedroom and went to the dresser and began pulling out his shirts and underclothes and socks.

"I hate you," I yelled, throwing his things out into the living room. "You're a cold, unfeeling monster! I'm going to leave you. I won't stay married to someone who doesn't care where his wife is this late at night!"

I was being silly and I knew it, but I couldn't stop. I didn't mean anything that I said, but I couldn't unsay it—not without losing face.

Bob glared at me for a moment, and I had never seen him so angry, his fists clenched at his sides. I got a little scared when he started to make a move, but he didn't come near me or touch me. He stepped over the clothes all over the living-room floor, went to the closet and took out a blanket, then turned off the light and lay down on the couch.

"Oh!" I screamed, slamming the bedroom door.

I threw myself down on the bed dramatically. But my clothes were wet and uncomfortable, so I got up and took them off, took a hot bath, and got back in bed. *Serve him right if he catches a good cold out there,* I thought, snuggling down into the covers. *And it would serve him right if I meant what I said about leaving him.*

But just before I drifted off to sleep, I began to feel a bit ashamed of myself. I had acted like a four-year-old, screaming and making wild threats because my feelings were hurt.

But my pride wouldn't allow me to go out to my husband. And pride wouldn't allow him to come to me. The next morning, I really didn't hear him get up and leave the house. It must have been very early, though, because when I went out into the kitchen and looked out the window to see what kind of day it was, I saw our car parked in the driveway.

That made me feel even worse, knowing Bob must have walked or taken a bus to where I'd left the car, and then somehow got gas for it. That's when you really feel awful, you know—when you've hurt someone and he turns around and does something nice for you. To top it off, I knew he hadn't had any breakfast because nothing was disturbed in the kitchen.

It was a Friday. I usually did my weekend shopping on Friday mornings. That morning, I felt particularly restless in the house and got out as fast as I could. Marion saw me and called to me.

"Kay, will you do me a favor?" she asked. "Pete's gone off with the car and won't be back until late tonight. I'm without transportation. Can I come along and do a little shopping?"

"Sure," I said. "I'll bring the car around in front of your house."

It took her ten minutes to put the kids into clothes and get them to the car. And it took us another hour to do the shopping, because it wasn't easy pushing two carts around the supermarket and keeping track of Marion's three kids.

"Honestly," Marion said, piling the kids and groceries into the car, "this is the one job I hate. If that big lug of a husband of mine had to do it, I'll bet he'd throw in the towel the first day."

"Bob doesn't mind shopping for me when he has the car and I don't," I said. "But then, I don't have a family yet. I mean, we don't buy as many groceries."

"Your husband's a doll," Marion said. "He came over and helped me bring my bundles into the house last week while my Pete was watching TV."

"He told me he'd had a beer with Pete," I said.

"Well, Pete believes in relaxing when he's home," she said. "But I love the brute. Gee, this was nice of you, Kay."

"Any time," I told her.

But I'd barely got back in my car when Pete drove up.

"Hiya, Kay," he yelled to me.

Marion heard him and came to the door. "What are you doing back?" she called out.

"Got halfway to the lake and one of the guys got sick," he told her. "So we turned right around and came home. No big deal. Now I can go bowling tonight."

"Why don't you forget about that, honey," Marion was saying as they went toward their house, and from the way Pete's arm tightened around her, I figured he very well might.

I went into our house. I unpacked the groceries and then went about setting the house straight. As I picked up the clothes I'd tossed out into the living room the night before, my feeling of shame returned. I'd had no right to do that, actually. And Bob had every reason to be upset at me. I wondered if he'd remember my threats about leaving him. I really felt sorry for the scene I had created and wanted to tell him that. But how?

My chance came sooner than I expected. . . .

About the time they'd built the development houses, they'd also put in a sewer. But there had been a lot of trouble on our block because they'd run into quicksand and had had to dig down for twenty-five feet. Then they'd built an artificial bed for the pipelines, and for a while, there had been the most awful odor of gas where one of the gas lines had been dragged down by the weight of the sewer. But that, too, had been taken care of.

We hadn't had any trouble on the block since, and to tell the truth, I'd forgotten all about it. After all, it was just something we'd heard about from our neighbors. That's why I didn't think of an explosion when I heard a kind of swoosh just as Bob's car pulled into the driveway that night. I peered out the kitchen window and saw Bob turn and start running toward the street, and my first thought was that it was a car accident. I went to the front door, and people were hurrying out of their houses and kids were scrambling down the walks.

"Get back! Everyone get back!" I heard Bob yell. "Someone call the gas company, quick!"

I ran down the walk, and Marion came out of her house, asking what had happened. I heard her calling to her husband to come quick.

Bob and some of the other men were huddling, and then Bob seemed to take over. "Let's get the kids off the block fast!" he said. "Come on—kids go first. Go up to the Presbyterian Church and wait there. We think a gas main collapsed, but we don't want to take chances on anything blowing up."

There was such a scramble and screeching then. I ran back to our house, turned off the gas burners, pulled on a coat, and started outdoors to see what I could do. Marion was herding her kids outside, and she kept yelling for Pete. Suddenly, he came out of their house, carrying a strongbox in his hands.

"Pete!" Marion called to him. "Help me with the kids. We've got to get them out of here."

"Okay, kids, run for your lives!" he said. He was hanging on to his strongbox, and he started racing up the street. He didn't even wait for Marion and the kids, and he didn't stop to help the men who were trying to get everyone off the block. I stared, unable to believe that a big, strong guy like Pete could get so scared he would think only of saving his own skin.

Then I looked around for Bob. I saw him dashing up to front doors and yelling, "Everybody out here?"

I felt tears sting my eyes. He wasn't even wearing a coat. He'd catch his death of cold, racing around like that. But Bob didn't seem to think of his own skin at all. My Bob—my gentle, considerate, kind husband—was more of a man than Pete would ever be!

I turned and ran back into our house, grabbing Bob's coat. Then I ran up the street toward him, calling his name. By then, the gas-company people were there, and the place was chaos. I caught up with Bob at the house next door.

"Your coat," I said through chattering teeth. "Put it on."

"Honey!" He grabbed my arms, and the strength I felt told me that here was man enough for any woman! "I thought you left. Go—run! Get out of here!"

"You come, too!" I cried. "I won't go without you."

"I'll come as soon as I know everyone's okay here," he said firmly. "Go on, I'll meet you at your mother's."

I went. I ran all the way to Mother's, and then I waited and waited. In about two hours, Bob came for me. He was dirty and tired, but I could tell everything was all right. There had been a gas leak, he told me, and the men were going to work all night to take care of it. But they knew where and what it was, and it was safe for all of us to go back to our houses.

"Stay here," Mother said. "I'll fix you something to eat, Bob."

"No, we'll go home," I said, taking my husband's hand. "I have dinner ready—if there's anything left of it."

We walked home, past the searchlights on the gas-company trucks. The repairmen called out to Bob, recognizing him as the one who'd taken charge during the emergency.

That night when my husband drew me close in his arms, I knew his gentleness-covered strength. I knew that I was married to a man who didn't have to prove his masculinity with cave-man lovemaking.

That was the night, too, when I became a woman. At last, I'd outgrown my teenage dreams of an "exciting" marriage and learned what a really satisfying marriage is like. I knew, finally, that it's based on respect as well as passion, on a way of expressing love that's natural and right for the two people involved. Bob could no more be like Pete than Pete could be like Bob! And, suddenly, I knew I wouldn't want Bob to be that kind of man.

Now, when I see Pete next door kissing Marion lustily and making like a male man, I feel sorry for her. Bedroom bravery isn't enough! I'd rather have a man like my Bob! THE END

TRUE STORY
SUBSCRIBE & SAVE 50%

YES, please enter my subscription to *True Story* for 12 issues at $24.00.

Call
1-800-666-8783
With Your
Credit Card
In Hand

PLEASE NOTE: Credit card payments for your subscription will appear on your statement as *Dorchester Media*, *not* as the magazine name.

Please allow 6-8 weeks for delivery of first issue. Annual newsstand price is $47.88